Henrik Ibsen was born on 20 March 1826 at Skien, Norway. Eight years later his father, a merchant, went bankrupt, reducing the family to poverty. Ibsen left school at the age of fifteen and was apprenticed to an apothecary for five years. During that time he began studying to enter university to do medicine but found his interests turning more towards writing. He had written some poems, and also a play, *Catalina*, which was published unsuccessfully in 1850 under a pseudonym. Later that year he moved to Christiana, and worked as a journalist before being appointed stage manager to the Bergen theatre in 1851. In 1857 he became director of the newly founded Norwegian Theatre in Christiana, but the theatre went bankrupt, and the plays Ibsen had produced over the previous years had not met with any great success. In 1863 he was awarded a scholarship which enabled him to travel to Rome where he wrote *Brand* (1866) and *Peer Gynt* (1867). He continued to live abroad, mainly in Germany and Italy, and began to write the series of plays which established his international reputation as a dramatist: *Pillars of Society* (1877), *A Doll's House* (1879), *Ghosts* (1881), *An Enemy of the People* (1882), *The Wild Duck* (1884), *The Lady from the Sea* (1888), *Hedda Gabler* (1890) and *The Master Builder* (1892). Ibsen was introduced to English audiences by Sir Edmund Gosse, who enthusiastically reviewed and wrote about Ibsen's work, and William Archer, who translated many of the plays. Ibsen returned to Norway in 1891, and died at Christiana on 12 May 1906.

HENRIK IBSEN

A Doll's House

The Wild Duck

The Lady from the Sea

Translated by R. Farquharson Sharp
and Eleanor Marx-Aveling

Printed in Great Britain by
The Guernsey Press Co. Ltd, Guernsey, C.I. for
J. M. Dent & Sons Ltd
Orion Publishing Group, Orion House,
5 Upper St. Martin's Lane, London WC2H 9EA
and
Charles E. Tuttle Co., Inc.
28, South Main Street
Rutland, Vermont
05701, U.S.A.

This edition was first published in
Everyman's Library in 1910
Revised edition 1958
Reissued 1992
Reprinted 1992

ISBN 0 460 87135 8

Everyman's Library
Reg. U.S. Patent Office

INTRODUCTION

HENRIK IBSEN was born, on 20th March 1828, at Skien, a small Norwegian town which concerned itself solely with the timber trade. About eight years later his father's means, which had originally been easy, were suddenly and disastrously reduced. The family had to remove to humbler quarters and live in a very small way, and thus the boy had an early initiation into the privation that was to be his lot in life for many years. One of his few pleasures in these early days was the possession, which was allowed to him undisturbed, of an attic in his father's house. Here he could rummage at will, we are told by Mr Gosse, amongst 'some dreary old books, amongst others Harrison's folio *History of the City of London*, as well as a paint-box, an hour-glass, and an extinct eight-day clock, properties which were faithfully introduced, half a century later, into *The Wild Duck*.'

As a youth, Ibsen displayed some talent for painting, and, when he left school at fifteen, was anxious to be an artist. But poverty forbade, and for five years he was apprenticed to an apothecary. By the end of that time his literary gifts had begun to assert themselves, and his soul, stirred by the revolutionary wave that was spreading over Europe, unburdened itself in poetry. It was not long before the irksomeness of life in a small country town became insupportable by one who had ambitions, and in 1850 Ibsen managed to get to Christiania, where he eked out an existence by humble journalistic work. He had taken with him to Christiania a three-act blank verse tragedy, *Catilina*, which was published (under a pseudonym) in 1850 and fell still-born from the press. The efforts of friends, however, procured him an appointment as 'stage-poet' to the Bergen theatre; and after five years there (during which time one or two immature plays of his own were performed) he returned to Christiania to be 'artistic director' of the new Norwegian theatre that had been established in rivalry with the old house. Except for the fact that his duties brought him some valuable experience of the technical side of the drama, the Christiania venture was disastrous to him. Ill luck and rebuffs pursued him; his theatre went bankrupt; and he was driven often back upon his painting to earn the price of a meal. Eventually he was forced to accept an offer of employment at the old theatre. He made repeated efforts to obtain a civil-list pension, but this was for a long time refused him, owing to the soreness produced in official quarters by the freedom with which Ibsen had, in his writings, satirized officialdom.

Having, by his uncompromising independence of temperament, made Norway too hot to hold him, Ibsen became a voluntary exile in 1864, and did not return to his own country (save for two brief visits) till some five and twenty years afterwards. The first four of these years were spent in Italy, the others mainly in Germany. The effect of a wider life was not long in making itself evident. From Italy *Brand* and *Peer Gynt*, two magnificent 'dramatic poems,' came in successive years to astonish Ibsen's compatriots and make him famous. The long demanded pension could no longer be withheld, and Ibsen's time of penury was over. In 1877 he began to write the series of prose plays on which his wider reputation rests, the last of them being published in 1900, when their author was an old man of seventy-two.

Ibsen returned to his own people in 1891 and settled in Christiania. Returning with a European reputation, he somewhat grimly enjoyed the hero-worship showered upon him by a people who had formerly made an outcast of him. In 1898 his seventieth birthday was celebrated with enthusiastic honours, and in the following year a statue of him was erected outside the Christiania theatre. When he died, after a long illness, in May 1906, he was accorded a public funeral.

A Doll's House (*Et Dukkehjem*), the earliest of Ibsen's 'social dramas,' was the first of his works to compel attention outside of Scandinavia. His reputation at home had gradually grown through a series of romantic and historical plays of less eventual importance, and had been sealed by the immense success of his *Brand*, which was published in 1866. From that point in his career, his work took mainly the form of political or social satire, for which he found an abundance of themes in the narrow and self-satisfied provincialism of Norwegian town life. *A Doll's House* was written in 1879, when Ibsen was fifty-one, and published in December of that year. Shortly afterwards it was acted in Copenhagen. It was first seen in London in 1889, and

in Paris in 1894; subsequently it has been widely translated, and
the part of Nora (its heroine) has been included in the repertory
of more than one world-famous actress.

The theme of the play, with its insistence on the woman's
right to individual self-development, provoked a storm of discussion, and, in many quarters, an outpouring of violent abuse.
The latter was possibly a good deal due to the fact that in this
play (as, afterwards, in *Ghosts*) Ibsen seems unable to keep away
from the topic of disease in its hereditary aspect.   In *A Doll's
House*, however, the topic is by no means essential to the scheme
of the play as it is in *Ghosts*.   The subject of *A Doll's House*—
the awakening to the sense of individual responsibility on the
part of a woman who has always been treated as a spoilt child—
was of itself sufficient matter for any amount of discussion.
Whether Nora acted rightly or wrongly, naturally or unnaturally,
in leaving husband, home, and children in order to develop her
own 'individuality'; whether her casting herself adrift was
indispensable to her development—all this was hotly debated.
Though it may seem to some that, in his statement of the case,
Ibsen thinks too much of a woman's rights and too little of her
duties, it must be born in mind that in all his 'social plays' he
contented himself with stating problems as they appeared to him,
and did not attempt to answer them.   His reply to those who
accused him of a merely destructive philosophy was that his task,
as he conceived it, was to point out the weaknesses of the social
fabric, and to leave constructive philosophy to those who were
not dramatists.   He diagnosed, and left the cure to others.
Moreover, however sound or unsound his theory of Nora's action
may seem to us, it must be remembered to his credit that Ibsen,
in spite of his enthusiastic advocacy of a woman's right to the
development of her own individuality, would never give any
countenance to the self-styled 'emancipated' woman.   He had
no patience with those whose idea of self-development seems to
consist chiefly in the abandonment of the sphere in which woman
is pre-eminent and the invasion of spheres for which she is
organically unsuited.   Women, he used to maintain, must
inevitably in the future have an immense influence in the
practical world; but as mothers, and as mothers only.

In the matter of technique, *A Doll's House* marks a turning-
point in the history of European drama.   Twenty years have
made us so accustomed to the results of the revolution worked by
Ibsen's dramatic method, that it is not easy to realize how com-

plete the revolution was. Naturalness of dialogue and situation;
adherence to the 'unities' of time and place; the disappearance of
such artificialities as the soliloquy; the avoidance of a happy
ending when such an outcome is illogical—all this has become so
familiar to us, and so inevitably a condition of any drama to be
written nowadays, that we are apt to forget that the change dates
from the year when an enthusiastic band of pioneers gave the
first performance of *A Doll's House* outside of Scandinavia.

The Wild Duck (*Vildanden*), which was published in 1884 and
first acted early in 1885, represents a different mental attitude on
Ibsen's part. In the five years which had elapsed since the
appearance of *A Doll's House*, the controversy which that play
had aroused had been intensified a hundredfold by *Ghosts*, which
followed it. Ibsen was the target for the fiercest attacks from his
own people, to whom in retort he sent *An Enemy of the People*,
a play charged with a mordant satire that added fuel to the
flames. *The Wild Duck* seems to have been written in a condition of mental reaction after the heat of battle, when Ibsen
was able to appreciate the irony of the situation. The play is,
in effect, substantially a satire on some of his most fervently
expressed theories, and, incidentally, of the 'Ibsenites.' The
character of Gregers Werle satirizes the unthinking reformers
who would enforce an unpractical ideal of absolute sincerity and
truthfulness. In his obedience to the 'demand of the ideal,'
Gregers brings about a misery which ends in tragedy. A truthfulness that admits of no compromise wrecks a family's peace;
insistence on the beauty of self-sacrifice leads to the suicide of a
young and innocent life. In the end the reformer is confronted
with the hard fact that, in this world, the ideal and the practical
often can only be reconciled by compromise, and that the well-
meaning busybody is responsible for a deal of mischief. It can
scarcely be doubted that there are, in the exposition of Gregers's
character, many sly hits at Ibsen himself and his usually uncompromising philosophy of life. Even such details as Gregers's
unfortunate attempt to 'do everything for himself' in his room,
suggest some of the author's idiosyncrasies. Ibsen used to
insist on sewing on his own buttons when they came off his
clothes, maintaining that women could not sew them on firmly.
(His wife, however, divulged the fact that she used to go surrep-
titiously to his room when he had done, and 'finish them off'—
a process, very necessary to the durability of the sewing, that he
usually forgot!) On one occasion he considerably startled a

friend of his, late in life, by asking him suddenly whether he blacked his own boots.

The whole trend of *The Wild Duck* suggests that the storm of controversy that had raged round *A Doll's House* and *Ghosts* had awakened Ibsen to the inevitableness of compromise in daily existence, if disaster is to be averted. In technical skill the play is his masterpiece; indeed, it would be difficult to name any modern drama that is its superior in construction, characterization, and absolute naturalness and aptness of dialogue. The skill with which, as the play progresses, the audience is made aware, little by little, of the tragedy that is past before the play opens, is the more striking the more it is examined; and it is accomplished without any sacrifice of probability in action or speech. The only weak point in the play lies in the 'symbolism' of the Wild Duck itself. Symbolism, especially when it descends to detail, is usually a mistake in the acted drama, and in this case its purport is too vague for it to be of any value. It is by no means clear which of the characters the Wild Duck is meant to symbolize; moreover, the symbolism is not essential to the development of the play, which would be the only justification for its use.

A more general and less detailed symbolism may produce a dramatic effect in the way of general 'atmosphere,' as it does to some extent (though, again, by no means as an indispensable ingredient) in the third play in this collection. *The Lady from the Sea* (*Fruen fra Havet*) was only published in 1888, but had been planned long before *The Wild Duck*, a fact which may explain its inferiority to that play in dramatic quality. It is not of the same stuff as Ibsen's 'social dramas.' It is a mixture of psychology and poetic fancy surrounding one of Ibsen's haunting principles—that an action is only valuable and reasonable if it be the spontaneous outcome of the individual will. The 'Lady from the Sea's' shadowy sense of the attraction of the sea, coupled with the incident of the half-betrothal to the mysterious 'Stranger' and her temporary infatuation to leave her husband for him, are really only embroideries round the theme of the play. That theme is the psychological development of an idle woman who has nothing particular to occupy her life. She frets at the restrictions of wifely duty upon which her husband would insist; until, when he realizes the situation sufficiently to remove his restrictions, and the idea of compulsion is gone, the woman's mental attitude correspondingly alters. She now finds no attraction in forbidden fruit, and a strong attraction in her obvious duty.

The translation of *The Lady from the Sea* is that of Mrs Marx-Aveling; for those of *A Doll's House* and *The Wild Duck* I am responsible.

R. Farquharson Sharp.

For the 1958 reprint the translations were revised by Torgrim and Linda Hannås.

SELECT BIBLIOGRAPHY

SEPARATE PLAYS (titles in English; dates of first Norwegian editions). *Catilina*, 1850: *The Warrior's Barrow*, 1850; *Norma*, 1851: *Olaf Liljekrans*, 1856; *The Feast at Solhoug*, 1856; *Lady Inger of Østeraad*, 1857; *The Vikings at Helgeland*, 1858; *Love's Comedy*, 1862; *The Pretenders*, 1864; *Brand*, 1866; *Peer Gynt*, 1867; *The League of Youth*, 1869; *Emperor and Galilean*, 1873; *The Pillars of Society*, 1877; *A Doll's House*, 1879; *Ghosts*, 1881; *An Enemy of the People*, 1882; *The Wild Duck*, 1884; *Rosmersholm*, 1886; *The Lady from the Sea*, 1888; *Hedda Gabler*, 1890; *The Master Builder*, 1892; *Little Eyolf*, 1894; *John Gabriel Borkman*, 1896; *When We Dead Awaken*, 1899.

COLLECTED EDITIONS. *The Complete Major Prose Plays*, translated and introduced by Rolf Fielde, 1978; *Letters and Speeches*, edited by Evert Sprinchorn, 1965; *Ibsen's Poems*, in versions by John Northam, 1986.

BIOGRAPHY AND CRITICISM. G. B. Shaw, *The Quintessence of Ibsenism*, 1891 (expanded 1913); E. W. Gosse, *Henrik Ibsen* (Literary Lives Series), 1907; B. W. Downs, *Ibsen: The Intellectual Background*, 1946; J. Lavrin, *Ibsen: an Approach*, 1950; B. W. Downs, *A Study of Six Plays by Ibsen*, 1950; J. R. Northam, *Ibsen's Dramatic Method*, 1951; B. Ibsen, *The Three Ibsens*, translated by G. Schjelderup, 1951; G. Wilson Knight, *Ibsen* (Writers and Critics Series), 1962; M. C. Bradbrook, *Ibsen the Norwegian: A Revaluation*, 1966; R. Fjelde, *Ibsen* (Twentieth Century Views Series), 1966; J. W. McFarlane (ed.), *Henrik Ibsen*, 1970; Michael Egan (ed.), *Ibsen* (Critical Heritage Series), 1972; John Northam, *Ibsen: A Critical Study*, 1973; M. Meyer, *Ibsen*, (n.e.) 1985; E. Beyer, *Ibsen: The Man and His Work*, 1978; H. Clurman, *Ibsen*, 1978; E. Durbach, *Ibsen and the Theatre*, 1980; J. S. Chamberlain, *Ibsen: The Open Vision*, 1982; David Thomas, *Henrik Ibsen* (Modern Dramatists Series), 1983; *William Archer on Ibsen: the major essays, 1889–1919*, 1984; M. Meyer (ed.), *Ibsen* (Writers on File Series), 1985.

CONTENTS

A DOLL'S HOUSE

DRAMATIS PERSONAE

Torvald Helmer.
Nora, his wife.
Doctor Rank.
Mrs Linde.
Nils Krogstad.
Helmer's three young children
Anne, their nurse.
· A Housemaid.
A Porter.

(The action takes place in Helmer's house.)

A DOLL'S HOUSE

ACT I

(SCENE.—*A room furnished comfortably and tastefully, but not extravagantly. At the back, a door to the right leads to the entrance-hall, another to the left leads to Helmer's study. Between the doors stands a piano. In the middle of the left-hand wall is a door, and beyond it a window. Near the window are a round table, arm-chairs, and a small sofa. In the right-hand wall, at the farther end, another door; and on the same side, nearer the footlights, a stove, two easy chairs, and a rocking-chair; between the stove and the door, a small table. Engravings on the walls; a cabinet with china and other small objects; a small book-case with well-bound books. The floors are carpeted, and a fire burns in the stove. It is winter.*

A bell rings in the hall; shortly afterwards the door is heard to open. Enter NORA, *humming a tune and in high spirits. She is in outdoor dress and carries a number of parcels; these she lays on the table to the right. She leaves the outer door open after her, and through it is seen a* PORTER *who is carrying a Christmas-tree and a basket, which he gives to the* MAID *who has opened the door.*)

Nora. Hide the Christmas-tree carefully, Helen. Make sure the children don't see it till this evening, when it is decorated. (*To the* PORTER, *taking out her purse.*) How much?

Porter. Sixpence.

Nora. There is a shilling. No, keep the change. (*The* PORTER *thanks her, and goes out.* NORA *shuts the door. She is laughing to herself, as she takes off her hat and coat. She takes a packet of macaroons from her pocket and eats one or two; then goes cautiously to her husband's door and listens.*) Yes, he is in. (*Still humming, she goes to the table on the right.*)

Helmer (*calls out from his room*). Is that my little lark twittering out there?

Nora (*busy opening some of the parcels*). Yes, it is!

Helmer. Is it my little squirrel scurrying around?

Nora. Yes!

Helmer. When did my squirrel come home?

Nora. Just now. (*Puts the bag of macaroons into her pocket and wipes her mouth.*) Come in here, Torvald, and see what I have bought.

Helmer. Don't disturb me. (*A little later, he opens the door and looks into the room, pen in hand.*) Bought, did you say? All these things? Has my little spendthrift been wasting money again?

Nora. Yes but, Torvald, this year we really can let ourselves go a little. This is the first Christmas that we have not needed to economize.

Helmer. Still, you know, we can't spend money recklessly.

Nora. Yes, Torvald, we can be a wee bit more reckless now, can't we? Just a tiny wee bit! You are going to have a big salary and earn lots and lots of money.

Helmer. Yes, after the New Year; but then it will be a whole quarter before the salary is due.

Nora. Pooh! we can borrow till then.

Helmer. Nora! (*Goes up to her and takes her playfully by the ear.*) The same little featherbrain! Suppose, now, that I borrowed fifty pounds to-day, and you spent it all in the Christmas week, and then on New Year's Eve a slate fell on my head and killed me, and——

Nora (*putting her hands over his mouth*). Oh! don't say such horrid things.

Helmer. Still, suppose that happened—what then?

Nora. If that were to happen, I don't suppose I should care whether I owed money or not.

Helmer. Yes, but what about the people who had lent it?

Nora. Them? Who would bother about them? I shouldn't know who they were.

Helmer. That is like a woman! But seriously, Nora, you know what I think about that. No debt, no borrowing. There can be no freedom or beauty about a home life that depends on borrowing and debt. We two have kept bravely on the straight road so far, and we will go on the same way for the short time longer that there need be any struggle.

Nora (*moving towards the stove*). As you please, Torvald.

Helmer (*following her*). Come, come, my little skylark must not droop her wings. What is this! Is my little squirrel upset? (*Taking out his purse.*) Nora, what do you think I have got here?

Nora (*turning round quickly*). Money!

Helmer. There you are. (*Gives her some money.*) Do you think I don't know what a lot is wanted for housekeeping at Christmas-time?

Nora (*counting*). Ten shillings—a pound—two pounds! Thank you, thank you, Torvald; that will keep me going for a long time.

Helmer. Indeed it must.

Nora. Yes, yes, it will. But come here and let me show you what I have bought. And all so cheap! Look, here is a new suit for Ivar, and a sword; and a horse and a trumpet for Bob; and a doll and a doll's bed for Emmy—they are very plain, but anyway she will soon break them to pieces. And here are dress-lengths and handkerchiefs for the maids; old Anne ought really to have something better.

Helmer. And what is in this parcel?

Nora (*crying out*). No, no! you mustn't see that till this evening.

Helmer. Very well. But now tell me, you extravagant little person, what would you like for yourself?

Nora. For myself? Oh, I am sure I don't want anything.

Helmer. Yes, but you must. Tell me something reasonable that you would particularly like to have.

Nora. No, I really can't think of anything—unless, Torvald——

Helmer. Yes?

Nora (*playing with his coat buttons, and without raising her eyes to his*). If you really want to give me something, you might —you might——

Helmer. Well, out with it!

Nora (*speaking quickly*). You might give me money, Torvald. Only just as much as you can afford; and then one of these days I will buy something with it.

Helmer. But, Nora——

Nora. Oh, do! dear Torvald; please, please do! Then I will wrap it up in a beautiful gilt paper and hang it on the Christmas-tree. Wouldn't that be fun?

Helmer. What are little people called that are always wasting money?

Nora. Spendthrifts—I know. Let's do as you suggest. Torvald, and then I shall have time to think what I am most in need of. That is a very sensible plan, isn't it?

Helmer (*smiling*). Indeed it is—that is to say, if you were really to save out of the money I give you, and then really buy something for yourself. But if you spend it all on the house-keeping and any number of unnecessary things, then I merely have to pay up again.

Nora. Oh but, Torvald——

Helmer. You can't deny it, my dear little Nora. (*Puts his arm round her waist.*) It's a sweet little spendthrift, but she uses up a lot of money. It's almost unbelievable how expensive such little persons are!

Nora. You shouldn't say that. I do really save all I can.

Helmer (laughing). That's very true—all you can. But you can't save anything!

Nora (smiling quietly and happily). You haven't any idea how many expenses we skylarks and squirrels have, Torvald.

Helmer. You are an odd little soul. Very like your father. You always find some new way of wheedling money out of me, and, as soon as you have got it, it seems to melt in your hands. You never know where it has gone. Still, one must take you as you are. It's in the blood; for it is true that you can inherit these things, Nora.

Nora. Oh, I wish I had inherited many of father's qualities.

Helmer. And I would not wish you to be anything but just what you are, my sweet little skylark. But, you know, it strikes me that you are looking rather—what shall I say—rather uneasy to-day?

Nora. Do I?

Helmer. You do, really. Look straight at me.

Nora (looks at him). Well?

Helmer (wagging his finger at her). Hasn't Miss Sweet-Tooth been breaking rules in town to-day?

Nora. No; what makes you think that?

Helmer. Hasn't she paid a visit to the confectioner's?

Nora. No, I assure you, Torvald——

Helmer. Not been nibbling sweets?

Nora. No, certainly not.

Helmer. Not even taken a bite at a macaroon or two?

Nora. No, Torvald, I assure you really——

Helmer. There, there, you know I was only joking.

Nora (going to the table on the right). I shouldn't think of going against your wishes.

Helmer. No, I am sure of that; besides, you gave me your word—— (*Going up to her.*) Keep your little Christmas secrets to yourself, my darling. They will all be revealed to-night when the Christmas-tree is lit, no doubt.

Nora. Did you remember to invite Doctor Rank?

Helmer. No. But there is no need; he will come to dinner with us as a matter of course. However, I will ask him when he comes in this morning. I have ordered some good wine. Nora, you can't think how I am looking forward to this evening.

Nora. So am I! And how the children will enjoy themselves, Torvald!

Helmer. It is wonderful to feel that one has a perfectly safe job, and a big enough income. It's delightful to think of, isn't it?

Nora. It's wonderful!

Helmer. Do you remember last Christmas? For quite three weeks beforehand you shut yourself up every evening till long after midnight, making ornaments for the Christmas-tree, and all the other fine things that were to be a surprise to us. It was the dullest three weeks I ever spent!

Nora. I didn't find it dull.

Helmer (*smiling*). But there was precious little result, Nora.

Nora. Oh, you shouldn't tease me about that again. How could I help the cat's going in and tearing everything to pieces?

Helmer. Of course you couldn't, poor little girl. You had the best of intentions to please us all, and that's the main thing. But it is a good thing that our hard times are over.

Nora. Yes, it is really wonderful.

Helmer. This time I needn't sit here and be dull all alone, and you needn't ruin your dear eyes and your pretty little hands——

Nora (*clapping her hands*). No, Torvald, I needn't any longer, need I! It's wonderfully lovely to hear you say so! (*Taking his arm.*) Now I will tell you how I have been thinking we ought to arrange things, Torvald. As soon as Christmas is over—— (*A bell rings in the hall.*) There's the bell. (*She tidies the room a little.*) There's someone at the door. What a nuisance!

Helmer. If it is a caller, remember I am not at home.

Maid (*in the doorway*). A lady to see you, ma'am—a stranger.

Nora. Ask her to come in.

Maid (*to* HELMER). The doctor came at the same time, sir.

Helmer. Did he go straight into my room?

Maid. Yes, sir.

(HELMER *goes into his room.   The* MAID *ushers in* Mrs LINDE, *who is in outdoor clothes, and shuts the door*.)

Mrs Linde (*in a dejected and timid voice*). How do you do, Nora?

Nora (*doubtfully*). How do you do——

Mrs Linde. You don't recognize me, I suppose.

Nora. No, I don't know—yes, of course, I seem to—— (*Suddenly*.) Yes! Christine! Is it really you?

Mrs Linde. Yes, it is I.

Nora. Christine! To think of my not recognizing you! And yet how could I——   (*In a gentle voice*.) How you have altered, Christine!

Mrs Linde. Yes, I have indeed.   In nine, ten long years——

Nora. Is it so long since we met?   I suppose it is.   The last eight years have been a happy time for me, I can tell you.   And so now you have come into the town, and have taken this long journey in winter—that was brave of you.

Mrs Linde. I arrived by steamer this morning.

Nora. To have some fun at Christmas-time, of course.   How lovely!   We'll have such fun together!   But take off your things.   You are not cold, I hope. (*Helps her*.) Now let's sit down by the stove, and be cosy.   No, take this arm-chair; I'll sit here in the rocking-chair.   (*Takes her hands*.)   Now you look like your old self again; it was only the first moment—— You are a little paler, Christine, and perhaps a little thinner.

Mrs Linde. And much, much older, Nora.

Nora. Perhaps a little older; very, very little; certainly not much.   (*Stops suddenly and speaks seriously*.)   What a thoughtless creature I am, chattering away like this.   My poor, dear Christine, do forgive me.

Mrs Linde. What do you mean, Nora?

Nora (*gently*). Poor Christine, you are a widow.

Mrs Linde. Yes; it is three years ago now.

Nora. Yes, I knew; I saw it in the papers.   I assure you, Christine, I meant ever so often to write to you at the time, but I always put it off and something always prevented me.

Mrs Linde. I quite understand, dear.

Nora. It was very bad of me, Christine.   Poor thing, how you must have suffered.   And he left you nothing?

Mrs Linde. No.

Nora. And no children?

Mrs Linde. No.

Nora. Nothing at all, then.

Mrs Linde. Not even any sorrow or grief to live upon.

Nora (looking incredulously at her). But, Christine, is that possible?

Mrs Linde (smiles sadly and strokes her hair). It sometimes happens, Nora.

Nora. So you are quite alone. How dreadfully sad that must be. I have three lovely children. You can't see them just now. They are out with their nurse. But now you must tell me all about it.

Mrs Linde. No, no; I want to hear about you.

Nora. No, you must begin. I mustn't be selfish to-day; to-day I must only think of your affairs. But there is one thing I must tell you. Do you know we have just had a great piece of good luck?

Mrs Linde. No, what is it?

Nora. Imagine, my husband has been made manager of the Bank!

Mrs Linde. Your husband? What good luck!

Nora. Yes, tremendous! A barrister's profession is such an uncertain thing, especially if he won't undertake unsavoury cases; and naturally Torvald has never been willing to do that, and I quite agree with him. You can imagine how pleased we are! He is to take up his work in the Bank at the New Year, and then he will have a big salary and lots of commissions. After this we can live quite differently—we can do just as we like. I feel so relieved and so happy, Christine! It will be wonderful to have heaps of money and no worries, won't it?

Mrs Linde. Yes, anyhow I think it would be delightful to have what one needs.

Nora. No, not only what one needs, but heaps and heaps of money.

Mrs Linde (smiling). Nora, Nora, haven't you learnt sense yet? At school you were always a great spendthrift.

Nora (laughing). Yes, that is what Torvald says now. (*Wags her finger at her.*) But 'Nora, Nora' is not so silly as you think. We have not been in a position for me to waste money. We have both had to work.

Mrs Linde. You too?

Nora. Yes; odds and ends, needlework, crotchet-work, embroidery, and that kind of thing. (*Dropping her voice.*) And other things as well. You know Torvald left his office when we were married? There was no prospect of promotion there, and he had to try and earn more than before. But during the first year he overworked himself dreadfully. You see, he had to make money every way he could, and he worked early and late; but he couldn't stand it, and became dreadfully ill, and the doctors said he must go south.

Mrs Linde. You spent a whole year in Italy, didn't you?

Nora. Yes. It was no easy matter to get away, I can tell you. It was just after Ivar was born; but naturally we had to go. It was a wonderfully beautiful journey, and it saved Torvald's life. But it cost a tremendous lot of money, Christine.

Mrs Linde. So I should think.

Nora. It cost about two hundred and fifty pounds. That's a lot, isn't it?

Mrs Linde. Yes, and in emergencies like that it is lucky to have the money.

Nora. I ought to tell you that we had it from father.

Mrs Linde. Oh, I see. It was just about that time that he died, wasn't it?

Nora. Yes; and do you know, I couldn't go and nurse him. I was expecting little Ivar's birth every day and I had my poor sick Torvald to look after. My dear, kind father—I never saw him again, Christine. That was the saddest time I have known since our marriage.

Mrs Linde. I know how fond you were of him. And then you went off to Italy?

Nora. Yes; you see we had money then, and the doctors insisted on our going, so we started a month later.

Mrs Linde. And your husband came back quite well?

Nora. As sound as a bell!

Mrs Linde. But—the doctor?

Nora. What doctor?

Mrs Linde. I thought your maid said the gentleman who arrived here just as I did was the doctor?

Nora. Yes, that was Doctor Rank, but he doesn't come here professionally. He is our greatest friend, and comes in at least once every day. No, Torvald has not had an hour's illness since then, and our children are strong and healthy and so am I. (*Jumps up and claps her hands.*) Christine! Christine! it's good to be alive and happy!—But how horrid of me; I am talking of nothing but my own affairs. (*Sits on a stool near her, and rests her arms on her knees.*) You mustn't be angry with me. Tell me, is it really true that you did not love your husband? Why did you marry him?

Mrs Linde. My mother was alive then, and was bedridden and helpless, and I had to provide for my two younger brothers; so I did not think I was justified in refusing his offer.

Nora. No, perhaps you were quite right. He was rich at that time, then?

Mrs Linde. I believe he was quite well off. But his business was a precarious one; and, when he died, it all went to pieces and there was nothing left.

Nora. And then?——

Mrs Linde. Well, I had to turn my hand to anything I could find—first a small shop, then a small school, and so on. The last three years have seemed like one long working-day, with no rest. Now it is ended, Nora. My poor mother needs me no more, she is gone; and the boys do not need me either; they have got jobs and can fend for themselves.

Nora. What a relief you must feel it——

Mrs Linde. No, indeed; I only feel my life unspeakably empty. No one to live for any more. (*Gets up restlessly.*) That was why I could not stand the life in my little backwater any longer. I hope it may be easier here to find something which will busy me and occupy my thoughts. If only I could be lucky enough to get some regular work—office work of some kind——

Nora. But, Christine, that is so frightfully tiring, and you look tired out now. You had far better go away to the seaside.

Mrs Linde (*walking to the window*). I have no father to give me money for a journey, Nora.

Nora (*rising*). Oh, don't be angry with me.

Mrs Linde (*going up to her*). It is you that must not be angry with me, dear. The worst of a position like mine is that it makes one so bitter. No one to work for, and yet obliged to be always on the look-out for chances. One must live, and so one becomes selfish. When you told me of the happy turn your fortunes have taken—you will hardly believe it—I was delighted not so much on your account as on my own.

Nora. How do you mean?—Oh, I understand. You mean that perhaps Torvald could get you something to do.

Mrs Linde. Yes, that was what I was thinking of.

Nora. He must, Christine. Just leave it to me; I will broach the subject very cleverly—I will think of something that will please him very much. It will make me so happy to be of some use to you.

Mrs Linde. How kind you are, Nora, to be so anxious to help me! It is doubly kind in you, for you know so little of the burdens and troubles of life.

Nora. I——? I know so little of them?

Mrs Linde (*smiling*). My dear! Small household cares and that sort of thing!—You are a child, Nora.

Nora (*tosses her head and crosses the stage*). You ought not to be so superior.

Mrs Linde. No?

Nora. You are just like the others. They all think that I am incapable of anything really serious——

Mrs Linde. Come, come——

Nora. —that I have gone through nothing in this world of cares.

Mrs Linde. But, my dear Nora, you have just told me all your troubles.

Nora. Pooh!—those were trifles. (*Lowering her voice.*) I have not told you the important thing.

Mrs Linde. The important thing? What do you mean?

Nora. You look down upon me altogether, Christine—but you ought not to. You are proud, aren't you, of having worked so hard and so long for your mother?

Mrs Linde. Indeed, I don't look down on anyone. But it is true that I am both proud and glad to think that I was privileged to make the end of my mother's life almost free from care.

Nora. And you are proud to think of what you have done for your brothers.

Mrs Linde. I think I have the right to be.

Nora. I think so, too. But now, listen to this; I too have something to be proud and glad of.

Mrs Linde. I have no doubt you have. But what do you refer to?

Nora. Speak quietly. Suppose Torvald were to hear! He mustn't on any account—no one in the world must know, Christine, except you.

Mrs Linde. But what is it?

Nora. Come here. (*Pulls her down on the sofa beside her.*) Now I will show you that I too have something to be proud and glad of. It was I who saved Torvald's life.

Mrs Linde. 'Saved'? How?

Nora. I told you about our trip to Italy. Torvald would never have recovered if he had not gone there——

Mrs Linde. Yes, but your father gave you the necessary funds.

Nora (*smiling*). Yes, that is what Torvald and all the others think, but——

Mrs Linde. But——

Nora. Father didn't give us a shilling. I was the one who found the money.

Mrs Linde. You? All that large sum?

Nora. Two hundred and fifty pounds. What do you think of that?

Mrs Linde. But, Nora, how could you possibly do it? Did you win a prize in the Lottery?

Nora (*contemptuously*). In the Lottery? There would have been no credit in that.

Mrs Linde. But where did you get it from, then?

Nora (*humming and smiling with an air of mystery*). Hm, hm! Aha!

Mrs Linde. Because you couldn't have borrowed it.

Nora. Couldn't I? Why not?

Mrs Linde. No, a wife cannot borrow without her husband's consent.

Nora (*tossing her head*). Oh, if it is a wife who has any head for business—a wife who has the wit to be a little bit clever——

Mrs Linde. I don't understand it at all, Nora.

Nora. There is no need for you to. I never said I had borrowed the money. I may have got it some other way. (*Lies back on the sofa.*) Perhaps I got it from some other admirer. When anyone is as attractive as I am——

Mrs Linde. You are a mad creature.

Nora. Now, you know you're full of curiosity, Christine.

Mrs Linde. Listen to me, Nora dear. Haven't you been a little bit imprudent?

Nora (*sits up straight*). Is it imprudent to save your husband's life?

Mrs Linde. It seems to me imprudent, without his knowledge, to——

Nora. But it was absolutely necessary that he should not know! My goodness, can't you understand that? It was necessary he should have no idea what a dangerous condition he was in. It was to me that the doctors came and said that his life was in danger, and that the only thing to save him was to live in the south.   Do you suppose I didn't try, first of all, to get what I wanted as if it were for myself?   I told him how much I should love to travel abroad like other young wives; I tried tears and entreaties with him; I told him that he ought to remember the condition I was in, and that he ought to be kind and indulgent to me; I even hinted that he might raise a loan. That nearly made him angry, Christine.   He said I was thoughtless, and that it was his duty as my husband not to indulge me in my whims and caprices—as I believe he called them.   Very well, I thought, you must be saved—and that was how I came to devise a way out of the difficulty——

Mrs Linde. And did your husband never get to know from your father that the money had not come from him?

Nora. No, never.   Father died just at that time.   I had meant to let him into the secret and beg him never to reveal it. But he was so ill then—there never was any need to tell him.

Mrs Linde. And since then have you never told your secret to your husband?

Nora. Good Heavens, no!   How could you think I would? A man who has such strong views about these things!   And besides, how painful and humiliating it would be for Torvald, with his manly independence, to know that he owed me anything!   It would upset our mutual relations altogether; our beautiful happy home would no longer be what it is now.

Mrs Linde. Do you never mean to tell him about it?

Nora (*meditatively, and with a half smile*). Yes—some day, perhaps, after many years, when I am no longer as pretty as I am now.   Don't laugh at me!   I mean, of course, when Torvald is no longer as devoted to me as he is now; when my dancing and dressing-up and reciting have palled on him; then it may be a good thing to have something in reserve—— (*Breaking off.*) What nonsense!   That time will never come.   Now, what do you think of my great secret, Christine?   Do you still think I am useless?   I can tell you, too, that this affair has been terribly worrying.   It has been by no means easy for me to meet my commitments punctually.   I may tell you that there is something that is called, in business, quarterly interest, and another thing called payment in instalments, and it is always so dreadfully difficult to manage them.   I have had to save a little here and there, where I could, you understand.   I haven't been able to put aside much from my housekeeping money, for Torvald likes good food.   I couldn't let my children be shabbily dressed; I have felt I must use up all he gave me for them, the sweet little darlings!

Mrs Linde. So it has all had to come out of your own necessaries of life, poor Nora?

Nora. Of course. Besides, I was the one responsible for it. Whenever Torvald has given me money for new dresses and things like that, I have never spent more than half of it; I have always bought the simplest and cheapest things. Thank Heaven, any clothes look well on me, and so Torvald has never noticed it. But it was often very hard on me, Christine—because it is so nice to be really well dressed, isn't it?

Mrs Linde. Yes, of course.

Nora. Well, then I have found other ways of earning money. Last winter I was lucky enough to get a lot of copying to do; so I locked myself up and sat writing every evening until quite late at night. Often I was desperately tired; but all the same it was a tremendous pleasure to sit there working and earning money. It was like being a man.

Mrs Linde. How much have you been able to pay off in that way?

Nora. I can't tell you exactly. You see, it is very difficult to keep an account of a business matter of that kind. I only know that I have paid every penny that I could scrape together. Quite often I was at my wits' end. (*Smiles.*) Then I used to sit here and imagine that a rich old gentleman had fallen in love with me——

Mrs Linde. What! Who was it?

Nora. Be quiet!—that he had died; and that when his will was opened it contained, written in big letters, the instruction: 'The lovely Mrs Nora Helmer is to have all I possess paid over to her at once in cash.'

Mrs Linde. But, my dear Nora—who could the man be?

Nora. Good gracious, can't you understand? There was no old gentleman at all; it was only something that I used to sit here and imagine, when I couldn't think of any way of procuring money. But it doesn't matter now; the tiresome old man can stay where he is, as far as I am concerned; I don't bother about him or his will either. I am free from care now. (*Jumps up.*) My goodness, it's wonderful to think of, Christine! Free from care! To be able to be free from care, quite free from care; to be able to play and romp with the children; to be able to keep the house beautifully and have everything just as Torvald likes it!

And, think of it, soon the spring will come and the big blue sky! Perhaps we shall be able to take a little trip—perhaps I shall see the sea again! Oh, it's a wonderful thing to be alive and be happy. (*A bell is heard in the hall.*)

Mrs Linde (*rising*). There is the bell; perhaps I had better go.

Nora. No, don't go; no one will come in here; it is sure to be for Torvald.

Servant (*at the hall door*). Excuse me, ma'am—there is a gentleman to see the master, and as the doctor is with him——

Nora. Who is it?

Krogstad (*at the door*). It is- I, Mrs Helmer. (Mrs LINDE *starts, trembles, and turns to the window.*)

Nora (*takes a step towards him, and speaks in a strained, low voice*). You? What is it? What do you want to see my husband about?

Krogstad. Bank business—in a way. I have a small post in the Bank, and I hear your husband is to be our chief now——

Nora. Then it is——

Krogstad. Nothing but dry business matters, Mrs Helmer; absolutely nothing else.

Nora. Will you please go into the study, then. (*She bows indifferently to him and shuts the door into the hall; then comes back and makes up the fire in the stove.*)

Mrs Linde. Nora—who was that man?

Nora. A lawyer, of the name of Krogstad.

Mrs Linde. Then it really was he.

Nora. Do you know the man?

Mrs Linde. I used to—many years ago. At one time he was a solicitor's clerk in our town.

Nora. Yes, he was.

Mrs Linde. He has altered a lot.

Nora. He made a very unhappy marriage.

Mrs Linde. He is a widower now, isn't he?

Nora. With several children. There now, it is burning up. (*Shuts the door of the stove and moves the rocking-chair aside.*)

Mrs Linde. They say he carries on various kinds of business.

Nora. Really! Perhaps he does; I don't know anything about it. But don't let us think of business; it is so tiresome.

Doctor Rank (*comes out of* HELMER'*s study. Before he shuts the door he calls to him*). No, my dear fellow, I won't disturb you; I would rather go in to your wife for a little while. (*Shuts*

the door and sees Mrs LINDE.)   I beg your pardon; I am afraid
I am disturbing you too.

Nora. No, not at all. (*Introducing him.*) Doctor Rank,
Mrs Linde.

Rank. I have often heard Mrs Linde's name mentioned here.
I think I passed you on the stairs when I arrived, Mrs Linde?

Mrs Linde. Yes, I go up very slowly; I can't manage stairs
well.

Rank. Ah! some slight internal weakness?

Mrs Linde. No, the fact is I have been overworking myself.

Rank. Nothing more than that?   Then I suppose you have
come to town to amuse yourself with our entertainments?

Mrs Linde. I have come to look for work.

Rank. Is that a good cure for overwork?

Mrs Linde. One must live, Doctor Rank.

Rank. Yes, the general opinion seems to be that it is necessary.

Nora. Look here, Doctor Rank—you know you want to live.

Rank. Certainly.   However wretched I may feel, I want to
prolong the agony as long as possible.   All my patients are
like that.   And so are those who are morally diseased; one of
them, and a bad case too, is at this very moment with Helmer——

Mrs Linde (*sadly*). Ah!

Nora. Whom do you mean?

Rank. A lawyer by the name of Krogstad, a fellow you don't
know at all.   He suffers from a diseased moral character, Mrs
Helmer; but even he began talking of its being highly important
that he should live.

Nora. Did he?   What did he want to speak to Torvald
about?

Rank. I have no idea; I only heard that it was something
about the Bank.

Nora. I didn't know this—what's his name—Krogstad had
anything to do with the Bank.

Rank. Yes, he has some sort of post there.   (*To* Mrs LINDE.)
I don't know whether you find also in your part of the world
that there are certain people who go zealously snuffing about to
smell out moral corruption, and, as soon as they have found
some, put the person concerned into some lucrative position
where they can keep their eye on him.   Healthy natures are left
out in the cold.

Mrs Linde. Still I think the sick are those who most need
taking care of.

Rank (*shrugging his shoulders*). Yes, there you are.   That is the sentiment that is turning Society into a sick-house.

(NORA, *who has been absorbed in her thoughts, breaks out into smothered laughter and claps her hands.*)

Rank. Why do you laugh at that?   Have you any notion what Society really is?

Nora. What do I care about silly old Society?   I am laughing at something quite different, something extremely amusing. Tell me, Doctor Rank, are all the people who are employed in the Bank dependent on Torvald now?

Rank. Is that what you find so extremely amusing?

Nora (*smiling and humming*). That's my affair! (*Walking about the room.*)   It's perfectly glorious to think that we have— that Torvald has so much power over so many people. (*Takes the packet from her pocket.*)   Doctor Rank, what do you say to a macaroon?

Rank. What, macaroons?   I thought they were forbidden here.

Nora. Yes, but these are some Christine gave me.

Mrs Linde. What! I——

Nora. Oh, well, don't be alarmed!   You couldn't know that Torvald had forbidden them.   I must tell you that he is afraid they will spoil my teeth.   But, gracious!—once in a way——   That's so, isn't it, Doctor Rank?   Excuse me! (*Puts a macaroon into his mouth.*)   You must have one too, Christine.   And I shall have one, just a little one—or at most two. (*Walking about.*)   I am tremendously happy.   There is just one thing in the world now that I should dearly love to do.

Rank. Well, what is that?

Nora. It's something I should dearly love to say, if Torvald could hear me.

Rank. Well, why can't you say it?

Nora. No, I daren't; it's so shocking.

Mrs Linde. Shocking?

Rank. Well, I should not advise you to say it.   Still, with us you might.   What is it you would so much like to say if Torvald could hear you?

Nora. I should just love to say—Well, I'm damned!

Rank. Are you mad?

Mrs Linde. Nora, dear——!

Rank. Say it, here he is!

Nora (*hiding the packet*). Hush!   Hush!   Hush!   (HELMER

*comes out of his room, with his coat over his arm and his hat in
his hand.*)

Nora. Well, Torvald dear, have you got rid of him?

Helmer. Yes, he has just gone.

Nora. Let me introduce you—this is Christine, who has come
to town.

Helmer. Christine——?   I'm sorry, but I don't know——

Nora. Mrs Linde, dear; Christine Linde.

Helmer. Of course.   A school friend of my wife's, I presume?

Mrs Linde. Yes, we have known each other since then.

Nora. And just think, she has come a long way in order
to see you.

Helmer. What do you mean?

Mrs Linde. No, really, I——

Nora. Christine is tremendously clever at book-keeping, and
she is frightfully anxious to work under some clever man, so as
to perfect herself——

Helmer. Very sensible, Mrs Linde.

Nora. And when she heard you had been appointed manager
of the Bank—the news was telegraphed, you know—she
travelled here as quick as she could.   Torvald, I am sure you
will be able to do something for Christine, for my sake, won't
you?

Helmer. Well, it is not altogether impossible.   I presume you
are a widow, Mrs Linde?

Mrs Linde. Yes.

Helmer. And have had some experience of book-keeping?

Mrs Linde. Yes, a fair amount.

Helmer. Ah! well, it's very likely I may be able to find
something for you——

Nora (*clapping her hands*). What did I tell you?   What did
I tell you?

Helmer. You have just come at a fortunate moment, Mrs
Linde.

Mrs Linde. How am I to thank you?

Helmer. There is no need. (*Puts on his coat.*)   But to-day
you must excuse me——

Rank. Wait a minute; I will come with you. (*Brings his
fur coat from the hall and warms it at the fire.*)

Nora. Don't be away long, Torvald dear.

Helmer. About an hour, not more.

Nora. Are you going too, Christine?

Mrs Linde (*putting on her cloak*). Yes, I must go and look for a room.

Helmer. Oh, well then, we can walk down the street together.

Nora (*helping her*). What a pity it is we are so short of space here; I am afraid it is impossible for us——

Mrs Linde. Please don't think of it! Good-bye, Nora dear, and many thanks.

Nora. Good-bye for the present. Of course you will come back this evening. And you too, Dr Rank. What do you say? If you are well enough? Oh, you must be! Wrap yourself up well. (*They go to the door all talking together. Children's voices are heard on the staircase.*)

Nora. There they are! There they are! (*She runs to open the door. The* NURSE *comes in with the children.*) Come in! Come in! (*Stoops and kisses them.*) Oh, you sweet blessings! Look at them, Christine! Aren't they darlings?

Rank. Don't let us stand here in the draught.

Helmer. Come along, Mrs Linde; the place will only be bearable for a mother now!

(RANK, HELMER, *and* MRS LINDE *go downstairs. The* NURSE *comes forward with the children; NORA shuts the hall door.*)

Nora. How fresh and well you look! Such red cheeks!— like apples and roses. (*The children all talk at once while she speaks to them.*) Have you had great fun? That's splendid! What, you pulled both Emmy and Bob along on the sledge? —both at once?—that *was* good. You are a clever boy, Ivar. Let me take her for a little, Anne. My sweet little baby doll! (*Takes the baby from the* MAID *and dances it up and down.*) Yes, yes, mother will dance with Bob too. What! Have you been snowballing? I wish I had been there too! No, no, I'll take their things off, Anne; please let me do it, it is such fun. Go in now, you look half frozen. There is some hot coffee for you on the stove.

(*The* NURSE *goes into the room on the left.* NORA *takes off the children's things and throws them about, while they all talk to her at once.*)

Nora. Really! Did a big dog run after you? But it didn't bite you? No, dogs don't bite nice little dolly children. You mustn't look at the parcels, Ivar. What are they? Ah, I dare say you would like to know. No, no—it's something nasty! Come, let us have a game! What shall we play at? Hide and Seek? Yes, we'll play Hide and Seek. Bob shall hide first. Must I hide? All right, I'll hide first. (*She and the children laugh and shout, and romp in and out of the room; at last* NORA *hides under the table, the children rush in and out, looking for her, but do not see her; they hear her smothered laughter, run to the table, lift up the cloth, and find her. Shouts of laughter. She crawls forward and pretends to frighten them. Fresh laughter. Meanwhile there has been a knock at the hall door, but none of them has noticed it. The door is half opened, and* KROGSTAD *appears. He waits a little; the game goes on.*)

Krogstad. Excuse me, Mrs Helmer.

Nora (*with a stifled cry, turns round and gets up on to her knees*). Oh! what do you want?

Krogstad. Forgive me, the outer door was ajar; I suppose someone forgot to shut it.

Nora (*rising*). My husband is out, Mr Krogstad.

Krogstad. I know that.

Nora. What do you want here, then?

Krogstad. A word with you.

Nora. With me?—— (*To the children, gently.*) Go in to nurse. What? No, the strange man won't do mother any harm. When he has gone we will have another game. (*She takes the children into the room on the left, and shuts the door after them.*) You want to speak to me?

Krogstad. Yes, I do.

Nora. To-day? It is not the first of the month yet.

Krogstad. No, it's Christmas Eve, and it will depend on *you* what sort of a Christmas you will spend.

Nora. What do you mean? To-day it is absolutely impossible for me——

Krogstad. We won't talk about that till later on. This is something different. I presume you can give me a moment?

Nora. Yes—yes, I can—although——

Krogstad. Good. I was in Olsen's Restaurant and saw your husband going down the street——

Nora. Yes?

Krogstad. With a lady.

Nora. What then?

Krogstad. May I inquire if it was a Mrs Linde?

Nora. It was.

Krogstad. Just arrived in town?

Nora. Yes, to-day.

Krogstad. She is a great friend of yours, isn't she?

Nora. She is.   But I don't see——

Krogstad. I knew her too, once upon a time.

Nora. I am aware of that.

Krogstad. Are you?   So you know all about it; I thought as much.   Then I can ask you, without beating about the bush —is Mrs Linde to have a job in the Bank?

Nora. What right have you to question me, Mr Krogstad? —You, one of my husband's subordinates!   But since you ask, you shall know.   Yes, Mrs Linde *is* to have a job.   And it was I who pleaded her cause, Mr Krogstad, let me tell you that.

Krogstad. I was right in what I thought, then.

Nora (*walking up and down the stage*).   Sometimes one has a tiny little bit of influence, I should hope.   Because one is a woman, it does not necessarily follow that——   When anyone is in a subordinate position, Mr Krogstad, they should really be careful to avoid offending anyone who—who——

Krogstad. Who has influence?

Nora. Exactly.

Krogstad (*changing his tone*).   Mrs Helmer, you will kindly use your influence on my behalf.

Nora. What?   What do you mean?

Krogstad. You will kindly see that I am allowed to keep my subordinate position in the Bank.

Nora. What do you mean by that?   Who proposes to take your post away from you?

Krogstad. Oh, there is no necessity to keep up the pretence of ignorance.   I can quite understand that your friend is not very anxious to expose herself to the chance of rubbing shoulders with me; and I quite understand, too, whom I have to thank for being turned off.

Nora. But I assure you——

Krogstad. Very likely; but, to come to the point, the time has come when I should advise you to use your influence to prevent that.

Nora. But, Mr Krogstad, I *have* no influence.

Krogstad. Haven't you?   I thought you said yourself just now——

Nora. Naturally I did not mean you to put that construction on it.   I!   What should make you think I have any influence of that kind with my husband?

Krogstad. Oh, I have known your husband from our student

days. I don't suppose he is any more unassailable than other husbands.

Nora. If you speak slightingly of my husband, I shall turn you out of the house.

Krogstad. You are bold, Mrs Helmer.

Nora. I am not afraid of you any longer. As soon as the New Year comes, I shall be free of the whole thing in a very short time.

Krogstad (controlling himself). Listen to me, Mrs Helmer. If necessary, I am prepared to fight for my small job in the Bank as if I were fighting for my life.

Nora. So it seems.

Krogstad. It's not only for the sake of the money; as a matter of fact, that weighs least with me in the matter. There is another reason—well, I may as well tell you. My position is this. I dare say you know, like everybody else, that once, many years ago, I was guilty of an indiscretion.

Nora. I think I have heard something of the kind.

Krogstad. The matter never came into court; but every way seemed to be closed to me after that. So I took to the business that you know of. I had to do something; and, honestly, I don't think I've been one of the worst. But now I must cut myself free from all that. My sons are growing up; for their sake I must try and win back as much respect as I can in the town. This job in the Bank was like the first step up for me— and now your husband is going to kick me downstairs again into the mud.

Nora. But you must believe me, Mr Krogstad; it is not in my power to help you at all.

Krogstad. Then it is because you haven't the will; but I have means to compel you.

Nora. You don't mean that you will tell my husband that I owe you money?

Krogstad. Hm!—suppose I were to tell him?

Nora. It would be perfectly infamous of you. (*Sobbing.*) To think of his learning my secret, which has been my pride and joy, in such an ugly, clumsy way—that he should learn it from you! And it would put me in a horribly disagreeable position——

Krogstad. Only disagreeable?

Nora (impetuously). Well, do it, then!—and it will be the worse for you. My husband will see for himself what a blackguard you are, and you certainly won't keep your job then.

Krogstad. I asked you if it was only a disagreeable scene at home that you were afraid of?

Nora. If my husband does get to know of it, of course he will at once pay you what is still owing, and we shall have nothing more to do with you.

Krogstad (*coming a step nearer*). Listen to me, Mrs Helmer. Either you have a very bad memory or you know very little of business. I shall have to remind you of a few details.

Nora. What do you mean?

Krogstad. When your husband was ill, you came to me to borrow two hundred and fifty pounds.

Nora. I didn't know anyone else to go to.

Krogstad. I promised to get you that amount——

Nora. Yes, and you did so.

Krogstad. I promised to get you that amount, on certain conditions. Your mind was so taken up with your husband's illness, and you were so anxious to get the money for your journey, that you seem to have paid no attention to the conditions of our bargain. Therefore it will not be amiss if I remind you of them. Now, I promised to get the money on the security of a bond which I drew up.

Nora. Yes, and which I signed.

Krogstad. Good. But below your signature there were a few lines constituting your father a surety for the money; those lines your father should have signed.

Nora. Should? He did sign them.

Krogstad. I had left the date blank; that is to say, your father should himself have inserted the date on which he signed the paper. Do you remember that?

Nora. Yes, I think I remember——

Krogstad. Then I gave you the bond to send by post to your father. Isn't that so?

Nora. Yes.

Krogstad. And you naturally did so at once, because five or six days afterwards you brought me the bond with your father's signature. And then I gave you the money.

Nora. Well, haven't I been paying it off regularly?

Krogstad. Fairly regularly, yes. But—to come back to the matter in hand—that must have been a very trying time for you, Mrs Helmer?

Nora. It was, indeed.

Krogstad. Your father was very ill, wasn't he?

Nora. He was very near his end.

Krogstad. And died soon afterwards?

Nora. Yes.

Krogstad. Tell me, Mrs Helmer, can you by any chance remember what day your father died?—on what day of the month, I mean.

Nora. Father died on the 29th of September.

Krogstad. That is correct; I have ascertained it for myself. And, as that is so, there is a discrepancy (*taking a paper from his pocket*) which I cannot account for.

Nora. What discrepancy?   I don't know——

Krogstad. The discrepancy consists, Mrs Helmer, in the fact that your father signed this bond three days after his death.

Nora. What do you mean?   I don't understand——

Krogstad. Your father died on the 29th of September.   But, look here; your father has dated his signature the 2nd of October. It is a discrepancy, isn't it?   (NORA *is silent.*)   Can you explain it to me?   (NORA *is still silent.*)   It is a remarkable thing, too, that the words '2nd of October,' as well as the year, are not written in your father's handwriting but in one that I think I know.   Well, of course it can be explained; your father may have forgotten to date his signature, and someone else may have dated it haphazard before they knew of his death.   There is no harm in that.   It all depends on the signature of the name; and *that* is genuine, I suppose, Mrs Helmer?   It was your father himself who signed his name here?

Nora (*after a short pause, throws her head up and looks defiantly at him*). No, it was not.   It was I who wrote father's name.

Krogstad. Are you aware that is a dangerous confession?

Nora. In what way?   You shall have your money soon.

Krogstad. Let me ask you a question; why did you not send the paper to your father?

Nora. It was impossible; father was so ill.   If I had asked him for his signature, I should have had to tell him what the money was to be used for; and when he was so ill himself I couldn't tell him that my husband's life was in danger—it was impossible.

Krogstad. It would have been better for you if you had given up your trip abroad.

Nora. No, that was impossible.   That trip was to save my husband's life; I couldn't give that up.

Krogstad. But did it never occur to you that you were committing a fraud on me?

Nora. I couldn't take that into account; I didn't trouble myself about you at all.   I couldn't bear you, because you put so many heartless difficulties in my way, although you knew what a dangerous condition my husband was in.

Krogstad. Mrs Helmer, you evidently do not realize clearly what it is that you have been guilty of.   But I can assure you that my one false step, which lost me all my reputation, was nothing more or nothing worse than what you have done.

Nora. You?   Do you ask me to believe that you were brave enough to run a risk to save your wife's life?

Krogstad. The law cares nothing about motives.

Nora. Then it must be a very foolish law.

Krogstad. Foolish or not, it is the law by which you will be judged, if I produce this paper in court.

Nora. I don't believe it.   Is a daughter not to be allowed to spare her dying father anxiety and care?   Is a wife not to be allowed to save her husband's life?   I don't know much about law; but I am certain that there must be laws permitting such things as that.   Have you no knowledge of such laws—you who are a lawyer?   You must be a very poor lawyer, Mr Krogstad.

Krogstad. Maybe.   But matters of business—such business as you and I have had together—do you think I don't understand that?   Very well.   Do as you please.   But let me tell you this—if I lose my position a second time, you shall lose yours with me.   (*He bows, and goes out through the hall.*)

Nora (*appears buried in thought for a short time, then tosses her head*).   Nonsense!   Trying to frighten me like that!— I am not as silly as he thinks.   (*Begins to busy herself putting the children's things in order.*)   And yet——?   No, it's impossible!   I did it for love's sake.

The Children (*in the doorway on the left*).   Mother, the stranger man has gone out through the gate.

Nora. Yes, dears, I know.   But, don't tell anyone about the stranger man.   Do you hear?   Not even father.

Children. No, mother; but will you come and play again?

Nora. No, no—not now.

Children. But, mother, you promised us.

Nora. Yes, but I can't now.   Run along in; I have such a lot to do.   Run along in, my sweet little darlings.   (*She gets them into the room by degrees and shuts the door on them; then sits down on the sofa, takes up a piece of needlework, and sews a few stitches, but soon stops.)* No! (*Throws down the work, gets up, goes to the hall door, and calls out.*) Helen! bring the tree in) (*Goes to the table on the left, opens a drawer, and stops again..* No, no! it is quite impossible!

Maid (*coming in with the tree*). Where shall I put it, ma'am?

Nora. Here, in the middle of the floor.

Maid. Shall I get you anything else?

Nora. No, thank you. I have all I want.   [*Exit* MAID.

Nora (*begins decorating the tree*). A candle here—and flowers here—— The horrible man! It's all nonsense—there's nothing wrong. The tree shall be marvellous! I will do everything I can think of to please you, Torvald!—I will sing for you, dance for you—— (HELMER *comes in with some papers under his arm.*) Oh! are you back already?

Helmer. Yes. Has anyone been here?

Nora. Here? No.

Helmer. That's strange. I saw Krogstad going out of the gate.

Nora. Did you? Oh yes, I forgot, Krogstad was here for a moment.

Helmer. Nora, I can see from your manner that he has been here begging you to say a good word for him.

Nora. Yes.

Helmer. And you were to appear to do it of your own accord; you were to conceal from me the fact of his having been here; didn't he beg that of you too?

Nora. Yes, Torvald, but——

Helmer. Nora, Nora, and you would be a party to that sort of thing? To have any talk with a man like that, and give him any sort of promise? And to tell me a lie into the bargain?

Nora. A lie——?

Helmer. Didn't you tell me no one had been here? (*Shakes his finger at her.*) My little song-bird must never do that again. A song-bird must have a clean beak to chirp with—no false notes! (*Puts his arm round her waist.*) That is so, isn't it? Yes, I am sure it is. (*Lets her go.*) We will say no more about it. (*Sits down by the stove.*) How warm and snug it is here! (*Turns over his papers.*)

Nora (*after a short pause, during which she busies herself with the Christmas-tree.*) Torvald!

Helmer. Yes.

Nora. I am looking forward tremendously to the fancy-dress ball at the Stenborgs' the day after to-morrow.

Helmer. And I am tremendously curious to see what you are going to surprise me with.

Nora. It was very silly of me to want to do that.

Helmer. What do you mean?

Nora. I can't hit upon anything that will do; everything I think of seems so silly and insignificant.

Helmer. Does my little Nora acknowledge that at last?

Nora (*standing behind his chair with her arms on the back of it*). Are you very busy, Torvald?

Helmer. Well——

Nora. What are all those papers?

Helmer. Bank business.

Nora. Already?

Helmer. I have got authority from the retiring manager to undertake the necessary changes in the staff and in the rearrangement of the work; and I must make use of the Christmas week for that, so as to have everything in order for the new year.

Nora. Then that was why this poor Krogstad——

Helmer. Hm!

Nora (*leans against the back of his chair and strokes his hair*). If you hadn't been so busy I should have asked you a tremendously big favour, Torvald.

Helmer. What is that? Tell me.

Nora. There is no one has such good taste as you. And I do so want to look nice at the fancy-dress ball. Torvald, couldn't you take me in hand and decide what I shall go as, and what sort of a dress I shall wear?

Helmer. Aha! so my obstinate little woman is obliged to get someone to come to her rescue?

Nora. Yes, Torvald, I can't get along a bit without your help.

Halmer. Very well, I will think it over, we shall manage to hit upon something.

Nora. That is nice of you. (*Goes to the Christmas-tree. A short pause.*) How pretty the red flowers look—— But, tell me, was it really something very bad that this Krogstad was guilty of?

Helmer. He forged someone's name. Have you any idea what that means?

Nora. Isn't it possible that he was driven to do it by necessity?

Helmer. Yes; or, as in so many cases, by imprudence. I am

not so heartless as to condemn a man altogether because of a single false step of that kind.

Nora. No, you wouldn't, would you, Torvald?

Helmer. Many a man has been able to retrieve his character, if he has openly confessed his fault and taken his punishment.

Nora. Punishment——?

Helmer. But Krogstad did nothing of that sort; he got himself out of it by a cunning trick, and that is why he has gone under altogether.

Nora. But do you think it would——?

Helmer. Just think how a guilty man like that has to lie and play the hypocrite with everyone, how he has to wear a mask in the presence of those near and dear to him, even before his own wife and children. And about the children—that is the most terrible part of it all, Nora.

Nora. How?

Helmer. Because such an atmosphere of lies infects and poisons the whole life of a home. Each breath the children take in such a house is full of the germs of evil.

Nora (coming nearer him). Are you sure of that?

Helmer. My dear, I have often seen it in the course of my life as a lawyer. Almost everyone who has gone to the bad early in life has had a deceitful mother.

Nora. Why do you only say—mother?

Helmer. It seems most commonly to be the mother's influence, though naturally a bad father's would have the same result. Every lawyer is familiar with the fact. This Krogstad, now, has been persistently poisoning his own children with lies and dissimulation; that is why I say he has lost all moral character. *(Holds out his hands to her.)* That is why my sweet little Nora must promise me not to plead his cause. Give me your hand on it. Come, come, what is this? Give me your hand. There now, that's settled. I assure you it would be quite impossible for me to work with him; I literally feel physically ill when I am in the company of such people.

Nora (takes her hand out of his and goes to the opposite side of the Christmas-tree). It's terribly hot in here; and I have such a lot to do.

Helmer (getting up and putting his papers in order). Yes, and I must try and read through some of these before dinner; and I must think about your costume, too. And it is just possible I may have something ready in gold paper to hang up on the tree. (*Puts his hand on her head.*) My precious little singing-bird! (*He goes into his room and shuts the door after him.*)

Nora (*after a pause, whispers*). No, no—it isn't true. It's impossible; it must be impossible.

(*The* NURSE *opens the door on the left.*)

Nurse. The little ones are begging so hard to be allowed to come in to mother.

Nora. No, no, no! Don't let them come in to me! You stay with them, Anne.

Nurse. Very well, ma'am. (*Shuts the door.*)

Nora (*pale with terror*). Deprave my little children? Poison my home? (*A short pause. Then she tosses her head.*) It's not true. It can't possibly be true.

ACT II

(THE SAME SCENE.—*The Christmas-tree is in the corner by the piano, stripped of its ornaments and with burnt-down candle-ends on its dishevelled branches.* NORA's *cloak and hat are lying on the sofa. She is alone in the room, walking about uneasily. She stops by the sofa and takes up her cloak.*)

Nora (*drops her cloak*). Someone is coming now! (*Goes to the door and listens.*) No—it's no one. Of course, no one will come to-day, Christmas Day—nor to-morrow either. But, perhaps—(*opens the door and looks out*). No, nothing in the letter-box; it's quite empty. (*Comes forward.*) What rubbish! of course he can't be in earnest about it. Such a thing couldn't happen; it is impossible—I have three little children.

(*Enter the* NURSE *from the room on the left, carrying a big cardboard box.*)

Nurse. At last I have found the box with the fancy dress.

Nora. Thanks; put it on the table.

Nurse (*doing so*). But it is very much in need of mending.

Nora. I should like to tear it into a hundred thousand pieces.

Nurse. What an idea! It can easily be put in order—just a little patience.

Nora. Yes, I will go and get Mrs Linde to come and help me with it.

Nurse. What, out again? In this horrible weather? You will catch cold, ma'am, and make yourself ill.

Nora. Well, worse than that might happen. How are the children?

Nurse. The poor little souls are playing with their Christmas presents, but——

Nora. Do they ask much for me?

Nurse. You see, they are so accustomed to have their mother with them.

Nora. Yes, but, nurse, I shall not be able to be so much with them now as I was before.

Nurse. Oh well, young children easily get accustomed to anything.

Nora. Do you think so? Do you think they would forget their mother if she went away altogether?

Nurse. Good heavens!—went away altogether?

Nora. Nurse, I want you to tell me something I have often wondered about—how could you have the heart to put your own child out among strangers?

Nurse. I was obliged to, if I wanted to be little Nora's nurse.

Nora. Yes, but how could you be willing to do it?

Nurse. What, when I was going to get such a good place by it? A poor girl who has got into trouble should be glad to. Besides, that wicked man didn't do a single thing for me.

Nora. But I suppose your daughter has quite forgotten you.

Nurse. No, indeed she hasn't. She wrote to me when she was confirmed, and when she was married.

Nora (*putting her arms round her neck*). Dear old Anne, you were a good mother to me when I was little.

Nurse. Little Nora, poor dear, had no other mother but me.

Nora. And if my little ones had no other mother, I am sure you would—— What nonsense I am talking! (*Opens the box.*) Go in to them. Now I must—— You will see to-morrow how lovely I shall look.

Nurse. I am sure there will be no one at the ball as lovely as you, ma'am. (*Goes into the room on the left.*)

Nora (*begins to unpack the box, but soon pushes it away from her*). If only I dared go out. If only no one would come. If only I could be sure nothing would happen here in the meantime. How absurd! No one will come. Only I mustn't think about it. I will brush my muff. What pretty, pretty gloves! Out of my thoughts, out of my thoughts! One, two, three, four, five, six—— (*Screams.*) Oh! there is someone coming—— (*Makes a movement towards the door, but stands irresolute.*)

(*Enter* Mrs Linde *from the hall, where she has taken off her cloak and hat.*)

Nora. Oh, it's you, Christine. There is no one else out there, is there? How good of you to come!

Mrs Linde. I heard you were up asking for me.

Nora. Yes, I was passing by. As a matter of fact, it is something you could help me with. Let us sit down here on the sofa. Look here. To-morrow evening there is to be a fancy-dress ball at the Stenborgs', who live above us; and Torvald wants me to go as a Neapolitan fisher-girl, and dance the Tarantella that I learnt at Capri.

Mrs Linde. I see; you are going to keep up the character.

Nora. Yes, Torvald wants me to. Look, here is the dress; Torvald had it made for me there, but now it is all so torn, and I haven't any idea——

Mrs Linde. We will easily put that right. It is only some of the trimming come unsewn here and there. Needle and cotton? Now then, that's all we want.

Nora. It *is* nice of you.

Mrs Linde (*sewing*). So you are going to be dressed up to-morrow, Nora. I'll tell you what—I shall come in for a moment and see you in your fine feathers. But I have completely forgotten to thank you for a delightful evening yesterday.

Nora (*gets up, and crosses the stage*). Well, I don't think yesterday was as pleasant as usual. You ought to have come to town a little earlier, Christine. Certainly Torvald does understand how to make a house dainty and attractive.

Mrs Linde. And so do you, it seems to me; you are not your father's daughter for nothing. But tell me, is Doctor Rank always as depressed as he was yesterday?

Nora. No; yesterday it was very noticeable. You see he suffers from a very dangerous disease. He has tuberculosis of the spine, poor creature. His father was a horrible man who committed all sorts of excesses; and that is why his son was sickly from childhood, do you understand?

Mrs Linde (*dropping her sewing*). But, my dearest Nora, how do you know anything about such things?

Nora (*walking about*). Pooh! When you have three children, you get visits now and then from—from married women, who know something of medical matters, and they talk about one thing and another.

Mrs Linde (*goes on sewing. A short silence*). Does Doctor Rank come here every day?

Nora. Every day regularly. He is Torvald's most intimate friend, and a great friend of mine too. He is just like one of the family.

Mrs Linde. But tell me this—is he perfectly sincere? I mean, isn't he the kind of man who is very anxious to make himself agreeable?

Nora. Not in the least. What makes you think that?

Mrs Linde. When you introduced him to me yesterday, he declared he had often heard my name mentioned in this house; but afterwards I noticed that your husband hadn't the slightest idea who I was. So how could Doctor Rank——?

Nora. That's quite right, Christine. Torvald is so absurdly fond of me that he wants me absolutely to himself, as he says. At first he used to seem almost jealous if I mentioned any of the dear folk at home, so naturally I gave up doing so. But I often talk about such things with Doctor Rank, because he likes hearing about them.

Mrs Linde. Listen to me, Nora. You are still very like a child in many things, and I am older than you in many ways and have a little more experience. Let me tell you this—you ought to make an end of it with Doctor Rank.

Nora. What ought I to make an end of?

Mrs Linde. Of two things, I think. Yesterday you talked some nonsense about a rich admirer who was to leave you money——

Nora. An admirer who doesn't exist, unfortunately! But what then?

Mrs Linde. Is Doctor Rank a man of means?

Nora. Yes, he is.

Mrs Linde. And has no one to provide for?

Nora. No, no one; but——

Mrs Linde. And comes here every day?

Nora. Yes, I told you so.

Mrs Linde. But how can this well-bred man be so tactless?

Nora. I don't understand you at all.

Mrs Linde. Don't prevaricate, Nora. Do you suppose I don't guess who lent you the two hundred and fifty pounds?

Nora. Are you out of your senses? How can you think of such a thing! A friend of ours, who comes here every day! Do you realize what a horribly painful position that would be?

Mrs Linde. Then it really isn't him?

Nora. No, certainly not. It would never have entered my head for a moment. Besides, he had no money to lend then; he came into his money afterwards.

Mrs Linde. Well, I think that was lucky for you, my dear Nora.

Nora. No, it would never have come into my head to ask Doctor Rank. Although I am quite sure that if I had asked him——

Mrs Linde. But of course you won't.

Nora. Of course not. I have no reason to think it could possibly be necessary. But I am quite sure that if I told Doctor Rank——

Mrs Linde. Behind your husband's back?

Nora. I must make an end of it with the other one, and that will be behind his back too. I *must* make an end of it with him.

Mrs Linde. Yes, that is what I told you yesterday, but——

Nora (*walking up and down*). A man can put a thing like that straight much easier than a woman——

Mrs Linde. One's husband, yes.

Nora. Nonsense! (*Standing still.*) When you pay off a debt you get your bond back, don't you?

Mrs Linde. Yes, as a matter of course.

Nora. And can tear it into a hundred thousand pieces, and burn it up—the nasty dirty paper!

Mrs Linde (*looks hard at her, lays down her sewing, and gets up slowly*). Nora, you are concealing something from me.

Nora. Do I look as if I were?

Mrs Linde. Something has happened to you since yesterday morning. Nora, what is it?

Nora (*going nearer to her*). Christine! (*Listens.*) Hush! there's Torvald come home. Do you mind going in to the children for the present? Torvald can't bear to see dressmaking going on. Let Anne help you.

Mrs Linde (*gathering some of the things together*). Certainly—but I am not going away from here till we have had it out with one another. (*She goes into the room on the left, as* HELMER *comes in from the hall.*)

Nora (*going up to* HELMER). I have wanted you so much, Torvald dear.

Helmer. Was that the dressmaker?

Nora. No, it was Christine; she is helping me to put my dress in order.   You will see I shall look quite smart.

Helmer. Wasn't that a happy thought of mine, now?

Nora. Splendid!   But don't you think it is nice of me, too, to do as you wish?

Helmer. Nice?—because you do as your husband wishes? Well, well, you little rogue, I am sure you didn't mean it in that way.   But I am not going to disturb you; you will want to be trying on your dress, I expect.

Nora. I suppose you are going to work.

Helmer. Yes.   (*Shows her a bundle of papers.*)   Look at that. I have just been into the Bank.   (*Turns to go into his room.*)

Nora. Torvald.

Helmer. Yes.

Nora. If your little squirrel were to ask you for something very, very prettily——?

Helmer. What then?

Nora. Would you do it?

Helmer. I should like to hear what it is, first.

Nora. Your squirrel would run about and do all her tricks if you would be nice, and do what she wants.

Helmer. Speak plainly.

Nora. Your skylark would chirp about in every room, with her song rising and falling——

Helmer. Well, my skylark does that anyhow.

Nora. I would play the fairy and dance for you in the moonlight, Torvald.

Helmer. Nora—you surely don't mean that request you made to me this morning?

Nora (*going near him*). Yes, Torvald, I beg you so earnestly——

Helmer. Have you really the courage to open up that question again?

Nora. Yes, dear, you *must* do as I ask; you *must* let Krogstad keep his post in the Bank.

Helmer. My dear Nora, it is his post that I have arranged Mrs Linde shall have.

Nora. Yes, you have been awfully kind about that; but you could just as well dismiss some other clerk instead of Krogstad.

Helmer. This is simply incredible obstinacy!   Because you chose to give him a thoughtless promise that you would speak for him, I am expected to——

Nora. That isn't the reason, Torvald. It is for your own sake. This fellow writes in the most scurrilous newspapers; you have told me so yourself. He can do you an unspeakable amount of harm. I am frightened to death of him——

Helmer. Ah, I understand; it is recollections of the past that scare you.

Nora. What do you mean?

Helmer. Naturally you are thinking of your father.

Nora. Yes—yes, of course. Remember what these malicious creatures wrote in the papers about father, and how horribly they slandered him. I believe they would have procured his dismissal if the Ministry hadn't sent you over to inquire into it, and if you hadn't been so kindly disposed and helpful to him.

Helmer. My little Nora, there is an important difference between your father and me. Your father's reputation as a public official was not above suspicion. Mine is, and I hope it will continue to be so, as long as I hold my office.

Nora. You never can tell what mischief these men may contrive. We ought to be so well off, so snug and happy here in our peaceful home, and have no cares—you and I and the children, Torvald! That is why I beg you so earnestly——

Helmer. And it is just by interceding for him that you make it impossible for me to keep him. Is it already known at the Bank that I mean to dismiss Krogstad. Is it to get about now that the new manager has changed his mind at his wife's bidding——

Nora. And what if it did?

Helmer. Of course!—if only this obstinate little person can get her way! Do you suppose I am going to make myself ridiculous before my whole staff, to let people think that I am a man to be swayed by all sorts of outside influence? I should very soon feel the consequences of it, I can tell you! And besides, there is one thing that makes it quite impossible for me to have Krogstad in the Bank as long as I am manager.

Nora. Whatever is that?

Helmer. His moral failings I might perhaps have overlooked, if necessary——

Nora. Yes, you could—couldn't you?

Helmer. And I hear he is a good worker, too. But I knew him when we were boys. It was one of those rash friendships that so often prove an embarassment later. I may as well tell you plainly, we were once on very intimate terms with one another. But this tactless fellow has no restraint when other people are present. On the contrary, he thinks it gives him the right to adopt a familiar tone with me, and every minute it is 'I say, Helmer, old fellow!' and that sort of thing. I assure you it is extremely painful for me. He would make my position in the Bank intolerable.

Nora. Torvald, I don't believe you mean that.

Helmer. Don't you? Why not?

Nora. Because it is such a narrow-minded way of looking at things.

Helmer. What are you saying? Narrow-minded? Do you think I am narrow-minded?

Nora. No, just the opposite, dear—and it is exactly for that reason.

Helmer. It's the same thing. You say my point of view is narrow-minded, so I must be so too. Narrow-minded! Very well—I must put an end to this. (*Goes to the hall door and calls.*) Helen!

Nora. What are you going to do?

Helmer (*looking among his papers*). Settle it. (*Enter* MAID.) Look here; take this letter and go downstairs with it at once. Find a messenger and tell him to deliver it, and be quick. The address is on it, and here is the money.

Maid. Very well, sir. (*Exit with the letter.*)

Helmer (*putting his papers together*). Now then, little Miss Obstinate.

Nora (*breathlessly*). Torvald—what was that letter?

Helmer. Krogstad's dismissal.

Nora. Call her back, Torvald! There is still time. Oh Torvald, call her back! Do it for my sake—for your own sake—for the children's sake! Do you hear me, Torvald? Call her back! You don't know what that letter can bring upon us.

Helmer. It's too late.

Nora. Yes, it's too late.

Helmer. My dear Nora, I can forgive the anxiety you are in, although really it is an insult to me. It is, indeed. Isn't it an insult to think that I should be afraid of a starving pen-pusher's vengeance? But I forgive you nevertheless, because it is such eloquent witness to your great love for me. (*Takes her in his arms.*) And that is as it should be, my own darling Nora. Come what will, you may be sure I shall have both courage and strength if they be needed.   You will see I am man enough to take everything upon myself.

Nora (*in a horror-stricken voice*). What do you mean by that?

Helmer. Everything, I say——

Nora (*recovering herself*). You will never have to do that.

Helmer. That's right.   Well, we will share it, Nora, as man and wife should.   That is how it shall be. (*Caressing her.*) Are you content now?   There! there!—not these frightened dove's eyes!   The whole thing is only the wildest fancy!—— Now, you must go and play through the Tarantella and practise with your tambourine.   I shall go into the inner office and shut the door, and I shall hear nothing; you can make as much noise as you please. (*Turns back at the door.*)   And when Rank comes, tell him where he will find me. (*Nods to her, takes his papers and goes into his room, and shuts the door after him.*)

Nora (*bewildered with anxiety, stands as if rooted to the spot, and whispers*).   He was capable of doing it.   He will do it.   He will do it in spite of everything.—No, not that!   Never, never! Anything rather than that!   Oh, for some help, some way out of it! (*The doorbell rings.*)   Doctor Rank!   Anything rather than that—anything, whatever it is! (*She puts her hands over her face, pulls herself together, goes to the door, and opens it.   RANK is standing outside, hanging up his coat.   During the following dialogue it begins to grow dark.*)

Nora. Good afternoon, Doctor Rank.   I knew your ring. But you mustn't go in to Torvald now; I think he is busy with something.

Rank. And you?

Nora (*brings him in and shuts the door after him*).   Oh, you know very well I always have time for you.

Rank. Thank you.   I shall make use of as much of it as I can.

Nora. What do you mean by that?   As much of it as you can?

Rank. Well, does that alarm you?

Nora. It was such a strange way of putting it.   Is anything likely to happen?

Rank. Nothing but what I have long been prepared for.   But I certainly didn't expect it to happen so soon.

Nora (*gripping him by the arm*).   What have you found out? Doctor Rank, you must tell me.

Rank (*sitting down by the stove*).   It is all up with me.   And it can't be helped.

Nora (*with a sigh of relief*).   Is it about yourself?

Rank. Who else? It is no use lying to one's self. I am the most wretched of all my patients, Mrs Helmer. Lately I have been taking stock of my internal economy. Bankrupt! Probably within a month I shall lie rotting in the churchyard.

Nora. What an ugly thing to say!

Rank. The thing itself is cursedly ugly, and the worst of it is that I shall have to face so much more that is ugly before that. I shall only make one more examination of myself; when I have done that, I shall know pretty certainly when it will be that the horrors of dissolution will begin. There is something I want to tell you. Helmer's refined nature gives him an unconquerable disgust at everything that is ugly; I won't have him in my sick-room.

Nora. Oh, but, Doctor Rank——

Rank. I won't have him there. Not on any account. I bar my door to him. As soon as I am quite certain that the worst has come, I shall send you my card with a black cross on it, and then you will know that the loathsome end has begun.

Nora. You are quite absurd to-day. And I wanted you so much to be in a really good humour.

Rank. With death stalking beside me?—To have to pay this penalty for another man's sin! Is there any justice in that? And in every single family, in one way or another, some such inexorable retribution is being exacted——

Nora (*putting her hands over her ears*). Rubbish! Do talk about something cheerful.

Rank. Oh, it's a mere laughing matter, the whole thing. My poor innocent spine has to suffer for my father's youthful amusements.

Nora (*sitting at the table on the left*). I suppose you mean that he was too partial to asparagus and pâté de foie gras, don't you?

Rank. Yes, and to truffles.

Nora. Truffles, yes. And oysters too, I suppose?

Rank. Oysters, of course, that goes without saying.

Nora. And heaps of port and champagne. It is sad that all these nice things should take their revenge on our bones.

Rank. Especially that they should revenge themselves on the unlucky bones of those who have not had the satisfaction of enjoying them.

Nora. Yes, that's the saddest part of it all.

Rank (*with a searching look at her*). Hm!——

Nora (*after a short pause*). Why did you smile?

Rank. No, it was you that laughed.

Nora. No, it was you that smiled, Doctor Rank!

Rank (*rising*). You are a greater rascal than I thought.

Nora. I am in a silly mood to-day.

Rank. So it seems.

Nora (*putting her hands on his shoulders*). Dear, dear Doctor Rank, death mustn't take you away from Torvald and me.

Rank. It is a loss you would easily recover from. Those who are gone are soon forgotten.

Nora (*looking at him anxiously*). Do you believe that?

Rank. People form new ties, and then——

Nora. Who will form new ties?

Rank. Both you and Helmer, when I am gone. You yourself are already on the high road to it, I think. What did that Mrs Linde want here last night?

Nora. Oho!—you don't mean to say you are jealous of poor Christine?

Rank. Yes, I am. She will be my successor in this house. When I am done for, this woman will——

Nora. Hush! don't speak so loud. She is in that room.

Rank. To-day again. There, you see.

Nora. She has only come to sew my dress for me. Good gracious, how unreasonable you are! (*Sits down on the sofa.*) Be nice now, Doctor Rank, and to-morrow you'll see how beautifully I shall dance, and you can imagine I am doing it all for you —and for Torvald too, of course. (*Takes various things out of the box.*) Doctor Rank, come and sit down here, and I will show you something.

Rank (*sitting down*). What is it?

Nora. Just look at those!

Rank. Silk stockings.

Nora. Flesh-coloured. Aren't they lovely? It is so dark here now, but to-morrow—— No, no, no! you must only look at the feet. Oh well, you may have permission to look at the legs too.

Rank. Hm!——

Nora. Why are you looking so critical? Don't you think they will fit me?

Rank. I have no means of forming an opinion about that.

Nora (*looks at him for a moment*). Shame on you! (*Hits him lightly on the ear with the stockings.*) That's to punish you. (*Folds them up again.*)

Rank. And what other nice things am I to be allowed to see?

Nora. Not a single thing more, for being so naughty. (*She looks among the things, humming to herself.*)

Rank (*after a short silence*). When I am sitting here, talking to you as intimately as this, I cannot imagine for a moment what would have become of me if I had never come into this house.

Nora (*smiling*). I believe you do feel thoroughly at home with us.

Rank (*in a lower voice, looking straight in front of him*). And to have to leave it all——

Nora. Nonsense, you are not going to leave it.

Rank (*as before*). And not be able to leave behind one the slightest token of one's gratitude, barely a fleeting regret even—nothing but an empty place which the first comer can fill as well as any other.

Nora. And if I asked you now for a——? No!

Rank. For what?

Nora. For a big proof of your friendship——

Rank. Yes, yes!

Nora. I mean a tremendously big favour——

Rank. Would you really make me so happy for once?

Nora. Ah, but you don't know what it is yet.

Rank. No—but tell me.

Nora. I really can't, Doctor Rank. It is something out of all reason; it means advice, and help, and a favour——

Rank. The bigger a thing it is the better. I can't conceive what it is you mean. Do tell me. Haven't I your confidence?

Nora. More than anyone else. I know you are my truest and best friend, and so I will tell you what it is. Well, Doctor Rank, it is something you must help me to prevent. You know how devotedly, how inexpressibly deeply Torvald loves me; he would never for a moment hesitate to give his life for me.

Rank (*leaning towards her*). Nora—do you think he is the only one——?

Nora (*with a slight start*). The only one——?

Rank. The only one who would gladly give his life for your sake.

Nora (*sadly*). Is that it?

Rank. I was determined you should know it before I went away, and there will never be a better opportunity than this. Now you know it, Nora. And now you know, too, that you can trust me as you would trust no one else.

Nora (rises, deliberately and quietly). Let me pass.

Rank (makes room for her to pass him, but sits still). Nora!

Nora (at the hall door). Helen, bring in the lamp. (*Goes over to the stove.*) Dear Doctor Rank, that was really horrid of you.

Rank. To have loved you as much as anyone else does? Was that horrid?

Nora. No, but to go and tell me so. There was really no need——

Rank. What do you mean? Did you know——? (MAID *enters with lamp, puts it down on the table, and goes out.*) Nora—Mrs Helmer—tell me, had you any idea of this?

Nora. Oh, how do I know whether I had or whether I hadn't? I really can't tell you—— To think you could be so clumsy, Doctor Rank! We were getting on so nicely.

Rank. Well, at all events you know now that you can command me, body and soul. So won't you speak out?

Nora (looking at him). After what happened?

Rank. I beg you to let me know what it is.

Nora. I can't tell you anything now.

Rank. Yes, yes. You mustn't punish me in that way. Let me have permission to do for you whatever a man may do.

Nora. You can do nothing for me now. Besides, I really don't need any help at all. You will find that the whole thing is merely fancy on my part. It really is so—of course it is! (*Sits down in the rocking-chair, and looks at him with a smile.*) You are a nice sort of man, Doctor Rank!—don't you feel ashamed of yourself, now the lamp has come?

Rank. Not a bit. But perhaps I had better go—for ever?

Nora. No, indeed, you shall not. Of course you must come here just as before. You know very well Torvald can't do without you.

Rank. Yes, but you?

Nora. Oh, I am always tremendously pleased when you come.

Rank. It is just that, that put me on the wrong track. You are a riddle to me. I have often thought that you would almost as soon be in my company as in Helmer's.

Nora. Yes—you see there are some people one loves best, and others whom one would almost always rather have as companions.

Rank. Yes, there is something in that.

Nora. When I was at home, of course I loved father best. But I always thought it tremendous fun if I could steal down into the maids' room, because they never moralized at all, and talked to each other about such entertaining things.

Rank. I see—it is *their* place I have taken.

Nora (*jumping up and going to him*). Oh, dear, nice Doctor Rank, I never meant that at all. But surely you can understand that being with Torvald is a little like being with father——

(*Enter* MAID *from the hall.*)

Maid. If you please, ma'am. (*Whispers and hands her a card.*)

Nora (*glancing at the card*). Oh! (*Puts it in her pocket.*)

Rank. Is there anything wrong?

Nora. No, no, not in the least. It is only something—it is my new dress——

Rank. What? Your dress is lying there.

Nora. Oh, yes, that one; but this is another. I ordered it. Torvald mustn't know about it——

Rank. Oho! Then that was the great secret.

Nora. Of course. Do go in to him; he is sitting in the inner room. Keep him as long as——

Rank. Don't worry; I won't let him escape. (*Goes into* HELMER'S *room.*)

Nora (*to the* MAID). And he is standing waiting in the kitchen?

Maid. Yes; he came up the back stairs.

Nora. But didn't you tell him no one was in?

Maid. Yes, but it was no good.

Nora. He won't go away?

Maid. No; he says he won't until he has seen you, ma'am.

Nora. Well, let him come in—but quietly. Helen, you mustn't say anything about it to anyone. It is a surprise for my husband.

Maid. Yes, ma'am, I quite understand. (*Exit.*)

Nora. This dreadful thing is going to happen! It will happen in spite of me! No, no, no, it can't happen—it shan't happen! (*She bolts the door of* HELMER'S *room. The* MAID *opens the hall door for* KROGSTAD *and shuts it after him. He is wearing a fur coat, high boots, and a fur cap.*)

Nora (*advancing towards him*). Speak quietly—my husband is at home.

Krogstad. I don't care about that.

Nora. What do you want of me?

Krogstad. An explanation of something.

Nora. Hurry up then. What is it?

Krogstad. You know, I suppose, that I have got my dismissal.

Nora. I couldn't prevent it, Mr Krogstad. I fought as hard as I could on your side, but it was no good.

Krogstad. Does your husband love you so little, then? He knows what I can expose you to, and yet he ventures——

Nora. How can you suppose that he has any knowledge of the sort?

Krogstad. I didn't suppose so at all. It would not be the least like our dear Torvald Helmer to show so much courage——

Nora. Mr Krogstad, a little respect for my husband, please.

Krogstad. Certainly—all the respect he deserves. But since you have kept the matter so carefully to yourself, I can only suppose that you have a little clearer idea, than you had yesterday, of what it actually is that you have done?

Nora. More than you could ever teach me.

Krogstad. Yes, such a bad lawyer as I am.

Nora. What is it you want of me?

Krogstad. Only to see how you were, Mrs Helmer. I have been thinking about you all day long. A mere cashier, a pen-pusher, a—well, a man like me—even he has a little of what is called feeling, you know.

Nora. Show it, then; think of my little children.

Krogstad. Have you and your husband thought of mine? But never mind about that. I only wanted to tell you that you need not take this matter too seriously. In the first place there will be no accusation made on my part.

Nora. No, of course not; I was sure of that.

Krogstad. The whole thing can be arranged amicably; there is no reason why anyone should know anything about it. It will remain a secret between us three.

Nora. My husband must never get to know anything about it.

Krogstad. How will you be able to prevent it? Am I to understand that you can pay the balance that is owing?

Nora. No, not just at present.

Krogstad. Or perhaps that you have some expedient for raising the money soon?

Nora. No expedient that I mean to make use of.

Krogstad. Well, in any case, it would have been of no use to you now. If you stood there with ever so much money in your hand, I would never part with your bond.

Nora. Tell me what purpose you mean to put it to.

Krogstad. I shall only preserve it—keep it in my possession.

No one who is not concerned in the matter shall have the slightest hint of it. So that if the thought of it has driven you to any desperate resolution——

Nora. It has.

Krogstad. If you had it in your mind to run away from your home——

Nora. I had.

Krogstad. Or even something worse——

Nora. How could you know that?

Krogstad. Give up the idea.

Nora. How did you know I had thought of *that*?

Krogstad. Most of us think of that at first. I did, too—but I hadn't the courage.

Nora (*faintly*). Nor had I.

Krogstad (*in a tone of relief*). No, that's it, isn't it—you hadn't the courage either?

Nora. No, I haven't—I haven't.

Krogstad. Besides, it would have been a very foolish thing. Once the first storm at home is over—— I have a letter for your husband in my pocket.

Nora. Telling him everything?

Krogstad. In as lenient a manner as I possibly could.

Nora (*quickly*). He mustn't get the letter. Tear it up. I'll find some means of getting money.

Krogstad. Excuse me, Mrs Helmer, but I think I told you just now——

Nora. I am not speaking of what I owe you. Tell me what sum you are asking my husband for, and I will get the money.

Krogstad. I am not asking your husband for a penny.

Nora. What do you want, then?

Krogstad. I will tell you. I want to rehabilitate myself, Mrs Helmer; I want to get on; and in that your husband must help me. For the last year and a half I have not had a hand in anything dishonourable, and all that time I have been struggling in most restricted circumstances. I was content to work my way up step by step. Now I am turned out, and I am not going to be satisfied with merely being taken into favour again. I want to get on, I tell you. I want to get into the Bank again, in a higher position. Your husband must make a place for me——

Nora. That he will never do!

Krogstad. He will; I know him; he dare not protest. And as soon as I am in there again with him, then you will see! Within a year I shall be the manager's right hand. It will be Nils Krogstad and not Torvald Helmer who manages the Bank.

Nora. That's a thing you will never see!

Krogstad. Do you mean that you will——?

Nora. I have courage enough for it now.

Krogstad. Oh, you can't frighten me. A fine, spoilt woman like you——

Nora. You will see, you will see.

Krogstad. Under the ice, perhaps? Down into the cold, coal-black water? And then, in the spring, to float up to the surface, all horrible and unrecognizable, with your hair fallen out——

Nora. You can't frighten me.

Krogstad. Nor you me. People don't do such things, Mrs Helmer. Besides, what use would it be? I should have him completely in my power all the same.

Nora. Afterwards? When I am no longer——

Krogstad. Have you forgotten that it is I who have the keeping of your reputation? (NORA *stands speechlessly looking at him.*) Well, now, I have warned you. Don't do anything foolish. When Helmer has had my letter, I shall expect a message from him. And be sure you remember that it is your husband himself who has forced me into such ways as this again. I will never forgive him for that. Good-bye, Mrs Helmer. (*Exit through the hall.*)

Nora (*goes to the hall door, opens it slightly, and listens.*) He is going. He is not putting the letter in the box. Oh no, no! that's impossible! (*Opens the door by degrees.*) What is that? He is standing outside. He is not going downstairs. Is he hesitating? Can he——? (*A letter drops into the box; then* KROGSTAD'S *footsteps are heard, till they die away as he goes down-stairs.* NORA *utters a stifled cry, and runs across the room to the table by the sofa. A short pause.*)

Nora. In the letter-box. (*Steals across to the hall door.*) It's lying there—Torvald, Torvald, there is no hope for us now!

(Mrs LINDE *comes in from the room on the left, carrying the dress.*)

Mrs Linde. There, I can't see anything more to mend now. Would you like to try it on——?

Nora (*in a hoarse whisper*). Christine, come here.

Mrs Linde (*throwing the dress down on the sofa*). What is the matter with you? You look so agitated!

Nora. Come here. Do you see that letter? There, look—you can see it through the glass in the letter-box.

Mrs Linde. Yes, I see it.

Nora. That letter is from Krogstad.

Mrs Linde. Nora—it was Krogstad who lent you the money!

Nora. Yes, and now Torvald will know all about it.

Mrs Linde. Believe me, Nora, that's the best thing for both of you.

Nora. You don't know all. I forged a name.

Mrs Linde. Good heavens——!

Nora. I only want to say this to you, Christine—you must be my witness.

Mrs Linde. Your witness? What do you mean? What am I to——?

Nora. If I should go out of my mind—and it might easily happen——

Mrs Linde. Nora!

Nora. Or if anything else should happen to me—anything, for instance, that might prevent my being here——

Mrs Linde. Nora! Nora! you are quite out of your mind.

Nora. And if it should happen that there were someone who wanted to take all the responsibility, all the blame, you understand——

Mrs Linde. Yes, yes—but how can you suppose——?

Nora. Then you must be my witness, that it is not true, Christine. I am not out of my mind at all; I am in my right senses now, and I tell you no one else has known anything about it; I, and I alone, did the whole thing. Remember that.

Mrs Linde. I will, indeed. But I don't understand all this.

Nora. How should you understand it? A wonderful thing is going to happen!

Mrs Linde. A wonderful thing?

Nora. Yes, a wonderful thing!—But it is so terrible, Christine; it *mustn't* happen, not for all the world.

Mrs Linde. I will go at once and see Krogstad.

Nora. Don't go to him; he will do you some harm.

Mrs Linde. There was a time when he would gladly do anything for my sake.

Nora. He?

Mrs Linde. Where does he live?

Nora. How should I know——? Yes (*feeling in her pocket*), here is his card. But the letter, the letter——!

Helmer (*calls from his room, knocking at the door*). Nora!

Nora (*cries out anxiously*). Oh, what's that? What do you want?

Helmer. Don't be so frightened. We are not coming in; you have locked the door. Are you trying on your dress?

Nora. Yes, that's it. I look so nice, Torvald.

Mrs Linde (*who has read the card*). I see he lives at the corner here.

Nora. Yes, but it's no use. It is hopeless. The letter is lying there in the box.

Mrs Linde. And your husband keeps the key?

Nora. Yes, always.

Mrs Linde. Krogstad must ask for his letter back unread, he must find some excuse——

Nora. But it is just at this time that Torvald generally——

Mrs Linde. You must delay him. Go in to him in the meantime. I'll come back as soon as I can. (*She goes out hurriedly through the hall door.*)

Nora (*goes to* HELMER'*s door, opens it, and peeps in*). Torvald!

Helmer (*from the inner room*). Well? May I venture at last to come into my own room again? Come along, Rank, now you will see—— (*Halting in the doorway.*) But what is this?

Nora. What is what, dear?

Helmer. Rank led me to expect a splendid transformation.

Rank (*in the doorway*). I understood so, but evidently I was mistaken.

Nora. Yes, nobody is to have the chance of admiring me in my dress until to-morrow.

Helmer. But, my dear Nora, you look so worn out. Have you been practising too much?

Nora. No, I have not practised at all.

Helmer. But you will need to——

Nora. Yes, indeed I shall, Torvald. But I can't get on a bit without you to help me; I have absolutely forgotten the whole thing.

Helmer. Oh, we will soon work it up again.

Nora. Yes, help me, Torvald. Promise that you will! I am so nervous about it—all the people—— You must give yourself up to me entirely this evening. Not the tiniest bit of business—you mustn't even take a pen in your hand. Will you promise, Torvald dear?

Helmer. I promise. This evening I will be wholly and

absolutely at your service, you helpless little mortal. Ah, by the way, first of all I will just—— (*Goes towards the hall door.*)

Nora. What are you going to do there?

Helmer. Only to see if any letters have come.

Nora. No, no! don't do that, Torvald!

Helmer. Why not?

Nora. Torvald, please don't. There is nothing there.

Helmer. Well, let me look. (*Turns to go to the letter-box.* NORA, *at the piano, plays the first bars of the Tarantella.* HELMER *stops in the doorway.*) Aha!

Nora. I can't dance to-morrow if I don't practise with you.

Helmer (*going up to her*). Are you really so afraid of it, dear?

Nora. Yes, so dreadfully afraid of it. Let me practise at once; there is time now, before we go to dinner. Sit down and play for me, Torvald dear; criticize me, and correct me as you play.

Helmer. With great pleasure, if you wish me to. (*Sits down at the piano.*)

Nora (*takes out of the box a tambourine and a long variegated shawl. She hastily drapes the shawl round her. Then she springs to the front of the stage and calls out*). Now play for me! I am going to dance!

(HELMER *plays and* NORA *dances.* RANK *stands by the piano behind* HELMER, *and looks on.*)

Helmer (*as he plays*). Slower, slower!

Nora. I can't do it any other way.

Helmer. Not so violently, Nora!

Nora. This is the way.

Helmer (*stops playing*). No, no—that is not a bit right.

Nora (*laughing and swinging the tambourine*). Didn't I tell you so?

Rank. Let me play for her.

Helmer (*getting up*). Yes, do. I can correct her better then.

(RANK *sits down at the piano and plays.* NORA *dances more and more wildly.* HELMER *has taken up a position beside the stove, and during her dance gives her frequent instructions. She does not seem to hear him; her hair comes down and falls over her shoulders; she pays no attention to it, but goes on dancing. Enter* MRS LINDE.)

Mrs Linde (*standing as if spell-bound in the doorway*). Oh!——

Nora (*as she dances*). Such fun, Christine!

Helmer. My dear darling Nora, you are dancing as if your life depended on it.

Nora. So it does.

Helmer. Stop, Rank; this is sheer madness. Stop, I tell you! (RANK *stops playing, and* NORA *suddenly stands still.* HELMER *goes up to her.*) I could never have believed it. You have forgotten everything I taught you.

Nora (*throwing away the tambourine*). There, you see.

Helmer. You will want a lot of coaching.

Nora. Yes, you see how much I need it. You must coach me up to the last minute. Promise me that, Torvald!

Helmer. You can depend on me.

Nora. You must not think of anything but me, either to-day or to-morrow; you mustn't open a single letter—not even open the letter-box——

Helmer. Ah, you are still afraid of that fellow——

Nora. Yes, indeed I am.

Helmer. Nora, I can tell from your looks that there is a letter from him lying there.

Nora. I don't know; I think there is; but you mustn't read anything of that kind now. Nothing horrid must come between us till this is all over.

Rank (*whispers to* HELMER). You mustn't contradict her.

Helmer (*taking her in his arms*). The child shall have her way. But to-morrow night, after you have danced——

Nora. Then you will be free. (*The* MAID *appears in the doorway to the right.*)

Maid. Dinner is served, ma'am.

Nora. We will have champagne, Helen.

Maid. Very good, ma'am.   [*Exit.*

Helmer. Hallo!—are we going to have a banquet?

Nora. Yes, a champagne banquet till the small hours. (*Calls out.*) And a few macaroons, Helen—lots, just for once!

Helmer. Come, come, don't be so wild and nervous. Be my own little skylark, as you used.

Nora. Yes, dear, I will. But go in now, and you too, Doctor Rank. Christine, you must help me to do up my hair.

Rank (*whispers to* HELMER *as they go out*). I suppose there is nothing—she is not expecting anything?

Helmer. Far from it, my dear fellow; it is simply nothing more than this childish nervousness I was telling you of. (*They go into the right-hand room.*)

Nora. Well!

Mrs Linde. Gone out of town.

Nora. I could tell from your face.

Mrs Linde. He is coming home to-morrow evening. I wrote a note for him.

Nora. You should have let it alone; you must prevent nothing. After all, it is splendid to be waiting for a wonderful thing to happen.

Mrs Linde. What is it that you are waiting for?

Nora. Oh, you wouldn't understand. Go in to them, I will come in a moment. (Mrs LINDE *goes into the dining-room.* NORA *stands still for a little while, as if to compose herself. Then she looks at her watch.*) Five o'clock. Seven hours till midnight; and then twenty-four hours till the next midnight. Then the Tarantella will be over. Twenty-four and seven? Thirty-one hours to live.

Helmer (*from the doorway on the right*). Where's my little skylark?

Nora (*going to him with her arms outstretched*). Here she is!

ACT III

(THE SAME SCENE.—*The table has been placed in the middle of the stage, with chairs round it. A lamp is burning on the table. The door into the hall stands open. Dance music is heard in the room above.* Mrs LINDE *is sitting at the table idly turning over the leaves of a book; she tries to read, but does not seem able to collect her thoughts. Every now and then she listens intently for a sound at the outer door.*)

Mrs Linde (*looking at her watch*). Not yet—and the time is nearly up. If only he does not—— (*Listens again.*) Ah, there he is. (*Goes into the hall and opens the outer door carefully. Light footsteps are heard on the stairs. She whispers.*) Come in. There is no one here.

Krogstad (*in the doorway*). I found a note from you at home. What does this mean?

Mrs Linde. It is absolutely necessary that I should have a talk with you.

Krogstad. Really? And is it absolutely necessary that it should be here?

Mrs Linde. It is impossible where I live; there is no private entrance to my rooms. Come in; we are quite alone. The maid is asleep, and the Helmers are at the dance upstairs.

Krogstad (coming into the room). Are the Helmers really at a dance to-night?

Mrs Linde. Yes, why not?

Krogstad. Certainly—why not?

Mrs Linde. Now, Nils, let us have a talk.

Krogstad. Can we two have anything to talk about?

Mrs Linde. We have a great deal to talk about.

Krogstad. I shouldn't have thought so.

Mrs Linde. No, you have never properly understood me.

Krogstad. Was there anything else to understand except what was obvious to all the world—a heartless woman jilts a man when a more lucrative chance turns up?

Mrs Linde. Do you believe I am as absolutely heartless as all that? And do you believe that I did it with a light heart?

Krogstad. Didn't you?

Mrs Linde. Nils, did you really think that?

Krogstad. If it were as you say, why did you write to me as you did at the time?

Mrs Linde. I could do nothing else. As I had to break with you, it was my duty also to put an end to all that you felt for me.

Krogstad (wringing his hands). So that was it. And all this— only for the sake of money!

Mrs Linde. You mustn't forget that I had a helpless mother and two little brothers. We couldn't wait for you, Nils; your prospects seemed hopeless then.

Krogstad. That may be so, but you had no right to throw me over for anyone else's sake.

Mrs Linde. I really don't know. Often I used to ask myself if I had the right to do it.

Krogstad (more gently). When I lost you, it was as if all the solid ground went from under my feet. Look at me now—I am a shipwrecked man clinging to a bit of wreckage.

Mrs Linde. But help may be near.

Krogstad. It *was* near; but then you came and stood in my way.

Mrs Linde. Unintentionally, Nils. It was only to-day that I learnt it was your place I was going to take in the Bank.

Krogstad. I believe you, if you say so. But now that you know it, are you not going to give it up to me?

Mrs Linde. No, because that wouldn't benefit you in the least.

Krogstad. Oh, benefit, benefit—I would have done it, benefit or not.

Mrs Linde. I have learnt to act prudently. Life, and hard, bitter necessity have taught me that.

Krogstad. And life has taught me not to believe in fine speeches.

Mrs Linde. Then life has taught you something very sensible. But deeds you must believe in?

Krogstad. What do you mean by that?

Mrs Linde. You said you were like a shipwrecked man clinging to some wreckage.

Krogstad. I had good reason to say so.

Mrs Linde. Well, I am like a shipwrecked woman clinging to some wreckage—no one to mourn for, no one to care for.

Krogstad. It was your own choice.

Mrs Linde. There was no other choice—then.

Krogstad. Well, what now?

Mrs Linde. Nils, how would it be if we two shipwrecked people could join forces?

Krogstad. What are you saying?

Mrs Linde. Two on the same piece of wreckage would stand a better chance than each on their own.

Krogstad. Christine!

Mrs Linde. What do you suppose brought me to town?

Krogstad. Do you mean that you gave me a thought?

Mrs Linde. I could not endure life without work. All my life, as long as I can remember, I have worked, and it has been my greatest and only pleasure. But now I am quite alone in the world—my life is so dreadfully empty and I feel so forsaken. There is not the least pleasure in working for one's self. Nils, give me someone and something to work for.

Krogstad. I don't trust that. It is nothing but a woman's overstrained sense of generosity that prompts you to make such an offer of yourself.

Mrs Linde. Have you ever noticed anything of the sort in me?

Krogstad. Could you really do it? Tell me—do you know all about my past life?

Mrs Linde. Yes.

Krogstad. And do you know what they think of me here?

Mrs Linde. You seemed to me to imply that with me you might have been quite another man.

Krogstad. I am certain of it.

Mrs Linde. Is it too late now?

Krogstad. Christine, are you saying this deliberately? Yes, I am sure you are. I see it in your face. Have you really the courage, then——?

Mrs Linde. I want to be a mother to someone, and your children need a mother. We two need each other. Nils, I have faith in your real character—I can dare anything together with you.

Krogstad (*grasps her hands*). Thanks, thanks, Christine! Now I shall find a way to clear myself in the eyes of the world. Ah, but I forgot——

Mrs Linde (*listening*). Hush! The Tarantella! Go, go!

Krogstad. Why? What is it?

Mrs Linde. Do you hear them up there? When that is over, we can expect them back.

Krogstad. Yes, yes—I'll go. But it's all no use. Of course you don't know what steps I have taken in the matter of the Helmers.

Mrs Linde. Yes, I know all about that.

Krogstad. And in spite of that have you the courage to——?

Mrs Linde. I understand very well to what lengths a man like you might be driven by despair.

Krogstad. If I could only undo what I have done!

Mrs Linde. You cannot. Your letter is lying in the letter-box now.

Krogstad. Are you sure of that?

Mrs Linde. Quite sure, but——

Krogstad (*with a searching look at her*). Is that what it all means?—that you want to save your friend at any cost? Tell me frankly. Is that it?

Mrs Linde. Nils, a woman who has once sold herself for another's sake, doesn't do it a second time.

Krogstad. I will ask for my letter back.

Mrs Linde. No, no.

Krogstad. Yes, of course I will. I will wait here till Helmer comes; I will tell him he must give me my letter back—that it only concerns my dismissal—that he is not to read it——

Mrs Linde. No, Nils, you must not recall your letter.

Krogstad. But, tell me, wasn't it for that very purpose that you asked me to meet you here?

Mrs Linde. In my first moment of fright, it was. But twenty-four hours have passed since then, and in that time I have witnessed incredible things in this house. Helmer must know all about it. This unhappy secret must be disclosed; they must have a complete understanding between them, which is impossible with all this concealment and falsehood going on.

Krogstad. All right, if you will take the responsibility. But there is one thing I can do in any case, and I shall do it at once.

Mrs Linde (*listening*). You must be quick and go! The dance is over; we aren't safe a moment longer.

Krogstad. I'll wait for you below.

Mrs Linde. Yes, do. You must see me back to my door.

Krogstad. I have never had such an amazing piece of good fortune in my life! (*Goes out through the outer door. The door between the room and the hall remains open.*)

Mrs Linde (*tidying up the room and laying her hat and cloak ready*). What a difference! what a difference! Someone to work for and live for—a home to bring comfort into. That I will do, indeed. I wish they would be quick and come—— (*Listens.*) Ah, there they are now. I must put on my things. (*Takes up her hat and cloak.* HELMER's *and* NORA's *voices are heard outside; a key is turned, and* HELMER *brings* NORA *almost by force into the hall. She is in an Italian costume with a large black shawl round her; he is in evening dress, and a black domino which is flying open.*)

Nora (*hanging back in the doorway, and struggling with him*). No, no, no!—don't take me in. I want to go upstairs again; I don't want to leave so early.

Helmer. But, my dearest Nora——

Nora. Please, Torvald dear—please, *please*—only an hour more.

Helmer. Not a single minute, my sweet Nora. You know that was our agreement. Come along into the room; you are catching cold standing there. (*He brings her gently into the room, in spite of her resistance.*)

Mrs Linde. Good evening.

Nora. Christine!

Helmer. You here, so late, Mrs Linde?

Mrs Linde. Yes, you must forgive me; I was so anxious to see Nora in her dress. ·

Nora. Have you been sitting here waiting for me?

Mrs Linde. Yes, unfortunately I came too late, you had already gone upstairs; and I thought I couldn't go away again without having seen you.

Helmer (*taking off* NORA's *shawl*). Yes, take a good look at her. I think she is worth looking at.   Isn't she charming, Mrs Linde?

Mrs Linde. Yes, indeed she is.

Helmer. Doesn't she look remarkably pretty? Everyone thought so at the dance. But she is terribly self-willed, this sweet little person. What are we to do with her? You'll hardly believe that I almost had to bring her away by force.

Nora. Torvald, you will repent not having let me stay, even if it were only for half an hour.

Helmer. Listen to her, Mrs Linde! She had danced her Tarantella, and it had been a tremendous success, as it deserved —although possibly the performance was a trifle too realistic— a little more so, I mean, than was strictly compatible with the limitations of art. But never mind about that! The chief thing is, she had made a success—she had made a tremendous success. Do you think I was going to let her remain there after that, and spoil the effect? No, indeed! I took my charming little Capri maiden—my capricious little Capri maiden, I should say—on my arm; took one quick turn round the room; a curtsy on either side, and, as they say in novels, the beautiful apparition disappeared. An exit ought always to be effective, Mrs Linde; but that is what I cannot make Nora understand. Pooh! this room is hot. (*Throws his domino on a chair, and opens the door of his room.*) Hallo! it's all dark in here. Oh, of course— excuse me—— (*He goes in, and lights some candles.*)

Nora (*in a hurried and breathless whisper*). Well?

Mrs Linde (*in a low voice*). I have had a talk with him.

Nora. Yes, and——

Mrs Linde. Nora, you must tell your husband all about it.

Nora (*in an expressionless voice*). I knew it.

Mrs Linde. You have nothing to be afraid of as far as Krogstad is concerned; but you must tell him.

Nora. I won't tell him.

Mrs Linde. Then the letter will.

Nora. Thank you, Christine. Now I know what I must do. Hush——!

Helmer (*coming in again*). Well, Mrs Linde, have you admired her?

Mrs Linde. Yes, and now I will say good night.

Helmer. What, already? Is this yours, this knitting?

Mrs Linde (taking it). Yes, thank you, I had very nearly forgotten it.

Helmer. So you knit?

Mrs Linde. Of course.

Helmer. Do you know, you ought to embroider.

Mrs Linde. Really? Why?

Helmer. Yes, it's far more becoming. Let me show you. You hold the embroidery thus in your left hand, and use the needle with the right—like this—with a long, easy sweep. Do you see?

Mrs Linde. Yes, perhaps——

Helmer. But in the case of knitting—that can never be anything but ungraceful; look here—the arms close together, the knitting-needles going up and down—it has a sort of Chinese effect—— That was really excellent champagne they gave us.

Mrs Linde. Well—good night, Nora, and don't be self-willed any more.

Helmer. That's right, Mrs Linde.

Mrs Linde. Good night, Mr Helmer.

Helmer (accompanying her to the door). Good night, good night. I hope you will get home all right. I should be very happy to—but you haven't any great distance to go. Good night, good night. (*She goes out; he shuts the door after her, and comes in again.*) Ah!—at last we have got rid of her. She is a frightful bore, that woman.

Nora. Aren't you very tired, Torvald?

Helmer. No, not in the least.

Nora. Nor sleepy?

Helmer. Not a bit. On the contrary, I feel extraordinarily lively. And you?—you really look both tired and sleepy.

Nora. Yes, I am very tired. I want to go to sleep at once.

Helmer. There, you see it was quite right of me not to let you stay there any longer.

Nora. Everything you do is quite right, Torvald.

Helmer (kissing her on the forehead). Now my little skylark is speaking reasonably. Did you notice what good spirits Rank was in this evening?

Nora. Really? Was he? I didn't speak to him at all.

Helmer. And I very little, but I haven't for a long time seen him in such good form. (*Looks for a while at her and then goes nearer to her.*) It is wonderful to be at home by ourselves again, to be all alone with you—you fascinating, charming little darling!

Nora. Don't look at me like that, Torvald.

Helmer. Why shouldn't I look at my dearest treasure?—at all the beauty that is mine, all my very own?

Nora (*going to the other side of the table*). You mustn't say things like that to me to-night.

Helmer (*following her*). You have still got the Tarantella in your blood, I see. And it makes you more captivating than ever. Listen—the guests are beginning to go now. (*In a lower voice.*) Nora—soon the whole house will be quiet.

Nora. Yes, I hope so.

Helmer. Yes, my own darling Nora. Do you know, when I am out at a party with you like this, why I speak so little to you, why I keep away from you, and only send a stolen glance in your direction now and then?—do you know why I do that? It is because I make believe to myself that we are secretly in love, and you are my secretly promised bride, and that no one suspects there is anything between us.

Nora. Yes, yes—I know quite well your thoughts are with me all the time.

Helmer. And when we are leaving, and I am putting the shawl over your beautiful young shoulders—on your lovely neck —then I imagine that you are my young bride and that we have just come from the wedding, and I am bringing you for the first time into our home—to be alone with you for the first time— quite alone with my shy little darling! All this evening I have longed for nothing but you. When I watched the seductive figures of the Tarantella, my blood was on fire; I could endure it no longer, and that was why I brought you down so early——

Nora. Go away, Torvald! You must let me go. I won't——

Helmer. What's that? You're joking, my little Nora! You won't—you won't? Am I not your husband——? (*A knock is heard at the outer door.*)

Nora (*starting*). Did you hear——?

Helmer (*going into the hall*). Who is it?

Rank (*outside*). It's me. May I come in for a moment?

Helmer (*in a fretful whisper*). Oh, what does he want now? (*Aloud.*) Wait a minute! (*Unlocks the door.*) Well, that's kind of you not to pass by our door.

Rank. I thought I heard your voice, and felt as if I should like to look in. (*With a swift glance round.*) Ah, yes!—these dear familiar rooms.   You are very happy and cosy in here, you two.

Helmer. It seems to me that you looked after yourself pretty well upstairs too.

Rank. Excellently.   Why shouldn't I?   Why shouldn't one enjoy everything in this world?—at any rate as much as one can, and as long as one can.   The wine was capital——

Helmer. Especially the champagne.

Rank. So you noticed that too?   It is almost incredible how much I managed to put away!

Nora. Torvald drank a great deal of champagne to-night too.

Rank. Did he?

Nora. Yes, and he is always in such good spirits afterwards.

Rank. Well, why should one not enjoy a merry evening after a well-spent day?

Helmer. Well spent?   I am afraid I can't take credit for that.

Rank (*clapping him on the back*). But I can, you know!

Nora. Doctor Rank, you must have been occupied with some scientific investigation to-day.

Rank. Exactly.

Helmer. Just listen!—little Nora talking about scientific investigations!

Nora. And may I congratulate you on the result?

Rank. Indeed you may.

Nora. Was it favourable, then?

Rank. The best possible, for both doctor and patient—certainty.

Nora (*quickly and searchingly*). Certainty?

Rank. Absolute certainty.   So wasn't I entitled to make a merry evening of it after that?

Nora. Yes, you certainly were, Doctor Rank.

Helmer. I think so too, so long as you don't have to pay for it in the morning.

Rank. Oh well, one can't have anything in this life without paying for it.

Nora. Doctor Rank—do you like fancy-dress balls?

Rank. Yes, if there is a fine lot of pretty costumes.

Nora. Tell me—what shall we two wear at the next?

Helmer. Little featherbrain!—are you thinking of the next already?

Rank. We two?   Yes, I can tell you.   You shall go as a good fairy——

Helmer. Yes, but what do you suggest as an appropriate costume for that?

Rank. Let your wife go dressed just as she is in everyday life.

Helmer. That was really very nicely said. But can't you tell us what you will be?

Rank. Yes, my dear friend, I have quite made up my mind about that.

Helmer. Well?

Rank. At the next fancy-dress ball I shall be invisible.

Helmer. That's a good joke!

Rank. There is a big black hat—have you never heard of hats that make you invisible? If you put one on, no one can see you.

Helmer (*suppressing a smile*). Yes, you are quite right.

Rank. But I am clean forgetting what I came for. Helmer, give me a cigar—one of the dark Havanas.

Helmer. With the greatest pleasure. (*Offers him his case.*)

Rank (*takes a cigar and cuts off the end*). Thanks.

Nora (*striking a match*). Let me give you a light.

Rank. Thank you. (*She holds the match for him to light his cigar.*) And now good-bye!

Helmer. Good-bye, good-bye, dear old man!

Nora. Sleep well, Doctor Rank.

Rank. Thank you for that wish.

Nora. Wish me the same.

Rank. You? Well, if you want me to sleep well! And thanks for the light. (*He nods to them both and goes out.*)

Helmer (*in a subdued voice*). He has drunk more than he ought.

Nora (*absently*). Maybe. (HELMER *takes a bunch of keys out of his pocket and goes into the hall.*) Torvald! what are you going to do there?

Helmer. Empty the letter-box; it's quite full; there will be no room to put the newspaper in to-morrow morning.

Nora. Are you going to work to-night?

Helmer. You know quite well I'm not. What's this? Some-one has been at the lock.

Nora. At the lock——?

Helmer. Yes, someone has. What can it mean? I should never have thought the maid—— Here is a broken hairpin. Nora, it is one of yours.

Nora (*quickly*). Then it must have been the children——

Helmer. Then you must get them out of those ways. There,

at last I have got it open. (*Takes out the contents of the letter-box, and calls to the kitchen.*) Helen!—Helen, put out the light over the front door. (*Goes back into the room and shuts the door into the hall. He holds out his hand full of letters.*) Look at that —look what a heap of them there are. (*Turning them over.*) What on earth is that?

Nora (*at the window*). The letter—No! Torvald, no!

Helmer. Two cards—of Rank's.

Nora. Of Doctor Rank's?

Helmer (*looking at them*). Doctor Rank. They were on the top. He must have put them in when he went out.

Nora. Is there anything written on them?

Helmer. There is a black cross over the name. Look there— what an uncomfortable idea! It looks as if he were announcing his own death.

Nora. It is just what he is doing.

Helmer. What? Do you know anything about it? Has he said anything to you?

Nora. Yes. He told me that when the cards came it would be his leave-taking from us. He means to shut himself up and die.

Helmer. My poor old friend! I knew of course we shouldn't have him very long with us. But so soon! And so he hides himself away like a wounded animal.

Nora. If it has to happen, it is best it should be without a word—don't you think so, Torvald?

Helmer (*walking up and down*). He had so grown into our lives. I can't think of him as having gone out of them. With his sufferings and his loneliness, he was like a cloudy background to our sunlit happiness. Well, perhaps it is best so. For him, anyway. (*Standing still.*) And perhaps for us too, Nora. We two are thrown quite upon each other now. (*Puts his arms round her.*) My darling wife, I don't feel as if I could hold you tight enough. Do you know, Nora, I have often wished that you might be threatened by some great danger, so that I might risk my life's blood, and everything, for your sake.

Nora (*disengages herself, and says firmly and decidedly*). Now you must read your letters, Torvald.

Helmer. No, no; not to-night. I want to be with you, my darling wife.

Nora. With the thought of your friend's death——

Helmer. You are right, it has affected us both. Something

ugly has come between us—the thought of the horrors of death. We must try and rid our minds of that. Until then—we will each go to our own room.

Nora (hanging on his neck). Good night, Torvald—good night!

Helmer (kissing her on the forehead). Good night, my little singing-bird. Sleep well, Nora. Now I will read my letters through. (*He takes his letters and goes into his room, shutting the door after him.*)

Nora (gropes distractedly about, seizes HELMER's *domino, throws it round her, while she says in quick, hoarse, spasmodic whispers).* Never to see him again. Never! Never! (*Puts her shawl over her head.*) Never to see my children again either—never again. Never! Never!—oh! the icy, black water—the bottomless depths—If only it were over! He has got it now—now he is reading it. Good-bye, Torvald and my children! (*She is about to rush out through the hall, when* HELMER *opens his door hurriedly and stands with an open letter in his hand.*)

Helmer. Nora!

Nora. Oh!——

Helmer. What is this? Do you know what is in this letter?

Nora. Yes, I know. Let me go! Let me get out!

Helmer (holding her back). Where are you going?

Nora (trying to get free). You shan't save me, Torvald!

Helmer (reeling). True? Is this true, that I read here? Horrible! No, no—it's impossible that it can be true.

Nora. It is true. I have loved you above everything else in the world.

Helmer. Oh, don't let us have any silly excuses.

Nora (taking a step towards him). Torvald——!

Helmer. Miserable creature—what have you done?

Nora. Let me go. You shall not suffer for my sake. You shall not take it upon yourself.

Helmer. No tragedy airs, please. (*Locks the hall door.*) Here you shall stay and give me an explanation. Do you understand what you have done? Answer me! Do you understand what you have done?

Nora (looks steadily at him and says with a growing look of coldness in her face). Yes, now I am beginning to understand thoroughly.

Helmer (walking about the room). What a horrible awakening! All these eight years—she who was my pride and joy—a hypocrite, a liar—worse, worse—a criminal! The unutterable ugliness of it all!—What disgraceful behaviour! (NORA *is silent and looks steadily at him. He stops in front of her.*) I ought to have suspected that something of the sort would happen. I ought to have foreseen it. All your father's want of principle—be silent!—all your father's want of principle has come out in you. No religion, no morality, no sense of duty—— How I am punished for having winked at what he did! I did it for your sake, and this is how you repay me.

Nora. Yes, that's just it.

Helmer. Now you have destroyed all my happiness. You have ruined all my future. It is horrible to think of! I am in the power of an unscrupulous man; he can do what he likes with me, ask anything he likes of me, give me any orders he pleases—I dare not refuse. And I must sink to such miserable depths because of a thoughtless woman!

Nora. When I am out of the way, you will be free.

Helmer. No fine speeches, please. Your father had always plenty of those ready, too. What good would it be to me if you were out of the way, as you say? Not the slightest. He can make the affair known everywhere; and if he does, I may be falsely suspected of having been a party to your criminal action. Very likely people will think I was behind it all—that it was I who prompted you! And I have to thank you for all this—you whom I have cherished during the whole of our married life. Do you understand now what it is you have done for me?

Nora (*coldly and quietly*). Yes.

Helmer. It is so incredible that I can't take it in. But we must come to some understanding. Take off that shawl. Take it off, I tell you. I must try and appease him some way or another. The matter must be hushed up at any cost. And as for you and me, it must appear as if everything between us were just as before—but naturally only in the eyes of the world. You will still remain in my house, that is a matter of course. But I shall not allow you to bring up the children; I dare not trust them to you. To think that I should have to say this to one whom I have loved so dearly, and whom I still—— No, that is all over. From this moment happiness is not the question; all that concerns us is to save the remains, the fragments, the appearance——

(*A ring is heard at the front-door bell.*)

Helmer (*with a start*). What is that? So late! Can the

worst——? Can he——? Hide yourself, Nora. Say you
are ill.

(NORA *stands motionless.* HELMER *goes and unlocks the hall
door.*)

Maid (*half-dressed, comes to the door*). A letter for the mistress.

Helmer. Give it to me. (*Takes the letter, and shuts the door.*)
Yes, it is from him. You shall not have it; I will read it myself.

Nora. Yes, read it.

Helmer (*standing by the lamp*). I scarcely have the courage to
do it. It may mean ruin for both of us. No, I must know.
(*Tears open the letter, runs his eye over a few lines, looks at a paper
enclosed, and gives a shout of joy.*) Nora! (*She looks at him
questioningly.*) Nora!—No, I must read it once again—— Yes,
it is true! I am saved! Nora, I am saved!

Nora. And I?

Helmer. You too, of course; we are both saved, both you
and I. Look, he sends you your bond back. He says he regrets
and repents—that a happy change in his life—never mind what
he says! We are saved, Nora! No one can do anything to you.
Oh, Nora, Nora!—no, first I must destroy these hateful things.
Let me see—— (*Takes a look at the bond.*) No, no, I won't
look at it. The whole thing shall be nothing but a bad dream to
me. (*Tears up the bond and both letters, throws them all into the
stove, and watches them burn.*) There—now it doesn't exist any
longer. He says that since Christmas Eve you—— These
must have been three dreadful days for you, Nora.

Nora. I have fought a hard fight these three days.

Helmer. And suffered agonies, and seen no way out but——
No, we won't call any of the horrors to mind. We will only
shout with joy, and keep saying, 'It's all over! It's all over!'
Listen to me, Nora. You don't seem to realize that it is all over.
What is this?—such a cold, set face! My poor little Nora, I
quite understand; you don't feel as if you could believe that I
have forgiven you. But it is true, Nora, I swear it; I have
forgiven you everything. I know that what you did, you did out
of love for me.

Nora. That is true.

Helmer. You have loved me as a wife ought to love her husband. Only you had not sufficient knowledge to judge of the
means you used. But do you suppose you are any the less dear
to me, because you don't understand how to act on your own
responsibility? No, no; just lean on me; I will advise you and

direct you.   I shouldn't be a man if this womanly helplessness did not actually give you a double attractiveness in my eyes. You mustn't think any more about the hard things I said in my first moment of consternation, when I thought everything was going to overwhelm me.   I have forgiven you, Nora; I swear to you I have forgiven you.

Nora. Thank you for your forgiveness.   (*She goes out through the door to the right.*)

Helmer. No, don't go—— (*Looks in.*)   What are you doing in there?

Nora (*from within*). Taking off my fancy dress.

Helmer (*standing at the open door*). Yes, do.   Try and calm yourself, and make your mind easy again, my frightened little singing-bird.   Relax, and feel secure; I have broad wings to shelter you under.   (*Walks up and down by the door.*)   How warm and cosy our home is, Nora.   Here is shelter for you; here I will protect you like a hunted dove that I have saved from a hawk's claws; I will bring peace to your poor beating heart.   It will come, little by little, Nora, believe me.   To-morrow morning you will look upon it all quite differently; soon everything will be just as it was before.   Very soon you won't need me to assure you that I have forgiven you; you will yourself feel the certainty that I have done so.   Do you imagine I should ever think of such a thing as repudiating you, or even reproaching you?   You have no idea what a true man's heart is like, Nora. There is something so indescribably sweet and satisfying, to a man, in the knowledge that he has forgiven his wife—forgiven her freely, and with all his heart.   It seems as if that had made her, as it were, doubly his own; he has given her a new life, so to speak; and she has in a way become both wife and child to him. So you shall be for me after this, my little scared, helpless darling. Have no anxiety about anything, Nora; just be frank and open with me, and I will serve as will and conscience both to you—— What is this?   Not gone to bed?   Have you changed your things?

Nora (*in everyday dress*). Yes, Torvald, I have changed my things now.

Helmer. But what for?—as late as this.

Nora. I shan't sleep to-night.

Helmer. But, my dear Nora——

Nora (*looking at her watch*). It is not so very late.   Sit down here, Torvald.   You and I have a lot to say to one another. (*She sits down at one side of the table.*)

Helmer. Nora—what is this?—this cold, set face?

Nora. Sit down. It will take some time; I have a lot to talk over with you.

Helmer (*sits down at the opposite side of the table*). You alarm me, Nora!—and I don't understand you.

Nora. No, that is just it. You don't understand me, and I have never understood you either—before to-night. No, you mustn't interrupt me. You must simply listen to what I say. Torvald, this is a settling of accounts.

Helmer. What do you mean by that?

Nora (*after a short silence*). Isn't there one thing that strikes you as strange in our sitting here like this?

Helmer. What is that?

Nora. We have been married now eight years. Doesn't it occur to you that this is the first time we two, you and I, husband and wife, have had a serious conversation?

Helmer. What do you mean by serious?

Nora. In all these eight years—longer than that—from the very beginning of our acquaintance, we have never exchanged a word on any serious subject.

Helmer. Was it likely that I would be continually and for ever telling you about worries that you could not help me to bear?

Nora. I am not speaking about business matters. I say that we have never sat down in earnest together to try and get at the bottom of anything.

Helmer. But, dearest Nora, would it have been any good to you?

Nora. That is just it; you have never understood me. I have been greatly wronged, Torvald—first by father and then by you.

Helmer. What! By us two—by us two, who have loved you better than anyone else in the world?

Nora (*shaking her head*). You have never loved me. You have only thought it pleasant to be in love with me.

Helmer. Nora, what do I hear you saying?

Nora. It is perfectly true, Torvald. When I was at home with father, he told me his opinion about everything, and so I had the same opinions; and if I differed from him I concealed the fact, because he would not have liked it. He called me his doll-child, and he played with me just as I used to play with my dolls. And when I came to live with you——

Helmer. What sort of an expression is that to use about our

Nora (undisturbed). I mean that I was simply transferred from father's hands into yours. You arranged everything according to your own taste, and so I got the same tastes as you—or else I pretended to, I am really not quite sure which—I think sometimes the one and sometimes the other. When I look back on it, it seems to me as if I had been living here like a poor woman—just from hand to mouth. I have existed merely to perform tricks for you, Torvald. But you wanted it like that. You and father have committed a great sin against me. It is your fault that I have made nothing of my life.

Helmer. How unreasonable and how ungrateful you are, Nora! Haven't you been happy here?

Nora. No, I have never been happy. I thought I was, but it has never really been so.

Helmer. Not—not happy!

Nora. No, only merry. And you have always been so kind to me. But our home has been nothing but a playroom. I have been your doll-wife, just as at home I was father's doll-child; and here the children have been my dolls. I thought it great fun when you played with me, just as they thought it great fun when I played with them. That is what our marriage has been, Torvald.

Helmer. There is some truth in what you say—exaggerated and strained as your view of it is. But in future it will be different. Playtime is over, and lesson-time will begin.

Nora. Whose lessons? Mine, or the children's?

Helmer. Both yours and the children's, my darling Nora.

Nora. I'm afraid, Torvald, you are not the man to educate me into being a proper wife for you.

Helmer. And you can say that!

Nora. And I—how am I fitted to bring up the children?

Helmer. Nora!

Nora. Didn't you say so yourself a little while ago—that you dare not trust me to bring them up?

Helmer. In a moment of anger! Why do you take any notice of that?

Nora. Actually, you were perfectly right. I am not fit for the task. There is another task I must undertake first. I must try and educate myself—you are not the man to help me in that. I must do that for myself. And that is why I am going to leave you now.

Helmer (springing up). What are you saying?

Nora. I must stand quite alone, if I am to understand myself and everything about me. It is for that reason that I cannot remain with you any longer.

Helmer. Nora, Nora!

Nora. I am going away from here now, at once. I am sure Christine will take me in for the night——

Helmer. You are out of your mind! I won't allow it! I forbid you!

Nora. It is no use forbidding me anything any longer. I will take with me only what belongs to me. I will take nothing from you, either now or later.

Helmer. What sort of madness is this!

Nora. To-morrow I shall go home—I mean, to my old home. It will be easiest for me to find something to do there.

Helmer. You blind, foolish woman!

Nora. I must try and get some sense, Torvald.

Helmer. To desert your home, your husband, and your children! And you don't consider what people will say!

Nora. I cannot consider that at all. I only know that it is necessary for me.

Helmer. It's shocking. This is how you would neglect your most sacred duties.

Nora. What do you consider my most sacred duties?

Helmer. Do I need to tell you that? Are they not your duties to your husband and your children?

Nora. I have other duties just as sacred.

Helmer. Indeed you have not. What duties could those be?

Nora. Duties to myself.

Helmer. Before all else, you are a wife and a mother.

Nora. I don't believe that any longer. I believe that before all else I am a reasonable human being, just as you are—or, at all events, that I must try and become one. I know quite well, Torvald, that most people would think you right, and that views of that kind are to be found in books; but I can no longer content myself with what most people say, or with what is found in books. I must think over things for myself and get to understand them.

Helmer. Can you not understand your place in your own home? Have you not a reliable guide in such matters as that?— have you no religion?

Nora. I am afraid, Torvald, I do not exactly know what religion is.

Helmer. What are you saying?

Nora. I know nothing but what the clergyman said, when I went to be confirmed. He told us that religion was this, and that, and the other. When I am away from all this, and am alone, I will look into that matter too. I will see if what the clergyman said is true, or at all events if it is true for me.

Helmer. This is unheard of in a girl of your age! But if religion cannot lead you aright, let me try and awaken your conscience. I suppose you have some moral sense? Or—answer me—am I to think you have none?

Nora. I assure you, Torvald, that is not an easy question to answer. I really don't know. The thing perplexes me altogether. I only know that you and I look at it in quite a different light. I am learning, too, that the law is quite another thing from what I supposed; but I find it impossible to convince myself that the law is right. According to it a woman has no right to spare her old dying father, or to save her husband's life. I can't believe that.

Helmer. You talk like a child. You don't understand the conditions of the world in which you live.

Nora. No, I don't. But now I am going to try. I am going to see if I can make out who is right, the world or I.

Helmer. You are ill, Nora; you are delirious; I almost think you are out of your mind.

Nora. I have never felt my mind so clear and certain as to-night.

Helmer. And is it with a clear and certain mind that you forsake your husband and your children?

Nora. Yes, it is.

Helmer. Then there is only one possible explanation.

Nora. What is that?

Helmer. You do not love me any more.

Nora. No, that is just it.

Helmer. Nora!—and you can say that?

Nora. It gives me great pain, Torvald, because you have always been so kind to me, but I cannot help it. I don't love you any more.

Helmer (*regaining his composure*). Is that a clear and certain conviction too?

Nora. Yes, absolutely clear and certain. That is the reason why I will not stay here any longer.

Helmer. And can you tell me what I have done to forfeit your love?

Nora. Yes, indeed I can. It was to-night, when the wonderful thing did not happen; then I saw you were not the man I had thought you.

Helmer. Explain yourself better. I don't understand you.

Nora. I have waited so patiently for eight years; for, goodness knows, I knew very well that wonderful things don't happen every day. Then this horrible misfortune came upon me; and then I felt quite certain that the wonderful thing was going to happen at last. When Krogstad's letter was lying out there, never for a moment did I imagine that you would consent to accept this man's conditions. I was so absolutely certain that you would say to him: Publish the thing to the whole world. And when that was done——

Helmer. Yes, what then?—when I had exposed my wife to shame and disgrace?

Nora. When that was done, I was so absolutely certain, you would come forward and take everything upon yourself, and say: I am the guilty one.

Helmer. Nora——!

Nora. You mean that I would never have accepted such a sacrifice on your part? No, of course not. But what would my assurances have been worth against yours? That was the wonderful thing which I hoped for and feared; and it was to prevent that, that I wanted to kill myself.

Helmer. I would gladly work night and day for you, Nora— bear sorrow and want for your sake. But no man would sacrifice his honour for the one he loves.

Nora. It is a thing hundreds of thousands of women have done.

Helmer. Oh, you think and talk like a thoughtless child.

Nora. Maybe. But you neither think nor talk like the man I could bind myself to. As soon as your fear was over—and it was not fear for what threatened me, but for what might happen to you—when the whole thing was past, as far as you were concerned it was exactly as if nothing at all had happened. Exactly as before, I was your little skylark, your doll, which you would in future treat with doubly gentle care, because it was so brittle and fragile. (*Getting up.*) Torvald—it was then it dawned upon me that for eight years I had been living here with a strange man, and had borne him three children—— Oh, I can't bear to think of it! I could tear myself into little bits!

Helmer (sadly). I see, I see. An abyss has opened between us—there is no denying it. But, Nora, would it not be possible to fill it up?

Nora. As I am now, I am no wife for you.

Helmer. I have it in me to become a different man.

Nora. Perhaps—if your doll is taken away from you.

Helmer. But to part!—to part from you! No, no, Nora, I can't understand that idea.

Nora (going out to the right). That makes it all the more certain that it must be done. (*She comes back with her cloak and hat and a small bag which she puts on a chair by the table.*)

Helmer. Nora, Nora, not now! Wait till to-morrow.

Nora (putting on her cloak). I cannot spend the night in a strange man's room.

Helmer. But can't we live here like brother and sister——?

Nora (putting on her hat). You know very well that wouldn't last long. (*Puts the shawl round her.*) Good-bye, Torvald. I won't see the little ones. I know they are in better hands than mine. As I am now, I can be of no use to them.

Helmer. But some day, Nora—some day?

Nora. How can I tell? I have no idea what is going to become of me.

Helmer. But you are my wife, whatever becomes of you.

Nora. Listen, Torvald. I have heard that when a wife deserts her husband's house, as I am doing now, he is legally freed from all obligations towards her. In any case I set you free from all your obligations. You are not to feel yourself bound in the slightest way, any more than I shall. There must be perfect freedom on both sides. See, here is your ring back. Give me mine.

Helmer. That too?

Nora. That too.

Helmer. Here it is.

Nora. That's right. Now it is all over. I have put the keys here. The maids know all about everything in the house—better than I do. To-morrow, after I have left her, Christine will come here and pack up my own things that I brought with me from home. I will have them sent after me.

Helmer. All over! All over!—Nora, will you never think of me again?

Nora. I know I shall often think of you and the children and this house.

Helmer. May I write to you, Nora?

Nora. No—never. You must not do that.

Helmer. But at least let me send you——

Nora. Nothing—nothing——

Helmer. Let me help you if you are in want.

Nora. No. I can receive nothing from a stranger.

Helmer. Nora—can I never be anything more than a stranger to you?

Nora (*taking her bag*). Ah, Torvald, the most wonderful thing of all would have to happen.

Helmer. Tell me what that would be!

Nora. Both you and I would have to be so changed that—— Oh, Torvald, I don't believe any longer in wonderful things happening.

Helmer. But I will believe in it. Tell me! So changed that——?

Nora. That our life together would be a real marriage. Good-bye. (*She goes out through the hall.*)

Helmer (*sinks down on a chair at the door and buries his face in his hands*). Nora! Nora! (*Looks round, and rises.*) Empty. She is gone. (*A hope flashes across his mind.*) The most wonderful thing of all——?

(*The sound of a door shutting is heard from below.*)

THE WILD DUCK

DRAMATIS PERSONAE

Werle, a merchant and manufacturer.
Gregers Werle, his son.
Old Ekdal.
Hjalmar Ekdal, his son, a photographer.
Gina Ekdal, Hjalmar's wife.
Hedvig, their daughter, aged fourteen.
Mrs Sörby, the elder Werle's housekeeper.
Relling, a doctor.
Molvik, an ex-student of theology.
Graaberg, a bookkeeper in Werle's office.
Pettersen, Werle's servant.
Jensen, a hired waiter.
A Flabby Guest.
A Thin-haired Guest.
A Short-sighted Guest.
Six other Guests at Werle's dinner-party.
Several hired Servants.

(The first Act takes place in the elder Werle's house; the other four at Hjalmar Ekdal's.)

THE WILD DUCK

ACT I

(SCENE.—*A handsomely and comfortably furnished study in* WERLE's *house. Bookcases and upholstered furniture; a desk, covered with papers and documents, in the middle of the floor; the lamps are lit and have green shades, producing a soft light in the room. At the back are folding doors which have been thrown open and the portières drawn back. Through these is visible a large and well-appointed room, brightly lit with lamps and branch candle-sticks. A small private door, on the right-hand side of the study, leads to the office. On the left is a fireplace, with a cheerful fire, and beyond it folding doors leading to the dining-room.*

WERLE's *servant* PETTERSEN, *in livery, and the hired waiter* JENSEN *in black, are setting the study in order. In the large room at the back two or three other waiters are moving about, tidying the room and lighting more candles. From within the dining-room the noise of the guests' talking and laughing can be heard; someone raps on a glass with a knife, silence follows, and a toast is proposed; applause follows and the hum of conversation begins again.*)

Pettersen (*lighting a lamp on the mantelpiece and putting a shade over it*). Hark at 'em, Jensen; the old man's up now, making a long speech to propose Mrs Sörby's health.

Jensen (*moving a chair forward*). Do you think what people say about those two is true, that there's something between them?

Pettersen. Goodness knows.

Jensen. He's been a gay old dog in his time, hasn't he?

Pettersen. Maybe.

Jensen. They say this dinner-party is in honour of his son.

Pettersen. Yes, he came home yesterday.

Jensen. I never knew old Werle had a son.

Pettersen. Oh yes, he has a son, but he sticks up at the works at Höidal; he hasn't once been in the town all the years I have been in service here.

A waiter (*in the doorway to the other room*). Pettersen, there is an old chap here who——

Pettersen (muttering). Damn him, what's anyone coming now for!

(*Old* EKDAL *appears from the inner room. He is dressed in a weather-worn greatcoat with a high collar, carries a stick and a fur cap in his hands, and a paper parcel under his arm. He wears a dirty reddish-brown wig and a small grey moustache.*)

Pettersen (going towards him). Good Lord!—what do you want in here?

Ekdal (in the doorway). I so badly want to get into the office, Pettersen.

Pettersen. The office was closed an hour ago, and——

Ekdal. They told me that at the door, old man. But Graaberg is still there. Be a good chap, Pettersen, and let me slip in that way. (*Points to the private door.*) I've been that way before.

Pettersen. All right, you can go in. (*Opens the door.*) But, whatever you do, don't forget to go out the proper way, because we have got guests here.

Ekdal. Yes, yes—I know. Thanks, dear old Pettersen! My good old friend! Thanks! (*Under his breath.*) Idiot! (*Goes into the office.* PETTERSEN *shuts the door after him.*)

Jensen. Is that chap one of the clerks?

Pettersen. No, he only does odd jobs of copying when there is any wanted. But I can tell you old Ekdal was a fine fellow in his day.

Jensen. He looks as if he had seen better times.

Pettersen. That he has. He was a lieutenant, though you wouldn't think it.

Jensen. Good heavens, was he indeed!

Pettersen. True as I stand here. But he took to the timber trade, or something. They say he played old Werle a remarkably dirty trick once. The two of them were in partnership up at Höidal at that time. Oh, I know all about old Ekdal, I do. Many's the glass of bitters or bottle of beer we've drunk together at Mother Eriksen's.

Jensen. I shouldn't have thought he'd got much to stand you on.

Pettersen. Good Lord, Jensen, it's me who did the paying! Besides, I think one ought to be a bit civil to gentry that have come down in the world.

Jensen. Did he go bankrupt, then?

Pettersen. No, it was a good deal worse than that. He went to jail.

Jensen. To jail!

Pettersen. Or it may have been the penitentiary—— (*Listens.*) Sh! they are getting up from table now.

(*The dining-room doors are thrown open by a couple of servants. Mrs SÖRBY comes out, talking to two of the guests. The others follow her by degrees, with the elder WERLE amongst them. HJALMAR EKDAL and GREGERS WERLE come last.*)

Mrs Sörby (to the SERVANT, in passing). We will take coffee in the music-room, Pettersen.

Pettersen. Very good, ma'am.

(*Mrs SÖRBY and the two gentlemen go into the inner room and out to the right of it. PETTERSEN and JENSEN follow them.*)

The Flabby Guest (to the THIN-HAIRED GUEST). Whew!—it's hard work eating one's way through a dinner like that!

The Thin-haired Guest. Oh, with a little goodwill, it's amazing what you can get through in three hours.

The Flabby Guest. Yes, but afterwards, my dear sir, afterwards!

Another Guest. I believe the coffee and liqueurs are to be served in the music-room.

The Flabby Guest. Good! Then perhaps Mrs Sörby will play us something.

The Thin-haired Guest (in a low voice). So long as she doesn't make us dance to a tune we don't like.

The Flabby Guest. Not a bit of it; Bertha would never go back on her old friends. (*They laugh and go into the inner room.*)

Werle (in a low and depressed voice). I don't think anybody noticed it, Gregers.

Gregers (looking at him). What?

Werle. Didn't you notice it either?

Gregers. What was there to notice?

Werle. We were thirteen at table.

Gregers. Really? Were we?

Werle (with a look towards HJALMAR EKDAL). We are usually twelve at table. (*Turns to the other guests.*) Come along in here, gentlemen. (*He leads the way out through the inner room, and is followed by all the others except HJALMAR and GREGERS.*)

Hjalmar (who has heard what they were saying). You shouldn't have invited me, Gregers.

Gregers. What? This party is supposed to be in my honour. Why shouldn't I invite my best and only friend?

Hjalmar. But I don't believe your father likes it. I never come to the house.

Gregers. So I understand. But I wanted to see you and talk to you, because I expect to be going away again soon.—Well, we two old school friends have drifted a long way apart from each other, haven't we? We haven't met for sixteen or seventeen years.

Hjalmar. Is it as long as that?

Gregers. It is indeed. And how is the world treating you? You look well. You have become almost corpulent!

Hjalmar. Well, I should hardly call it corpulent; but probably I look more of a man than I did then.

Gregers. That you do; there is certainly more of your outer man.

Hjalmar (sadly). But the inner man, Gregers! Believe me, there is a vast difference there. You know what a disastrous blow has fallen on me and mine, since we two last met.

Gregers (lowering his voice). How is your father getting on now?

Hjalmar. My dear chap, don't let's talk about it. My poor unfortunate father lives at home with me, of course. He has not another creature in the world to cling to. But you can understand what torture it is to me to speak about it. Tell me, instead, how you have been getting on up there at the works.

Gregers. It has been splendidly lonely. I have had a fine opportunity to ruminate over all sorts of things. Come here, let's make ourselves more comfortable. (*He sits down in an arm-chair by the fire and pushes* HJALMAR *into another beside him.*)

Hjalmar (with feeling). Anyway, Gregers, I am grateful to you for asking me here; it shows that you no longer bear me any grudge.

Gregers (astonished). Whatever makes you think I had any grudge against you?

Hjalmar. At first you certainly had.

Gregers. When?

Hjalmar. After that miserable affair happened. And it was perfectly natural that you should, seeing that your own father was within a hair's breadth of being drawn into this—this terrible business.

Gregers. Was that any reason for my bearing you a grudge? Who put that idea into your head?

Hjalmar. I know you did, Gregers; your father told me so himself.

Gregers (*with a start*). My father!   Did he, indeed?   Ah!—
And so that's why you never let me hear from you—not a single
word?

Hjalmar. Yes.

Gregers. Not even when you went and turned yourself into a
photographer?

Hjalmar. Your father said I had better not write to you about
anything at all.

Gregers (*looking straight in front of him*). Well, perhaps he
was right.   But tell me now, Hjalmar, are you reasonably content
with your present position?

Hjalmar (*with a slight sigh*). Oh yes, oh yes; I think I can say
so, certainly.   It was a bit difficult for me at first, as you can
understand.   It was such an entirely new life to take up.   But
then the old life could never have been the same any more.   My
father's hopeless disaster—the shame and disgrace, Gregers——

Gregers (*feelingly*). Yes, yes—of course, of course.

Hjalmar. It was impossible to think of going on with my
studies; we hadn't a penny left—worse than that, there were
debts, most of them owed to your father, I believe——

Gregers. Hm!——

Hjalmar. So that it seemed to me the best thing was to drop
the old life and all its associations, once and for all.   It was
chiefly due to your father's advice that I did so; and as he was so
kind in helping me——

Gregers. My father was?

Hjalmar. Surely you know he was?   Where do you suppose
I could find the money to learn photography and set myself up
in a studio?   That costs a bit, I can tell you.

Gregers. And did my father pay for all this?

Hjalmar. Yes, my dear fellow, didn't you know that?   I
understood that he had written to you about it.

Gregers. He never said a word about its being his doing.   He
must have forgotten.   We have never written anything but
business letters to each other.   So it was really my father——!

Hjalmar. Yes, it was, indeed.   He has never wanted anyone
to know anything about it, but it was him.   And it was thanks to
him, too, that I was able to marry.   But perhaps that's news to
you too?

Gregers. I knew nothing whatever about it.   (*Takes him by
the arm.*)   I can't tell you, my dear Hjalmar, how glad all this
makes me—and how it hurts me too.   I may have been unjust

to my father after all, in some things. It shows at any rate that he has a heart. There is evidence of a conscience about it——

Hjalmar. Of a conscience——?

Gregers. Well, call it what you like. I can't tell you how glad I am to hear this about my father.—And so you are a married man, Hjalmar. It will be a long time before I shall be able to say that of myself. Well, I hope you are happy in your marriage.

Hjalmar. Very happy. I have as pretty and as capable a wife as a man could wish, and she is by no means without education either.

Gregers (slightly surprised). I should hope not!

Hjalmar. Well, life is an education, you see. Her daily companionship with me—and we see a few clever people now and then. I can assure you, you would hardly know it was the same Gina.

Gregers. Gina?

Hjalmar. Yes, don't you remember her name was Gina?

Gregers. What Gina? I don't know——

Hjalmar. Have you forgotten that she was in service in this house once?

Gregers (glancing at him). Is it Gina Hansen?

Hjalmar. Of course it's Gina Hansen.

Gregers. Who kept house for us that last year when my mother was ill?

Hjalmar. Yes, of course. But I thought, my dear chap, that your father had written to you about my marriage.

Gregers (rising). Yes, he did; but not that it was—— (*Walks up and down.*) Yes, wait a bit. I expect he did, now that I come to think of it. My father always writes me such brief letters. (*Sits down on the arm of* HJALMAR'S *chair.*) Tell me, Hjalmar—it's curious—how did you come to make Gina's—your wife's acquaintance?

Hjalmar. It was quite simple. Gina was not here for long. Everything was upside down in the house then with your mother's illness; Gina couldn't put up with it, so she took herself off. That was the year before your mother died—or I dare say it was the same year.

Gregers. It was the same year. I was up at the works then. And after that?

Hjalmar. Well, Gina went home to her mother, a very active and hard-working woman, who kept a small restaurant. And she had a room to let, a very nice, comfortable room——

Gregers. And you were fortunate enough to get it, I suppose?

Hjalmar. Yes, and in fact it was your father who put the idea into my head.   And that, you see, was the way I came to know Gina.

Gregers. And it ended in your falling in love?

Hjalmar. Yes.   Young people don't take long to fall in love, you know.

Gregers (rises again and walks about). Tell me, was it when you were engaged that my father induced you—I mean, was it then that you began to think of taking up photography?

Hjalmar. Yes, it was indeed.   I was so anxious to get some settled occupation, and both your father and I thought photography offered the best chances.   And Gina thought so too. Yes, and there was another reason, I must tell you; it turned out that, fortunately, Gina had taken some lessons in retouching.

Gregers. It was extraordinarily lucky altogether.

Hjalmar (in a pleased voice as he rises). Yes, wasn't it!   Don't you think everything turned out very luckily for me?

Gregers. I do, indeed.   It looks as if my father had been a sort of providence to you.

Hjalmar (heartily). He did not forsake his old friend's son in the day of trouble.   He has a heart, you see.

Mrs Sörby (coming in on the elder WERLE's *arm).* Don't be obstinate, dear Mr Werle.   You must not stay in there any longer staring at all those lights.   It is bad for your eyes.

Werle (slips his arm out of hers and passes his hand over his eyes). Well, I really believe you are right.

Mrs Sörby (to the guests, who are in the other room). If anyone would like a glass of punch, he must come in here and get it.

The Fat Guest (coming up to her). Is it really true that you are determined to deprive us of the sacred right of smoking?

Mrs Sörby. Yes, it's forbidden in here, in Mr Werle's sanctum.

The Thin-haired Guest. When did you enact this cruel law about tobacco, Mrs Sörby?

Mrs Sörby. After our last dinner, when certain persons allowed themselves to overstep the mark altogether.

The Thin-haired Guest. Mayn't we overstep it just a wee bit? —not the least bit?

Mrs Sörby. Not the least bit in any direction, Mr Balle.

(*Most of the* GUESTS *have come in by this time.   The* SERVANTS *hand round the punch.*)

Werle (to HJALMAR, *who is standing apart by a table).* What are you looking at there, Ekdal?

Hjalmar. I was just looking at an album, Mr Werle.

The Thin-haired Guest (who is wandering about the room). Ah, photographs! They must interest you, of course.

The Fat Guest (who has settled himself in an arm-chair). Haven't you brought any of your own with you?

Hjalmar. No, I haven't.

The Fat Guest. You should have; it's an excellent thing for the digestion to sit and look at pictures.

The Thin-haired Guest. And it contributes to the general entertainment, you know.

The Short-sighted Guest. And all contributions are thankfully received.

Mrs Sörby. They think that when one is asked out to dinner one ought to do something to earn it, Mr Ekdal.

The Fat Guest. Which is a real pleasure when one gets a good dinner for it.

The Thin-haired Guest. And when it is a case of a struggle for existence, then——

Mrs Sörby. You are right there! (*They go on laughing and joking.*)

Gregers (aside, to HJALMAR). You must join in, Hjalmar.

Hjalmar (wincing). How on earth can I join in?

The Fat Guest. Don't you think, Mr Werle, that Tokay may be considered a comparatively wholesome drink?

Werle (standing by the fire). I can vouch for the Tokay you had to-day, anyway; it is of one of the very finest years. But I have no doubt you noticed that.

The Fat Guest. Yes, it had a wonderfully delicate flavour.

Hjalmar (hesitatingly). Is there a difference between the years then?

The Fat Guest (laughing). Well, that's good!

Werle (with a smile). It's evidently waste of money to give him a fine wine.

The Thin-haired Guest. Tokay grapes are like photographs, Mr Ekdal; they need sunshine. Isn't that so?

Hjalmar. Yes, the light is a great point, certainly.

Mrs Sörby. Then it is just the same with all you gentlemen in official positions; you all like to bask in the sunshine of Court favour.

The Thin-haired Guest. Come, come!—that's a very ancient joke!

The Short-sighted Guest. Mrs Sörby is coming out!

The Fat Guest. And at our expense. (*Wags his finger.*) Madam Bertha!   Madam Bertha!

Mrs Sörby. Another thing that is true of you, too, is that different years' vintages may differ vastly.   The old vintages are the best.

The Short-sighted Guest. Do you reckon me among the old ones?

Mrs Sörby. Far from it.

The Thin-haired Guest. Listen to that!   But what about me, dear Mrs Sörby?

The Fat Guest. Yes, and me!   What vintage do you consider us?

Mrs Sörby. Very sweet years, both of you!   (*She puts a glass of punch to her lips; the* GUESTS *continue laughing and joking with her.*)

Werle. Mrs Sörby can always get out of a difficult position neatly, if she likes.   Don't put your glasses down; Pettersen, fill them up!—Gregers, come and have a glass with me. (GREGERS *does not move.*)   Won't you join us, Ekdal?   I had no opportunity of drinking with you at dinner.

(GRAABERG, *the bookkeeper, peeps into the room through the private door.*)

Graaberg. I beg your pardon, sir, but I can't get out.

Werle. Have you got locked in again?

Graaberg. Yes, and Flagstad has gone off with the keys.

Werle. All right, come out this way.

Graaberg. But I have someone with me——

Werle. Come along, come along, both of you.   Don't mind us.

(GRAABERG *and old* EKDAL *come out of the office.* WERLE *gives an involuntary exclamation of disgust; the laughing and joking stops suddenly.* HJALMAR *starts at the sight of his father, puts down his glass, and turns towards the fire-place.*)

Ekdal (*keeping his eyes on the ground and bowing awkwardly from side to side as he goes out, mumbling*). Excuse me!   Come the wrong way—door's locked—door's locked.—Excuse me!

[*Exit at the back, with* GRAABERG.

Werle (*between his teeth*). Confound that Graaberg!

Gregers (*with mouth hanging open and eyes staring, to* HJALMAR). Surely that was never——!

The Fat Guest. What is it?   Who was that?

Gregers. Nothing; only the bookkeeper and another man.

The Thin-haired Guest (*to* HJALMAR). Was he a friend of yours?

Hjalmar. I don't know—I didn't notice——

The Fat Guest (*rising*). What the deuce is all this about? (*He joins some of the others, who are talking under their breath.*)

Mrs Sörby (*whispers to the* SERVANT). Give him something to take away with him—something good.

Pettersen (*nodding*). I will.   [*Exit.*

Gregers (*in a low and shaking voice, to* HJALMAR). So it was really him?

Hjalmar. Yes.

Gregers. And yet you stood there and said you didn't know him!

Hjalmar (*in a loud whisper*). How could I——

Gregers. Acknowledge your own father?

Hjalmar (*bitterly*). If you were in my place, you would——

(*The* GUESTS, *who have been talking in low tones, now raise their voices with an obvious effort.*)

The Thin-haired Guest (*coming up genially to* HJALMAR *and* GREGERS). Well, I suppose you two are talking over old times at College, eh? Won't you smoke, Mr Ekdal? Shall I give you a light? Ah, I forgot, we mustn't smoke.

Hjalmar. Thank you, I won't now.

The Fat Guest. Can't you recite some charming little poem to us, Mr Ekdal? You used to have a great talent for that.

Hjalmar. I am sorry I cannot remember anything.

The Fat Guest. What a pity. Well, what shall we do, Balle? (*The two* GUESTS *go together into the other room.*)

Hjalmar (*sadly*). Gregers, I must go away. When Fate has dealt a man such a blow as it has done to me, you know—— Say good night to your father from me.

Gregers. Yes, yes. Are you going straight home?

Hjalmar. Yes. Why?

Gregers. Well, perhaps I might come along and see you presently.

Hjalmar. No, you mustn't do that. Don't come to my house. Mine is a sad home, Gregers—especially after a splendid entertainment like this. We can always find some place in the town to meet.

Mrs Sörby (*coming up to them, and speaking low*). Are you going, Mr Ekdal?

Hjalmar. Yes.

Mrs Sörby. Remember me to Gina.

Hjalmar. Thank you.

Mrs Sörby. And tell her I shall be up to see her some day soon.

Hjalmar. Yes, thanks. (*To* GREGERS.) Stay here. I will slip out unobserved. (*He goes out through the other room.*)

Mrs Sörby (*to the* SERVANT *who has come back*). Well, did you give the old man something to take with him?

Pettersen. Yes, ma'am; I gave him a bottle of brandy.

Mrs Sörby. Oh, you might have found something better than that to give him.

Pettersen. No, indeed, ma'am. Brandy is what he likes best, I know.

The Fat Guest (*standing in the doorway with a piece of music in his hand*). Shall we play a duet, Mrs Sörby?

Mrs Sörby. Yes, let's.

The Guests. Bravo! Bravo! (*They and all the* GUESTS *go out of the room.* GREGERS *remains standing by the fire. His father is looking for something on the desk and seems anxious for* GREGERS *to go; as* GREGERS *does not move,* WERLE *goes towards the door.*)

Gregers. Father, will you wait a moment?

Werle (*stopping*). What is it?

Gregers. I want a word with you.

Werle. Can't it wait till we are alone?

Gregers. No, it can't. We may never find ourselves alone.

Werle (*coming nearer him*). What do you mean by that?

(*During the following conversation the sound of the piano is heard faintly from the other room.*)

Gregers. How could you let that family come to grief so miserably?

Werle. You mean the Ekdals, I presume.

Gregers. Yes, I mean the Ekdals. Lieutenant Ekdal and you were once so intimate.

Werle. A great deal too intimate, unfortunately, and I have been paying for it for many years now. It is him I have to thank for the fact that my good name and reputation have suffered to some extent too.

Gregers (*in a low voice*). Was he really the only guilty one?

Werle. Who else, if you please!

Gregers. He and you were in partnership over that big purchase of timber——

Werle. But you know that it was Ekdal who made the map of the ground—that misleading map. He was responsible for the illegal felling of timber off Government property. In fact, he was responsible for the whole business. I had no knowledge of what Lieutenant Ekdal was undertaking.

Gregers. Lieutenant Ekdal seems to have had no knowledge himself of what he was undertaking.

Werle. Maybe.   But the fact remains that he was found guilty and I was acquitted.

Gregers. Yes, I am quite aware there were no proofs.

Werle. An acquittal is an acquittal.   Why are you raking up these horrible old stories, which have whitened my hair before its time?   Is this what your mind has been brooding over up there all these years?   I can assure you, Gregers, that here in town the whole story has been forgotten long ago, as far as I am concerned.

Gregers. But what about that wretched family?

Werle. What could you have expected me to do for them? When Ekdal regained his freedom he was a broken man, absolutely past help.   There are some men who go under entirely if Fate deals them even a slight blow, and never come to the surface again.   Believe me, Gregers, I could have done no more than I have, without exposing myself to all sorts of suspicion and gossip——

Gregers. Suspicion——?   Quite so.

Werle. I got Ekdal copying to do at the office, and I pay him a great deal more for his work than it is worth.

Gregers (without looking at him). I have no doubt of that.

Werle. You smile? Perhaps you don't believe it is true? I am quite aware it doesn't appear in my accounts; I never enter such payments as that.

Gregers (with a cold smile). I quite agree that there are certain expenses it is better not to enter in one's accounts.

Werle (with a start). What do you mean?

Gregers (in a more confident tone). Have you entered in your accounts what it cost you to have Hjalmar Ekdal taught photography?

Werle. I?   Why should I have entered that?

Gregers. I know now that it was you who paid for it.   And I know, too, that it was you who made it possible for him to settle down as he has done.

Werle. And, after all that, you say I have done nothing for the Ekdals!   I can assure you that family has caused me enough expense, in all conscience.

Gregers. Have you entered any one item of it in your accounts?

Werle. Why do you ask that?

Gregers. I have my reasons.   Tell me this—didn't your great solicitude for your old friend's son begin just at the time he was contemplating getting married?

Werle. Good Lord!—after all these years, how can I——?

Gregers. You wrote to me at the time—a business letter, naturally—and in a postscript, in just one or two words, you told me Hjalmar Ekdal had married a Miss Hansen.

Werle. Well, that was true; that was her name.

Gregers. But you never mentioned the fact that this Miss Hansen was Gina Hansen, our former housekeeper.

Werle (*laughs ironically, but in a constrained manner*). No, I didn't imagine you were so specially interested in our former housekeeper.

Gregers. Nor I was.   But (*lowering his voice*) there was some-one else in this house who *was* especially interested in her.

Werle. What do you mean?   (*In an angry voice.*)   You don't mean that you refer to me?

Gregers (*in a low voice, but firmly*). Yes, I refer to you.

Werle. And you dare——!   You have the audacity to——! And as for this ungrateful photographer chap—how dare he presume to come here and make such accusations!

Gregers. Hjalmar has never said a single word of the kind.   I don't believe that he has even a suspicion of anything of the sort.

Werle. Then where have you got it from?   Who could have told you such a thing?

Gregers. My poor unhappy mother told me, the last time I saw her.

Werle. Your mother!   I might have thought as much!   She and you were always together in everything.   It was she from the very first who drew you apart from me.

Gregers. No, it was the suffering and humiliation she had to undergo, till at last it broke her down and drove her to such a miserable end.

Werle. She had not the least suffering or humiliation to undergo—not more than many others, anyway!   But there is no dealing with sickly and hysterical folk.   I have good reason to know that.   And so you have been brooding over such a sus-picion as this!—you have been raking up all sorts of ancient rumours and slanders about your own father!—Let me tell you, Gregers, I really think at your age you might find something more useful to do.

Gregers. Yes, I think it is quite time I did.

Werle. And perhaps, if you did, you would be easier in your mind than you appear to be at present.   What possible point is there in your drudging away at the works, year in and year out, like the merest clerk, and refusing to accept a penny more than the ordinary wages?   It is simply folly on your part.

Gregers. Ah, if only I were as certain of that as you are!

Werle. I think I understand.   You want to be independent, not to be under the slightest obligation to me.   Well, now there happens to be an opportunity for you to become independent, to be your own master entirely.

Gregers. Indeed? and what may that be?

Werle. When I wrote to you that I had urgent reasons for asking you to come to town at once—well——

Gregers. Well, what is it exactly that you want?   I have been waiting all day for you to tell me.

Werle. I propose to offer you a partnership in the firm.

Gregers. Me!—a partner in your firm?

Werle. Yes.   It need not necessitate our always being together.   You might manage the business here in town, and I would go up to the works.

Gregers. You?

Werle. Yes.   You see, I am no longer as fit for my work as I used to be.   I have to be careful of my eyes, Gregers; they have begun to get a bit weak.

Gregers. They were always that.

Werle. Not as weak as they are now.   And, besides that, circumstances might make it desirable for me to live up there, at any rate for a while.

Gregers. Such an idea has never entered into my head.

Werle. Listen, Gregers; we seem to stand apart from each other in very many ways, but after all we are father and son.   It seems to me we ought to be able to come to some kind of an understanding with one another.

Gregers. To outward appearance, I suppose you mean?

Werle. Well, at any rate that would be something.   Think over it, Gregers.   Doesn't it appear to you as a possibility? Eh?

Gregers (*looking at him coldly*). There is something at the bottom of all this.

Werle. What do you mean?

Gregers. You probably intend to make use of me in some way.

Werle. Two people as closely connected as we are can always be of use to one another.

Gregers. Possibly.

Werle. I want you to stay at home with me for a bit. I am a lonely man, Gregers; I have always felt lonely, all my life, and I feel it more than ever now that I am no longer young. I need some companionship.

Gregers. You have Mrs Sörby.

Werle. Yes, that is so; and to tell you the truth, she has become almost indispensable to me. She is clever and easy-going, and livens up the house—and I need that sort of thing badly.

Gregers. Exactly; you seem to me to have just what you want.

Werle. Yes, but I am afraid it can't last. Under such circumstances a woman is easily put into a false position in the eyes of the world. Indeed, one might almost say that the man is not much safer.

Gregers. Oh, when a man gives such good dinners as you do, he can take considerable liberties with public opinion.

Werle. Yes, but what about her, Gregers? I am so afraid she won't put up with it any longer. And even if she did—if out of attachment to me she were to disregard gossip and scandal, and so on——? You have a very strong sense of justice, Gregers; doesn't it seem to you that——

Gregers (interrupting him). Tell me this, without beating about the bush; are you thinking of marrying her?

Werle. And if I were, what then?

Gregers. Exactly. What then?

Werle. Would it be a thing you would find it impossible to countenance?

Gregers. Not in the least. Not by any means.

Werle. Well, I was not sure whether perhaps, out of respect for your mother's memory, you——

Gregers. I am not overwrought.

Werle. Well, whether you are or not, you have at any rate lifted a heavy weight off my mind. It is an immense pleasure to me that I can count on your sympathy in this matter.

Gregers (looking intently at him). Now I understand how it is you want to make use of me.

Werle. Make use of you? What an expression!

Gregers. Oh, don't let us be so nice in our choice of words—at any rate when we are alone. (*With a short laugh.*) I see!

This was the reason why it was absolutely necessary for me to come to town—to help you to make a pretence of family life here for Mrs Sörby's edification!—a touching tableau, father and son! That would be something new.

Werle. How dare you take that tone with me!

Gregers. When was there any family life here? Never, as long as I can remember. But now, if you please, a little of that sort of thing is desirable. It would undoubtedly have a splendid effect if it could get about that the son has hastened home, on the wings of filial piety, to attend his old father's wedding. What becomes then of all the rumours of what his poor dead mother had suffered and endured? They are absolutely silenced; her son's action would do that.

Werle. Gregers—I don't believe there is anyone living towards whom you feel as bitterly as you do to me.

Gregers (*in a low voice*). I have seen you at too close quarters.

Werle. You have seen me through your mother's eyes. (*Lowering his voice a little.*) But you ought to remember that her eyes were—were—clouded now and then.

Gregers (*trembling*). I understand what you mean. But who is to blame for my mother's unfortunate weakness? You, and all your——! The last of them was this woman that was foisted upon Hjalmar Ekdal when you were tired of her. Ough!

Werle (*shrugging his shoulders*). Just the way your mother used to talk.

Gregers (*without paying any attention to him*). And there he is now, like a big unsuspecting child, in the middle of all this deceit; living under the same roof with a woman like that, without the slightest idea that what he calls his home is built on a lie. (*Taking a step nearer his father.*) When I look back on all you have done, it is like looking at a battle-field strewn on every side with ruined lives.

Werle. I am beginning to think the gulf between us is too wide to be bridged.

Gregers (*controls himself and bows*). I agree with you; and therefore I will take my hat and go.

Werle. Go? Out of the house?

Gregers. Yes, I see at last some object to live for.

Werle. What may that be?

Gregers. You would only laugh, if I told you.

Werle. A lonely man doesn't laugh so readily, Gregers.

Gregers (*pointing to the back of the room*). Look, father—Mrs

Sörby is playing blind man's buff with your guests.   Good night,
and good-bye. (*He goes out. The* GUESTS *are heard merrily
laughing as they come into the other room.*)

Werle (*muttering scornfully after* GREGERS). Ha! Ha! Poor
chap—and he says he is not overwrought!

ACT II

(SCENE.—HJALMAR EKDAL'S *studio, a fairly large attic room.
On the right, a sloping roof with large glass windows, half covered
by a blue curtain. The door leading into the room is in the right-
hand corner, and further forward on the same side is a door leading
to a sitting-room. In the left-hand wall are two doors, with a stove
between them. In the back wall are wide double doors, arranged so
as to slide back on either side. The studio is simply but comfortably
furnished. Between the doors on the right, near the wall, stands a
sofa with a table and some chairs; on the table a shaded lamp is lit.
An old arm-chair is drawn up by the stove. Photographic apparatus
and instruments are scattered here and there about the room.
Against the back wall, to the left of the double doors, is a bookcase,
containing some books, boxes, bottles of chemicals, and a variety of
instruments and tools. On the table are lying photographs, paint-
brushes, paper, and so forth.* GINA EKDAL *is sitting on a chair by
the table, sewing.* HEDVIG *is on the sofa reading a book, with her
thumbs in her ears and her hands shading her eyes.*)

Gina (*who has glanced several times at* HEDVIG *with restrained
anxiety, calls to her*). Hedvig! (HEDVIG *does not hear her.*)

Gina (*louder*). Hedvig!

Hedvig (*puts her hands down and looks up*). Yes, mother?

Gina. Hedvig, you must be good and not sit there reading any
longer.

Hedvig. Mayn't I read a little more, mother? Just a little?

Gina. No, no, you must put your book away. Your father
doesn't like it; he don't ever read in the evening himself.

Hedvig (*shutting her book*). No, father doesn't care very much
about reading.

Gina (*puts down her sewing and takes up a pencil and a little note-
book*). Do you remember how much we paid for the butter to-day?

Hedvig. One and ninepence.

Gina. That's right. (*Writes it down.*) It's frightful, the amount of butter we get through in this house. And then there was the smoked sausage and the cheese—let me see—(*writes*)—and then there was the ham—(*adds up*)—there, that lot alone comes to——

Hedvig. And then there's the beer.

Gina. Yes, of course. (*Puts it down.*) It soon mounts up, but it can't be helped.

Hedvig. But then you and I didn't need anything hot for dinner, as father was out.

Gina. No, that was lucky. And, what's more, I have taken eight and sixpence for photographs.

Hedvig. As much as that!

Gina. Yes, eight and sixpence exactly.

(*Silence.* GINA *resumes her sewing.* HEDVIG *takes a piece of paper and a pencil and begins a drawing, shading her eyes with her left hand.*)

Hedvig. Isn't it funny to think of father at a big dinner-party at Mr Werle's?

Gina. He is not, strictly speaking, Mr Werle's guest, it was the son who invited him. (*After a pause.*) We have nothing to do with Mr Werle.

Hedvig. I wish most awfully he would come home. He promised to ask Mrs Sörby for something nice to bring back to me.

Gina. Ah, there's plenty of good things going in that house, I can tell you.

Hedvig (*resuming her drawing*). And I believe I am a bit hungry too.

(*Old* EKDAL *comes in, a roll of papers under his arm and a parcel sticking out of his pocket.*)

Gina. How late you are to-night, grandfather——

Ekdal. They had locked up the office. I had to wait for Graaberg; and then I was obliged to go through—hm!

Hedvig. Did they give you some more copying, grandfather?

Ekdal. All this lot. Just look!

Gina. That's splendid.

Hedvig. And you have got a parcel in your pocket, too.

Ekdal. Have I? Oh, that's nothing, that's nothing. (*Puts down his stick in a corner of the room.*) This will keep me busy for a long time, Gina. (*Pulls one of the sliding doors at the back a little open.*) Hush! (*He looks in through the door for a moment and then shuts it again carefully.*)   Ha, ha!   They are all asleep, all of them in there.   And she has gone into the basket of her own accord.   Ha, ha!

Hedvig. Are you quite sure she isn't cold in the basket, grandfather?

Ekdal. What an idea!   Cold?   In all that straw?   (*Goes to the farther door on the left.*)   Are there matches here?

Gina. There's some on the chest of drawers.   (EKDAL *goes into his room.*)

Hedvig. Isn't it nice that grandfather has got all this new copying to do!

Gina. Yes, poor old grandfather; he will be able to make a little pocket-money.

Hedvig. And won't be able to sit all the morning at that horrid restaurant of Mrs Eriksen's over there.

Gina. Yes, that's another thing.

Hedvig (*after a short pause*). Do you think they are still at dinner?

Gina. Goodness knows.   Very likely they are.

Hedvig. Just think what a lovely dinner father must be having.   I know he will be in such a good temper when he comes home.   Don't you think so, mother?

Gina. Yes, but just think how nice it would be if we could tell him we had let the room.

Hedvig. We don't need that to-night.

Gina. Oh, every little helps.   And the room is standing empty.

Hedvig. I mean that we don't need to be able to tell him that to-night.   He will be in good spirits anyway.   We shall be all the more thankful for the news about the room for another time.

Gina (*looking at her*). Do you like having some good news to tell your father when he comes home in the evening?

Hedvig. Yes, because things seem to go pleasanter then.

Gina (*thoughtfully*). There's something in that, certainly.

(*Old* EKDAL *comes in again, and is going out by the nearer door on the left.*)

Gina (*turning in her chair*). Do you want something in the kitchen, grandfather?

Ekdal. Yes, I do.   Don't get up.   [*Exit.*

Gina. I hope he is not poking the fire in there. (*After a short pause.*)   Hedvig, do see what he's up to.

(EKDAL *returns with a little jug of hot water.*)

Hedvig. Have you been getting some hot water, grandfather?

Ekdal. Yes, I have. I want it for something—I have got some writing to do, and my ink is all dried up as thick as porridge—hm!

Gina. But you ought to have your supper first. It is all laid in there.

Ekdal. I can't bother about supper, Gina. I'm dreadfully busy, I tell you. I won't have anyone coming into my room, not anyone—hm! (*Goes into his room.* GINA *and* HEDVIG *exchange glances.*)

Gina (*in a low voice*). Can you imagine where he has got the money from?

Hedvig. I expect he has got it from Graaberg.

Gina. Not a bit of it. Graaberg always sends his pay to me.

Hedvig. Then he must have got a bottle on credit somewhere.

Gina. Poor grandfather, no one would give him credit.

(*Enter* HJALMAR EKDAL, *wearing an overcoat and a grey felt hat*).

Gina (*throws down her sewing and gets up*). Back already, Hjalmar?

Hedvig (*at the same time, jumping up*). Fancy your coming now, father!

Hjalmar (*taking off his hat*). Oh, most of the guests were leaving.

Hedvig. So early?

Hjalmar. Yes, it was a dinner-party, you know. (*Begins taking off his coat.*)

Gina. Let me help you.

Hedvig. And me too. (*They take off his coat;* GINA *hangs it on the wall.*) Were there many there, father?

Hjalmar. Oh no, not many. We were just twelve or fourteen at table.

Gina. And you had a chat with all of them?

Hjalmar. A little, yes; but Gregers practically monopolized me.

Gina. Is Gregers as ugly as ever?

Hjalmar. Well, he's not particularly handsome. Isn't the old man in yet?

Hedvig. Yes, grandfather is busy writing.

Hjalmar. Did he say anything?

Gina. No, what about?

Hjalmar. Didn't he say anything about——? I fancied I

heard he had been to Graaberg. I'll go in and see him for a moment.

Gina. No, no, it's not worth while.

Hjalmar. Why not? Did he say he didn't want me to go in?

Gina. He doesn't want anyone to go in to-night.

Hedvig (making signs to her). Hm—hm!

Gina (taking no notice). He came in and fetched himself some hot water.

Hjalmar. Then I suppose he is——?

Gina. Yes, that's it.

Hjalmar. Good heavens—my poor old grey-haired father! Well, anyway, let him have what little pleasure he can. (*Old* EKDAL *comes out of his room wearing a dressing-gown and smoking a pipe.*)

Ekdal. Ah, you are back. I thought I heard your voice.

Hjalmar. I have just come in.

Ekdal. You didn't see me, then?

Hjalmar. No, but they told me you had gone through—and so I thought I would come after you.

Ekdal. Nice of you, Hjalmar—hm! What were all those people?

Hjalmar. Oh, all sorts. Flor was there, and Balle, and Kaspersen, and what's-his-name—I don't remember—all of them gentry, you know.

Ekdal (nodding). Do you hear that, Gina? All of 'em gentry.

Gina. Yes, they are very grand in that house now.

Hedvig. Did any of them sing, father—or recite?

Hjalmar. No, they only talked nonsense. They wanted me to recite to them, but I wasn't going to do that.

Ekdal. You weren't going to do that, eh?

Gina. I think you might have done that.

Hjalmar. No, I don't think one ought to be at everybody's beck and call. (*Walking up and down.*) Anyway, I am not going to be.

Ekdal. No, no, Hjalmar's not that sort.

Hjalmar. I fail to see why I should be expected to amuse others if I happen to go out for once. Let the others exert themselves a little. These fellows go from one house to the next, eating and drinking, every day of their lives. I think they should take the trouble to do something in return for all the excellent meals they get.

Gina. But you didn't tell them that?

Hjalmar (*humming*). Hm—hm—hm; they heard something that astonished them, I can tell you.

Ekdal. And all of 'em gentry!

Hjalmar. That didn't save them. (*Casually*.) And then we had a little argument about Tokay.

Ekdal. Tokay, did you say? That's a grand wine, if you like!

Hjalmar. It *can* be a grand wine. But of course, you know, all vintages are not of the same quality; it entirely depends how much sunshine the vines have had.

Gina. There isn't anything you don't know, Hjalmar.

Ekdal. And did they want to argue about that?

Hjalmar. They tried to; but they were informed that it was just the same with gentry. All years are not equally good in their case either, they were told.

Gina. I don't know how you think of such things!

Ekdal. Ha—ha! They had to put that in their pipes and smoke it?

Hjalmar. We let them have it straight between the eyes.

Ekdal. Do you hear that, Gina? Straight between the eyes! —and gentry too!

Gina. Fancy that, straight between the eyes!

Hjalmar. Yes, but I don't want you to talk about it. One doesn't repeat those sort of things. The whole thing passed off quite amicably, of course. They were very genial, pleasant fellows. Why should I want to hurt their feelings? Not I.

Ekdal. But straight between the eyes——

Hedvig (*coaxingly*). How funny it is to see you in dress clothes. You look very nice in dress clothes, father.

Hjalmar. Yes, don't you think so? And this really fits me beautifully. It looks almost as if it had been made for me—a little tight in the armholes, perhaps—help me, Hedvig. (*Takes off the coat*.) I would rather put on my jacket. Where have you put my jacket, Gina?

Gina. Here it is. (*Brings the jacket and helps him on with it*.)

Hjalmar. That's better! Be sure you don't forget to let Molvik have the suit back to-morrow morning.

Gina (*folding it up*). I'll see to it.

Hjalmar (*stretching himself*). Ah, that's more comfortable. And I rather fancy a loose, easy coat like this suits my style better. Don't you think so, Hedvig?

Hedvig. Yes, father.

Hjalmar. Especially if I tie my cravat with flowing ends, like this—what do you think?

Hedvig. Yes, it goes so well with your beard and your thick curly hair.

Hjalmar. I don't know that I should call it curly; I should think 'wavy' was a better word.

Hedvig. Yes, it has beautiful waves in it.

Hjalmar. That's it—wavy.

Hedvig (*after a little pause, pulling his coat*). Father!

Hjalmar. Well, what is it?

Hedvig. You know quite well.

Hjalmar. No, indeed I don't.

Hedvig (*half laughing and half crying*). Father, you mustn't tease me any longer.

Hjalmar. But what is it?

Hedvig (*shaking him*). Don't pretend! Out with them, father—the good things you promised to bring home to me.

Hjalmar. There, just fancy my having forgotten all about it!

Hedvig. No, you are only teasing me, father! It's too bad. Where have you hidden it?

Hjalmar. Well, if I haven't forgotten all about it! But wait a bit, Hedvig, I have got something else for you. (*Rises, and hunts in the pockets of the dress coat.*)

Hedvig (*jumping and clapping her hands*). Oh, mother! mother!

Gina. You see, if you only give him time——

Hjalmar (*holding out a bit of paper*). Look, here it is.

Hedvig. That! It's only a piece of paper.

Hjalmar. It's the list of the different courses, my dear—the whole list. Here is 'Menu' at the top, that means the list of courses.

Hedvig. Is that all you have got?

Hjalmar. I forgot to bring anything else, I tell you. But I can tell you all these good things were a great treat. Sit down at the table now and read the list, and I will describe the taste of all the dishes to you. Look, Hedvig.

Hedvig (*gulping down her tears*). Thank you. (*She sits down, but does not read it.* GINA *makes signs to her, and* HJALMAR *notices it.*)

Hjalmar (*walking up and down*). It's incredible what the father of a family is expected to be able to think about; and if he forgets the slightest little thing, he is sure to see glum faces at once. Well, one gets accustomed even to that. (*Stands by the stove beside his father.*) Have you taken a peep in there this evening, father?

Ekdal. Of course I have.   She has gone into the basket.

Hjalmar. Has she gone into the basket?   She is beginning to get used to it, then.

Ekdal. Yes, I told you she would.   But, you know, there are some little matters——

Hjalmar. Little improvements, eh?

Ekdal. Yes, but we must see to them.

Hjalmar. Very well, let us talk over these improvements, father.   Come and sit on the sofa.

Ekdal. All right.   But I think I will just attend to my pipe first—it wants cleaning.   Hm!   (*Goes into his room.*)

Gina (*smiling at* HJALMAR). Clean his pipe!

Hjalmar. Come, come, Gina—let him be.   Poor, broken-down old fellow.   Yes, these improvements—we had better get them off our hands to-morrow.

Gina. You won't have time to-morrow, Ekdal.

Hedvig (*interrupting*). Oh yes, he will, mother!

Gina. Remember those prints that have got to be retouched. They have asked for them over and over again.

Hjalmar. Heavens above, those prints again!   I'll finish those off easily enough.   Are there any new orders?

Gina. No, worse luck.   There are only the two appointments you booked for to-morrow.

Hjalmar. Nothing else?   Well, of course, if people won't exert themselves——

Gina. But what am I to do?   I am sure I advertise as much as I can.

Hjalmar. Yes, you advertise!—and you see how much good it does.   I suppose nobody has been to look at the room either?

Gina. Not yet.

Hjalmar. What else could you expect?   If people won't keep their wits about them——   You really must pull yourself together, Gina.

Hedvig (*coming forward*). Shall I get your flute, father?

Hjalmar. No, no; I have no room for pleasures in my life. (*Walking about.*)   Work, work—I will show you what work means to-morrow, you may be sure of that.   I shall go on working as long as my strength holds out——

Gina. My dear Hjalmar, I didn't mean you to take me up that way.

Hedvig. Wouldn't you like me to bring you a bottle of beer, father?

Hjalmar. Certainly not, I don't want anything. (*Stops suddenly.*) Beer?—did you say beer?

Hedvig (*briskly*). Yes, father; lovely cool beer.

Hjalmar. Well, if you insist, I don't mind if you do bring me a bottle.

Gina. Yes, do, Hedvig; then we shall feel cosy.

(HEDVIG *runs towards the kitchen.* HJALMAR, *who is standing by the stove, stops her, looks at her, and draws her towards him.*)

Hjalmar. My little Hedvig!

Hedvig (*with tears of joy in her eyes*). Dear, kind father!

Hjalmar. No, you mustn't call me that. There was I, sitting at the rich man's table, enjoying myself, sitting there filling myself with all his good things—— I might at least have remembered——!

Gina (*sitting down at the table*). Don't be absurd, Hjalmar.

Hjalmar. It's true. But you mustn't think too much of that. You know, anyway, how much I love you.

Hedvig (*throwing her arms round him*). And we love you so awfully, father!

Hjalmar. And if sometimes I am unreasonable with you, you will remember—won't you—that I am a man beset by a host of cares. There, there! (*Wipes his eyes.*) No beer at such a moment as this. Give me my flute. (HEDVIG *runs to the bookcase and gets it for him.*) Thank you. That's better. With my flute in my hand, and you two beside me——! (HEDVIG *sits down at the table beside* GINA. HJALMAR *walks up and down, then resolutely begins playing a Bohemian country dance, but in very slow time and very sentimentally. He soon stops, stretches out his left hand to* GINA *and says in a voice full of emotion.*) No matter if we have to live poorly and frugally, Gina—this is our home; and I will say this, that it is good to be at home again. (*He resumes his playing; shortly afterwards a knock is heard at the door.*)

Gina (*getting up*). Hush, Hjalmar—I think there is someone at the door.

Hjalmar (*laying down his flute*). Of course!

(GINA *goes and opens the door.*)

Gregers Werle (*speaking outside the door*). I beg your pardon——

Gina (*retreating a little*). Ah!

Gregers (outside). Is this where Mr Ekdal the photographer lives?

Gina. Yes, it is.

Hjalmar (going to the door). Gregers! Is it you, after all? Come in, come in.

Gregers (coming in). I told you I would come up and see you.

Hjalmar. But to-night——? Have you left all your guests?

Gregers. I have left my guests and my home. Good evening, Mrs Ekdal. I don't suppose you recognize me?

Gina. Of course I do; you are not so difficult to recognize, Mr Werle.

Gregers. I suppose not; I am like my mother, and no doubt you remember her a little.

Hjalmar. Did you say that you had left your home?

Gregers. Yes, I have gone to an hotel.

Hjalmar. Indeed? Well, as you are here, take off your things and sit down.

Gregers. Thank you. *(He takes off his coat. He has changed his clothes, and is dressed in a plain grey suit of provincial cut.)*

Hjalmar. Sit down here on the sofa. Make yourself at home. (GREGERS *sits on the sofa and* HJALMAR *on the chair by the table.)*

Gregers (looking round him). So this is where you live, Hjalmar. Do you work here too?

Hjalmar. This is the studio, as you can see——

Gina. It is our largest room, and so we prefer sitting in here.

Hjalmar. We used to live in better quarters, but these have one great advantage, there is such a splendid amount of space——

Gina. And we have a room on the other side of the passage, which we can let.

Gregers (to HJALMAR). Ah!—have you any lodgers?

Hjalmar. No, not yet. It's not so easy, you know; one has to make an effort to get them. *(To* HEDVIG.) What about that beer? (HEDVIG *nods and goes into the kitchen.)*

Gregers. Is that your daughter?

Hjalmar. Yes, that is Hedvig.

Gregers. Your only child?

Hjalmar. Our only child, yes. She is the source of our greatest happiness and—*(lowering his voice)* also of our keenest sorrow.

Gregers. What do you mean?

Hjalmar. She is dangerously threatened with the loss of her sight.

Gregers. Going blind!

Hjalmar. Yes. There are only the first symptoms of it at present, and all may go well for some time yet. But the doctor has warned us. It is inevitable.

Gregers. What a terrible misfortune! What is the cause of it?

Hjalmar (sighing). It is hereditary, apparently.

Gregers (starting). Hereditary?

Gina. Hjalmar's mother had weak eyes too.

Hjalmar. Yes, so my father tells me; I can't remember her, you know.

Gregers. Poor child! And how does she take it?

Hjalmar. Oh well, as you can imagine we have not had the heart to tell her anything about it. She suspects nothing. She is as happy and careless as a bird, singing about the house, and so she is flitting through her life into the blackness that awaits her. *(Despairingly.)* It is terribly hard for me, Gregers.

(HEDVIG *comes in, bringing a tray with beer and glasses, and sets it down on the table.*)

Hjalmar (stroking her hair). Thank you, dear, thank you. (HEDVIG *puts her arms round his neck and whispers in his ear.*) No—no bread and butter, thanks—unless perhaps you would take some, Gregers?

Gregers (shaking his head). No, thanks.

Hjalmar (still speaking in a melancholy tone). Well, you may as well bring in a little, all the same. If you have a crusty piece, I should prefer it—and be sure to see that there is enough butter on it. (HEDVIG *nods happily and goes into the kitchen again.*)

Gregers (who has followed her with his eyes). She seems well and strong in other respects.

Gina. Yes, thank heaven, she is quite well in every other way.

Gregers. She looks as if she will be like you when she grows up, Mrs Ekdal. How old is she now?

Gina. Hedvig is almost fourteen; her birthday is the day after to-morrow.

Gregers. She is tall for her age.

Gina. Yes, she has grown a lot this last year.

Gregers. These young people growing up make us realize our own age. How long have you been married now?

Gina. We have been married—let me see—just fifteen years.

Gregers. Can it be so long as that!

Gina (looks at him watchfully). It is indeed.

Hjalmar. Yes, that it is. Fifteen years all but a few months. (*Changes the subject.*) They must have seemed long years to you up at the works, Gregers.

Gregers. They did seem long while I was getting through them; but now, looking back on them, I can scarcely believe it is all that time.

(*Old* EKDAL *comes in from his room, without his pipe, and wearing his old military cap. He walks a little unsteadily.*)

Ekdal. Now then, Hjalmar, we can sit down and talk over those—hm! What is it—what is it?

Hjalmar (going towards him). Father, someone is here—— Gregers Werle. I don't know whether you remember him?

Ekdal (looking at GREGERS, *who has risen).* Werle? Do you mean the son? What does he want with me?

Hjalmar. Nothing; it is me he has come to see.

Ekdal. Oh, then there is nothing the matter?

Hjalmar. No, of course not.

Ekdal (swinging his arms). I don't mind, you know; I am not afraid, but——

Gregers (going up to him). I only want to bring you a greeting from your old hunting-ground, Lieutenant Ekdal.

Ekdal. My hunting-ground?

Gregers. Yes, from up there round the Höidal works.

Ekdal. Ah, up there. I was well known up there once.

Gregers. You were a mighty hunter in those days.

Ekdal. Ah, that I was, believe me. You are looking at my cap. I need ask no one's leave to wear it here indoors. So long as I don't go into the streets with it on——

(HEDVIG *brings in a plate of bread and butter, and puts it on the table.*)

Hjalmar. Sit down, father, and have a glass of beer. Help yourself, Gregers.

(EKDAL *totters over to the sofa, mumbling.* GREGERS *sits down on a chair beside him.* HJALMAR *sits on the other side of* GREGERS. GINA *sits a little way from the table and sews;* HEDVIG *stands beside her* FATHER.)

Gregers. Do you remember, Lieutenant Ekdal, how Hjalmar and I used to come up and see you in the summer-time and at Christmas?

Ekdal. Did you? No—no—I don't remember that. But

I can tell you I was a fine sportsman in those days. I have shot bears, too—nine of 'em, I have shot.

Gregers (looking at him sympathetically). And now you get no more shooting.

Ekdal. Oh, I don't know about that. I get some sport still now and then. Not that sort of sport, of course. In the forests, you know—the forests, the forests——! (*Drinks.*) Are the forests looking fine up there now?

Gregers. Not so fine as in your day. A lot of them have been cut down.

Ekdal'(lowering his voice, as if afraid). That's a dangerous thing to do. That brings trouble. The forests avenge themselves.

Hjalmar (filling his FATHER'S *glass).* Now, father—a little more.

Gregers. How can a man like you, who were always used to being in the open, live in a stuffy town, boxed in by four walls like this?

Ekdal (looking at HJALMAR *with a quiet smile).* Oh, it is not so bad here, not bad at all.

Gregers. But think of all you were always used to—the cool, refreshing breezes, the free life in the woods and on the moors, among the animals and birds——

Ekdal (smiling). Hjalmar, shall we show it to him?

Hjalmar (hastily and with some embarrassment). No, no, father—not to-night.

Gregers. What does he want to show me?

Hjalmar. Oh, it is only a sort of—— You can see it some other time.

Gregers (continues talking to EKDAL). What I had in my mind, Lieutenant Ekdal, was that you should come back up to the works with me; I am going back there very soon. You could easily get some copying to do up there too; and here you haven't a single thing to give you pleasure or to amuse you.

Ekdal (staring at him in amazement). I haven't a single thing to——!

Gregers. Well, of course, you have Hjalmar; but then he has his own family ties. But a man like you, who has always felt so strongly the call of a free, unfettered life——

Ekdal (striking the table). Hjalmar, he *shall* see it!

Hjalmar. But, father, is it worth while now? It's dark, you know.

Ekdal. Nonsense, there is moonlight. (*Gets up.*) He *shall* see it, I say. Let me pass—and you come and help me, Hjalmar.

Hedvig. Yes, do, father!

Hjalmar (*getting up*). Very well.

Gregers (*to* GINA). What does he want me to see?

Gina. Oh, you mustn't expect to see anything very wonderful.

(EKDAL *and* HJALMAR *have gone to the back of the stage, and each of them pushes back one side of the sliding doors.* HEDVIG *helps the old man;* GREGERS *remains standing by the sofa;* GINA *sits quietly sewing. The open doors disclose a large, irregularly shaped attic, full of recesses and with two stove-pipes running up through it. Through the little roof-windows the bright moonlight is pouring in upon certain spots in the attic; the rest of it is in deep shadow.*)

Ekdal (*to* GREGERS). Come close and have a look.

Gregers (*going to him*). What is there for me to see?

Ekdal. Come and take a good look. Hm!

Hjalmar (*in a slightly constrained tone*). This is all my father's, you know.

Gregers (*comes to the door and looks into the attic*). You keep poultry then, Lieutenant Ekdal!

Ekdal. I should think we do keep poultry. They are roosting now; but you should just see them in the daytime!

Hedvig. And we have got a——

Ekdal. Hush! Hush! Don't say anything yet.

Gregers. You have got pigeons too, I see.

Ekdal. Yes, I shouldn't wonder if we had got pigeons too! They have nesting-boxes up there under the eaves, you see; pigeons like to roost well above ground, you know.

Gregers. They are not common pigeons, though.

Ekdal. Common pigeons! No, I should think not! We have got tumblers, and a pair of pouters too. But come and look here! Can you see that hutch over there against the wall?

Gregers. Yes, what is it for?

Ekdal. That's where the rabbits sleep at night.

Gregers. What, have you got rabbits too?

Ekdal. Yes, you bet we have rabbits! He is asking if we have got rabbits, Hjalmar! Hm! But now I will show you the great sight! Now you shall see it! Get out of the way, Hedvig. Just stand here; that's it; now look in there. Don't you see a basket with straw in it?

Gregers. Yes. And I can see a bird lying in the basket.

Ekdal. Hm!—a bird!

Gregers. Isn't it a duck?

Hjalmar. But what kind of a duck, should you say.

Hedvig. It isn't an ordinary duck.

Ekdal. Sh!

Gregers. It isn't a foreign bird either.

Ekdal. No, Mr—Werle, that is no foreign bird, because it is a wild duck.

Gregers. No! is it really? A wild duck?

Ekdal. Yes, that it is. The 'bird,' as you call it, is a wild duck. That's our wild duck.

Hedvig. My wild duck. It belongs to me.

Gregers. Is it possible it can live up here in the attic? Does it do well?

Ekdal. Of course it has a trough of water to splash about in.

Hjalmar. And gets fresh water every other day.

Gina (turning to HJALMAR). Hjalmar, dear, it is getting icy cold in here, you know.

Ekdal. Hm! we will shut it up then. We mustn't disturb their night's rest. Close them, Hedvig. (HJALMAR *and* HEDVIG *push the doors together.*) Some other time you shall see it properly. (*Sits down in the arm-chair by the stove.*) They are most remarkable birds, wild ducks, I can tell you.

Gregers. But how did you manage to capture it?

Ekdal. I didn't capture it. It is a certain person in the town here that we have to thank for it.

Gregers (with a slight start). I suppose that man is not my father, by any chance?

Ekdal. You have hit it. Your father and no one else. Hm!

Hjalmar. It's funny you should guess that, Gregers.

Gregers. You told me you were indebted to my father for so many different things; so I thought very likely——

Gina. But we didn't get the duck from Mr Werle himself——

Ekdal. It is Haakon Werle we have to thank for it all the same, Gina. (*To* GREGERS.) He was out in a boat, you see, and shot it. But your father's sight isn't good, you know, and it was only wounded.

Gregers. I see, it was only slightly hit.

Hjalmar. Yes, only in two or three places.

Hedvig. It was hit in the wing, so it couldn't fly.

Gregers. I see; then I suppose it dived down to the bottom?

Ekdal (sleepily, in a thick voice). Naturally. Wild duck always do that.   They stick down at the bottom—as deep as they can get—bite tight hold of the weed and wrack and all the rubbish that is down there.   And then they never come up again.

Gregers. But, Lieutenant Ekdal, your wild duck came up again.

Ekdal. He had an extraordinarily clever dog, your father. And the dog—it dived after it and hauled it up again.

Gregers (*turning to* HJALMAR). And then you got it?

Hjalmar. Not directly.   It was brought to your father's house first, but it didn't thrive there; so Pettersen asked permission to kill it——

Ekdal (*half asleep*). Hm!—Pettersen—yes—old idiot!——

Hjalmar (*lowering his voice*). That was how we got it, you see. Father knows Pettersen a little, and heard this about the wild duck, and managed to get it handed over to him.

Gregers. And now it thrives quite well in the attic there?

Hjalmar. Yes, perfectly well.   It has grown fat.   It has been so long in there now that it has forgotten all about its own wild life; and that was all that was necessary.

Gregers. You are right there, Hjalmar.   Only, never let it see the sky and the water.—But I mustn't stay any longer.   I think your father has gone to sleep.

Hjalmar. Oh, don't go because of that.

Gregers. But, by the way—you said you had a room to let, a room you don't use?

Hjalmar. Yes—why?   Do you happen to know anyone——?

Gregers. Can I have the room?

Hjalmar. You?

Gina. What, you, Mr Werle?

Gregers. Can I have the room?   If so, I will move in early to-morrow morning.

Hjalmar. Certainly, by all means——

Gina. But, Mr Werle, it really isn't the sort of room to suit you.

Hjalmar. Gina, how can you say that!

Gina. Well, it isn't big enough or light enough, and——

Gregers. That doesn't matter at all, Mrs Ekdal.

Hjalmar. I should call it a very nice room, and not too badly furnished either.

Gina. But remember the couple that lodge underneath.

Gregers. Who are they?

Gina. One of them used to be a private tutor——

Hjalmar. Mr Molvik—he has taken a degree——·

Gina. And the other is a doctor by the name of Relling.

Gregers. Relling? I know him a little; he used to practise up at Höidal at one time.

Gina. They are a regular pair of good-for-nothings. They are often out on the spree in the evening, and they come home late at night and not always quite——

Gregers. I should easily get used to that. I hope I shall settle down like the wild duck.

Gina. Well, I think you ought to sleep on it first, anyway.

Gregers. You don't seem to like the idea of having me in the house, Mrs Ekdal.

Gina. Gracious me! what makes you think that?

Hjalmar. I must say it is extremely odd of you, Gina. (*To* GREGERS.) Tell me, do you propose remaining here in town for the present?

Gregers (*putting on his overcoat*). Yes, now I propose to remain here.

Hjalmar. But not at home with your father? What do you intend to do with yourself?

Gregers. Ah, if only I knew that, it would all be plain sailing. But when one has had the misfortune to be christened 'Gregers' —'Gregers,' and 'Werle' to follow—did you ever hear anything so hideous?——

Hjalmar. It doesn't sound so to me.

Gregers (*shuddering*). I should feel inclined to spit on any fellow with a name like that. Once a man has had the misfortune to find himself saddled with the name of Gregers Werle, as I have——

Hjalmar (*laughing*). Ha, ha! Well, but if you weren't Gregers Werle, what would you like to be?

Gregers. If I could choose, I would rather be a clever dog than anything else.

Gina. A dog!

Hedvig (*involuntarily*). Oh no!

Gregers. Yes, an extraordinarily clever dog; the sort of dog that would go down to the bottom after wild duck, when they dive down and bite tight hold of the weed and wrack in the mud.

Hjalmar. I'll tell you something, Gregers—I don't understand a word of all this.

Gregers. No, and I don't suppose the meaning is very pretty either. Well, then, early to-morrow morning I will move in.

(*To* GINA.)   I shan't give you any trouble; I do everything for myself.   (*To* HJALMAR.)   We will finish our chat to-morrow. Good night, Mrs Ekdal.   (*Nods to* HEDVIG.)   Good night.

Gina. Good night, Mr Werle.

Hedvig. Good night.

Hjalmar (*who has lit a candle*). Wait a moment, I must give you a light; it is sure to be dark on the stairs. (GREGERS and HJALMAR *go out by the outer door.*)

Gina (*staring in front of her, with her sewing lying on her lap*). A funny idea, to want to be a dog!

Hedvig. Do you know, mother—I believe he meant something quite different by that.

Gina. What else could he mean?

Hedvig. I don't know; but I thought he seemed to mean something quite different from what he said—all the time.

Gina. Do you think so?   It certainly was queer.

Hjalmar (*coming back*). The lamp was still lit. (*Puts out the candle and lays it down.*)   Now, at last one can get a chance of something to eat. (*Begins to eat the bread and butter.*)   Well, you see, Gina—if only you keep your wits about you——

Gina. How do you mean, keep your wits about you?

Hjalmar. Well, anyway we have had a bit of luck, to succeed in letting the room at last.   And, besides, to a man like Gregers —a dear old friend.

Gina. Well, I really don't know what to say about it.

Hedvig. Oh mother, you will see it will be lovely.

Hjalmar. You certainly are very odd.   A little while ago you were so bent on letting the room, and now you don't like it.

Gina. Oh, I do, Hjalmar—if only it had been to someone else. What do you suppose his father will say?

Hjalmar. Old Werle?   It's no business of his.

Gina. But you may be sure things have gone wrong between them again, as the young man is leaving his father's house. You know the sort of terms those two are on.

Hjalmar. That may be all very true, but——

Gina. And it is quite likely his father may think that you are at the bottom of it all.

Hjalmar. Let him think what he likes!   Mr Werle has done a tremendous lot for me; I am the last to want to deny it.   But that is no reason why I should think myself bound to consult him in everything all my life.

Gina. But, Hjalmar dear, it might end in grandfather's

suffering for it; he might lose the little bit of money he gets from Graaberg.

Hjalmar. I feel almost inclined to say I wish he would! Don't you suppose it is a humiliating thing for a man like me, to see his grey-haired old father treated like an outcast? But I think that sort of thing is nearly at an end. (*Takes another piece of bread and butter.*) I have a mission in life, and I shall fulfil it!

Hedvig. Oh yes, father, do!

Gina. Sh! Don't wake him up.

Hjalmar (*lowering his voice*). I *shall* fulfil it, I say. The day will come when—when—— And that is why it is a good thing we got the room let; it puts me in a more independent position. And a man who has a mission in life must be independent of others. (*Stands by his father's chair and speaks with emotion.*) Poor old white-haired father! You may depend on your Hjalmar! He has broad shoulders—strong shoulders, at any rate. Some fine day you shall wake up, and—— (*To* GINA.) Don't you believe it?

Gina (*getting up*). Of course I do; but the first thing is to see about getting him to bed.

Hjalmar. Yes, come along then. (*They lift the old man carefully.*)

ACT III

(SCENE.—HJALMAR EKDAL'S *studio, the following morning. The sun is shining in through the big window in the sloping roof, where the curtain has been drawn back.* HJALMAR *is sitting at the table busy retouching a photograph. Various other portraits are lying in front of him. After a few moments* GINA *comes in by the outer door, in hat and cloak, and carrying a covered basket.*)

Hjalmar. Back already, Gina?

Gina. Yes, I've no time to waste. (*She puts the basket down on a chair and takes her things off.*)

Hjalmar. Did you look in on Gregers?

Gina. Yes, that I did; and a nice sight too! He had made the room in a pretty state as soon as he arrived.

Hjalmar. How?

Gina. He said he wanted to do everything for himself, you

know. So he tried to get the stove going; and what must he do but shut the regulator, so that the whole room was filled with smoke. Ouf!—there was a stink like——

Hjalmar. You don't mean it!

Gina. But that's not the best of it. He wanted to put the fire out then, so he emptied his washing water into the stove, and flooded the whole floor with a filthy mess.

Hjalmar. What a nuisance!

Gina. I have just got the porter's wife to clean up after him, the dirty tike; but the room won't be fit to go into till the afternoon.

Hjalmar. What is he doing with himself in the meantime?

Gina. He said he would go out for a bit.

Hjalmar. I went to see him, too, for a minute, after you went out.

Gina. So he told me. You have asked him to lunch.

Hjalmar. Just for a snack of lunch, you know. The first day he is here—we could hardly do less. You are sure to have something in the house.

Gina. I'll go and see what I can find.

Hjalmar. Don't be too scrimpy, though; because I fancy Relling and Molvik are coming up too. I happened to meet Relling on the stairs, you see, and so I had to——

Gina. Must we have those two as well?

Hjalmar. Good heavens!—a little bit more or less can't make much difference.

(*Old* EKDAL *opens his door and looks in.*)

Ekdal. Look here, Hjalmar—— (*Seeing* GINA.) Oh!

Gina. Do you want something, grandfather?

Ekdal. No, no—it doesn't matter. Hm! (*Goes into his room again.*)

Gina (*taking up her basket*). Keep your eye on him, and see he doesn't go out.

Hjalmar. Yes, yes, I will. I say, Gina—a little herring salad would be rather nice; I rather think Relling and Molvik were making a night of it last night.

Gina. So long as they don't come before I am ready——

Hjalmar. They won't do that. Take your time.

Gina. All right, and you can get a little work done in the meantime.

Hjalmar. Can't you see I *am* working? I am working as hard as I can.

Gina. You will be able to get those off your hands, you see. (*Takes her basket into the kitchen.* HJALMAR *resumes his work on the photographs with evident reluctance.*)

Ekdal (*peeps in, and, after looking round the studio, says in a low voice*). Have you finished that work?

Hjalmar. I am working away at these portraits——

Ekdal. Oh, well, it doesn't matter—if you are so busy—— Hm! (*Goes in again, but leaves his door open.* HJALMAR *goes on working for a little in silence; then lays down his brush and goes to the door.*)

Hjalmar. Are you busy, father?

Ekdal (*from within, in an aggrieved voice*). If you are busy, I'm busy too. Hm!

Hjalmar. Yes, of course. (*Returns to his work. After a few moments* EKDAL *comes out of his room again.*)

Ekdal. Hm! Look here, Hjalmar, I am not so busy as all that.

Hjalmar. I thought you were doing your copying.

Ekdal. Damn Graaberg! Can't he wait a day or two? It's not a matter of life and death, I suppose.

Hjalmar. No; and you are not his slave, anyway.

Ekdal. And there is that other matter in there——

Hjalmar. Exactly. Do you want to go in? Shall I open the doors for you?

Ekdal. I don't think it would be a bad idea.

Hjalmar (*rising*). And then we shall have got *that* off our hands.

Ekdal. Just so, yes. It must be ready by to-morrow morning early. We did say to-morrow, didn't we? Eh?

Hjalmar. Yes, to-morrow.

HJALMAR *and* EKDAL *each pull back a division of the sliding door. The morning sun is shining in through the top-lights of the attic; some of the pigeons are flying about, others sitting cooing on the rafters; from time to time the sound of hens cackling is heard from the recesses of the attic.*)

Hjalmar. There—now you can start, father.

Ekdal (*going in*). Aren't you coming, too?

Hjalmar. Well, I don't know—I think I—— (*Seeing* GINA *at the kitchen door.*) No, I haven't time; I must work. But we must use our patent arrangement. (*He pulls a cord and lowers a curtain, of which the bottom part is made out of a strip of old sailcloth, while the upper part is a fisherman's net stretched out.*

When it is down, the floor of the attic is no longer visible.)   That's it.   Now I can sit down in peace for a little.

Gina. Is he rummaging about in there again?

Hjalmar. Would you rather he had gone straight to the wine-shop? (*Sitting down.*) Is there anything you want? You look so——

Gina. I only wanted to ask if you thought we could have lunch in here?

Hjalmar. Yes; I suppose we have no sitters coming as early as that?

Gina. No, I don't expect anyone except the engaged couple who want to be taken together. .

Hjalmar. Why the devil can't they be taken together some other day!

Gina. It's all right, Hjalmar dear; I arranged to take them in the afternoon, when you are having your nap.

Hjalmar. That's fine! Yes, then, we will have lunch in here.

Gina. Very well, but there is no hurry about laying the lunch; you can have the table for a good while yet.

Hjalmar. Can't you see that I am taking every opportunity that I can to use the table!

Gina. Then you will be free afterwards, you see. (*Goes into the kitchen again.   Short pause.*)

Ekdal (*standing in the attic doorway, behind the net*).   Hjalmar!

Hjalmar. Yes?

Ekdal. I am afraid we must move the water-trough after all.

Hjalmar. Exactly what I have said all along.

Ekdal. Hm—hm—hm! (*Moves away from the door.*)

(HJALMAR *goes on with his work for a little, then glances at the attic, and is just getting up when* HEDVIG *comes in from the kitchen; thereupon he sits down again promptly.*)

Hjalmar. What do you want?

Hedvig. Only to come in to you, father.

Hjalmar (*after a moment's pause*). You seem to be very inquisitive.   Were you sent to watch me?

Hedvig. Of course not.

Hjalmar. What is your mother doing in there now?

Hedvig. She's busy making a herring salad. (*Goes up to the table.*) Isn't there any little thing I could help you with, father?

Hjalmar. No, no.   It is right that I should be the one to work away at it all—as long as my strength holds out.   There is no fear of my wanting help, Hedvig—at any rate so long as my health doesn't give way.

Hedvig. Oh, father—don't say such horrid things! (*She wanders about the room, then stands in the attic doorway and looks in.*)

Hjalmar. What is he doing in there?

Hedvig. I believe he is making a new path to the water-trough.

Hjalmar. He will never be able to manage that by himself. What a nuisance it is that I have got to sit here and——

Hedvig (*going to him*). Let me have the brush, father; I can do it, you know.

Hjalmar. Nonsense, you would only hurt your eyes.

Hedvig. Of course I shan't.   Give me the brush.

Hjalmar (*getting up*). Well, it certainly wouldn't take me more than a minute or two.

Hedvig. Pooh! What harm can it do me? (*Takes the brush from him.*) Now then. (*Sits down.*) I have got one here as a model, you know.

Hjalmar. But don't hurt your eyes! Do you hear? I won't be responsible; you must take the responsibility yourself, understand that.

Hedvig (*going on with the work*). Yes, yes, I will.

Hjalmar. Clever little girl! Just for a minute or two, you understand. (*He stoops under the net and goes into the attic.* HEDVIG *sits still, working.* HJALMAR's *voice and his* FATHER's *are heard discussing something.*)

Hjalmar (*coming to the net*). Hedvig, just give me the pincers; they are on the shelf. And the chisel. (*Looks back into the attic.*) Now you will see, father. Just let me show you first what I mean. (HEDVIG *has fetched the tools, and gives them to him.*) Thanks. I think it was a good thing I came, you know. (*Goes into the attic. Sounds of carpentering and talking are heard from within.* HEDVIG *stands looking after him. A moment later a knock is heard at the outer door, but she does not notice it.*)

Gregers Werle (*who is bareheaded and without an overcoat, comes in and stands for a moment in the doorway*). Ahem!

Hedvig (*turns round and goes to him*). Oh, good morning! Won't you come in?

Gregers. Thanks. (*Glances towards the attic.*) You seem to have workmen in the house.

Hedvig. No, it's only father and grandfather. I'll go and tell them.

Gregers. No, no, don't do that; I would rather wait a little. (*Sits down on the sofa.*)

Hedvig. It's so untidy here—— (*Begins to collect the photographs.*)

Gregers. Oh, let them be. Are they portraits that want finishing?

Hedvig. Yes, just a little job I was helping father with.

Gregers. Anyway, don't let me disturb you.

Hedvig. Oh, you don't. (*She draws the things to her again and sits down to her work.* GREGERS *watches her for a time without speaking.*)

Gregers. Has the wild duck had a good night?

Hedvig. Yes, thanks, I think it had.

Gregers (*turning towards the attic*). In the daylight it looks quite a different place from what it did in moonlight.

Hedvig. Yes, it has such a different look at different times. In the morning it looks quite different from in the evening, and when it rains you wouldn't think it was the same place as on a fine day.

Gregers. Ah, have you noticed that?

Hedvig. You couldn't help noticing it.

Gregers. Are you fond of being in there with the wild duck, too?

Hedvig. Yes, when I can——

Gregers. But I expect you haven't much time for that. I suppose you go to school?

Hedvig. No, I don't go to school any more. Father is afraid of my hurting my eyes.

Gregers. I see; I suppose he teaches you himself, then?

Hedvig. He has promised to teach me, but he hasn't had time so far.

Gregers. But isn't there anyone else to give you a little help?

Hedvig. Yes, there is Mr Molvik, but he isn't always exactly—quite—that is to say——

Gregers. Not quite sober?

Hedvig. That's it.

Gregers. I see; then you have a good deal of time to yourself. And, in there, I suppose, it is like a little world of its own, isn't it?

Hedvig. Yes, exactly. And there are such lots of wonderful things in there.

Gregers. Are there?

Hedvig. Yes, there are great cupboards full of books, and in lots of the books there are pictures.

Gregers. I see.

Hedvig. And then there is an old desk with drawers and flaps in it, and a huge clock with figures that ought to come out when it strikes. But the clock isn't going any longer.

Gregers. So time has ceased to exist in there—beside the wild duck.

Hedvig. Yes. And there is an old paint-box and things—and all the books.

Gregers. And you like reading the books?

Hedvig. Yes, when I can manage it. But the most of them are in English, and I can't read that; so then I look at the pictures. There is a great big book called *Harrison's History of London*; it's quite a hundred years old, and there's a tremendous lot of pictures in it. At the beginning there's a picture of Death, with an hour-glass, and a girl. I don't like that. But there are all the other pictures of churches, and castles, and streets, and big ships sailing on the sea.

Gregers. But, tell me, where did you get all these wonderful things from?

Hedvig. Oh, an old sea-captain lived here once, and he used to bring them home with him. They called him the Flying Dutchman; it was a funny thing to call him, because he wasn't a Dutchman at all.

Gregers. Wasn't he?

Hedvig. No. But one day he never came back, and all these things were left here.

Gregers. Tell me this—when you are sitting in there looking at the pictures, don't you want to get away out into the big world and see it for yourself?

Hedvig. No, not me! I want to stay at home here always and help father and mother.

Gregers. To finish photographs?

Hedvig. No, not only that. What I should like best of all would be to learn to engrave pictures like the ones in the English books.

Gregers. Hm! what does your father say to that?

Hedvig. I don't think father likes it; he is so funny about that. Would you believe it, he wants me to learn such absurd things as basket-making and straw-plaiting! I don't see any good in my doing that.

Gregers. Nor do I.

Hedvig. But father is right so far, that if I had learnt to make baskets, I could have made the new basket for the wild duck.

Gregers. Yes, so you could; and it was your business to see it was comfortable, wasn't it?

Hedvig. Yes, because it's my wild duck.

Gregers. Of course it is.

Hedvig. Yes, it's my very own.   But I lend it to father and grandfather as long as they like.

Gregers. I see, but what do they want it for?

Hedvig. Oh, they look after it, and build places for it, and all that sort of thing.

Gregers. I see; it is the most important person in there.

Hedvig. That it is, because it's a real, true wild duck.   Poor thing, it hasn't anyone to make friends with; isn't it a pity!

Gregers. It has no brothers and sisters, as the rabbits have.

Hedvig. No.   The hens have got lots of others there, that they were chickens with; but it has come right away from all its friends, poor thing.   It is all so mysterious about the wild duck. It hasn't any friends—and no one knows where it came from, either.

Gregers. And then it has been down to the ocean's depths.

Hedvig (*looks quickly at him, half smiles, and asks*). Why do you say 'the ocean's depths'?

Gregers. What else should I say?

Hedvig. You might have said 'the bottom of the sea.'

Gregers. Isn't it just the same if I say 'the ocean's depths'?

Hedvig. It sounds so funny to me to hear anyone else say 'the ocean's depths.'

Gregers. Why?   Tell me why.

Hedvig. No, I won't; it's only foolishness.

Gregers. It isn't.   Tell me why you smiled.

Hedvig. It is because whenever I happen to think all at once— suddenly—of what is in there, the whole room and all that's in it make me think of 'the ocean's depths.'   But that's all nonsense.

Gregers. No, don't say that.

Hedvig. Well, it's nothing but an attic.

Gregers (*looking earnestly at her*). Are you so sure of that?

Hedvig (*astonished*). Sure that it's an attic?

Gregers. Yes; are you so sure of that?

(HEDVIG *is silent and looks at him open-mouthed.*   GINA *comes in from the kitchen to lay the table.*)

Gregers (*rising*). I am afraid I have come too early.

Gina. Oh, well, you have got to be somewhere; and we shall very soon be ready. Clear up the table, Hedvig. (HEDVIG *gathers up the things; she and* GINA *lay the table during the following dialogue.* GREGERS *sits down in the arm-chair and turns over the pages of an album.*)

Gregers. I hear you can retouch photos, Mrs Ekdal.

Gina (*glancing at him*). Mhm! I can.

Gregers. That must have come in very handy.

Gina. How do you mean?

Gregers. As Hjalmar has taken to photography, I mean.

Hedvig. Mother can take photographs too.

Gina. Oh, yes, of course I got taught to do that.

Gregers. I suppose it is you who run the business, then?

Gina. Well, when Hjalmar hasn't time himself, I——

Gregers. His old father takes up a great deal of his time, I suppose?

Gina. Yes, and it isn't the sort of work for a man like Hjalmar to go taking rubbishin' portraits all day long.

Gregers. Exactly; but still, when he had once gone in for the thing——

Gina. I should like you to understand, Mr Werle, that Hjalmar is not an ordinary photographer.

Gregers. Quite, quite; but—— (*A shot is fired within the attic.* GREGERS *starts up.*) What's that!

Gina. Bah! now they are at their firing again.

Gregers. Do they use guns in there too?

Hedvig. They go out shooting.

Gregers. What on earth——? (*Goes to the attic door.*) Have you gone out shooting, Hjalmar?

Hjalmar (*inside the net*). Oh, are you there? I didn't know. I was so busy—— (*To* HEDVIG.) To think of your not telling us! (*Comes into the studio.*)

Gregers. Do you go shooting in there in the attic?

Hjalmar (*showing a double-barrelled pistol*). Oh, only with this old thing.

Gina. Yes, you and grandfather will do yourselves some harm one day with that there gun.

Hjalmar (*angrily*). I think I have mentioned that a firearm of this kind is called a pistol.

Gina. Well, that doesn't make it much better, that I can see.

Gregers. So you have become a sportsman too, Hjalmar?

Hjalmar. Oh, we only go after a rabbit or two now and then. It's principally to please my father, you know.

Gina. Men are funny creatures, they must always have something to bemuse them.

Hjalmar (*irritably*). Quite, quite; men must always have something to *a*muse them.

Gina. Well, that's exactly what I said.

Hjalmar. Well—ahem! (*To* GREGERS.) It happens very fortunately, you see, that the attic is so situated that no one can hear us shooting. (*Lays down the pistol on the top shelf of the bookcase.*) Don't touch the pistol, Hedvig; one barrel is loaded, remember.

Gregers (*looking through the net*). You have got a sporting gun too, I see.

Hjalmar. That is father's old gun. It won't shoot any longer, there is something gone wrong with the lock. But it's rather fun to have it there all the same; we can take it to pieces now and then and clean it, and grease it, and put it together again. Of course it's my father's toy, really.

Hedvig (*going to* GREGERS). Now you can see the wild duck properly.

Gregers. I was just looking at it. It seems to me to trail one wing a little.

Hjalmar. Well, no wonder; it was wounded.

Gregers. And it drags one foot a little—doesn't it?

Hjalmar. Perhaps just a tiny bit.

Hedvig. Yes, that was the foot the dog fixed its teeth into.

Hjalmar. But otherwise it hasn't the slightest blemish; and that really is remarkable when you consider that it has had a charge of shot in its wing and has been between a dog's teeth——

Gregers (*glancing at* HEDVIG). And has been down so long in the ocean's depths.

Hedvig (*with a smile*). Yes.

Gina (*standing by the table*). That blessed wild duck! The whole place is turned upside down for it.

Hjalmar. Ahem!—will you soon have finished laying the table?

Gina. Yes, very soon. Come and help me, Hedvig. (*She and* HEDVIG *go into the kitchen.*)

Hjalmar (*in an undertone*). I think perhaps you had better not stand there watching my father; he doesn't like it. (GREGERS *comes away from the attic door.*) And I had better shut the doors, before the others arrive. Sh! sh! Get in with you! (*He hoists up the netting and pulls the doors together.*) That contrivance is my own invention. It is really quite an amusement to have things to contrive and to repair when they go wrong. Besides, it is an absolute necessity, you see, because Gina wouldn't like to have rabbits and fowls wandering about the studio.

Gregers. Of course not, and I suppose the studio is really your wife's domain?

Hjalmar. I hand over the ordinary business as much as possible to her, for that enables me to shut myself up in the sitting-room and give my mind to more important matters.

Gregers. What are they, Hjalmar?

Hjalmar. I wonder you haven't asked that before. But perhaps you haven't heard anyone speak of the invention?

Gregers. The invention? No.

Hjalmar. Really? You haven't heard of it? Oh well, of course, up there in those outlandish parts——

Gregers. Then you have made an invention?

Hjalmar. Not exactly made it yet, but I am working hard on it. You can surely understand that when I decided to take up photography, it was not with the idea of merely taking ordinary portraits.

Gregers No, that is what your wife was saying to me just now.

Hjalmar. I vowed to myself that, if I devoted my powers to this trade, I would so dignify it that it would become both an art and a science. And so I decided to make this remarkable invention.

Gregers. And what is the nature of the invention? What is the idea?

Hjalmar. My dear fellow, you mustn't ask me for details yet. It takes time, you know. And you mustn't suppose it is vanity that impels me. I assure you I don't work for my own sake. No, no; it is the object of my life that is in my thoughts night and day.

Gregers. What object is that?

Hjalmar. Have you forgotten that poor old white-haired man?

Gregers. Your poor father? Yes, but what exactly can you do for him?

Hjalmar. I can revive his dead self-respect by restoring the name of Ekdal to honour and dignity.

Gregers. So that is the object of your life.

Hjalmar. Yes. I mean to rescue that poor shipwrecked being; for shipwrecked he was, when the storm broke over him. As soon as those horrible investigations were begun, he was no longer himself. That very pistol there—the very one that we use to shoot rabbits with—has played its part in the tragedy of the Ekdals.

Gregers. That pistol! Indeed?

Hjalmar. When the sentence of imprisonment was pronounced, he had his pistol in his hand——

Gregers. Did he mean to——?

Hjalmar. Yes, but he did not dare. He was a coward; so dazed and so broken in spirit he was by that time. Can you imagine it? He, a soldier, a man who had shot nine bears and was the descendant of two lieutenant-colonels—one after the other, of course—— Can you imagine it, Gregers?

Gregers. Yes, I can imagine it very well.

Hjalmar. I can't. And I will tell you how the pistol played a part in the history of our house a second time. When they had dressed him in prison clothes and put him under lock and key—that was a terrible time for me, my friend. I kept the blinds down on both my windows. When I peeped out, I saw the sun shining as usual. I couldn't understand it. I saw people going along the street, laughing and talking about casual matters. I could not understand that. It seemed to me as if the whole universe must be standing still as if it were eclipsed.

Gregers. I felt exactly like that when my mother died.

Hjalmar. It was at one of those moments that Hjalmar Ekdal pointed the pistol at his own heart.

Gregers. Then you too meant to——?

Hjalmar. Yes.

Gregers. But you didn't shoot?

Hjalmar. No. At that critical moment I gained the victory over myself. I went on living. But I can tell you it makes a call upon a man's courage to choose life under such conditions.

Gregers. Well, that depends how you look at it.

Hjalmar. No, there is no question about it. But it was best so, for now I shall soon have completed my invention; and Relling thinks, and so do I, that my father will be allowed to wear his uniform again. I shall claim that as my only reward.

Gregers. It is the matter of the uniform, then, that he——

Hjalmar. Yes, that is what he covets and yearns for most of all. You can't imagine how it cuts me to the heart. Every time we keep any little anniversary—such as our wedding-day, or anything of that sort—the old man comes in dressed in the uniform he used to wear in his happier days.   But if he hears so much as a knock at the door, he hurries into his room again as fast as his poor old legs will carry him—because, you see, he daren't show himself like that to strangers.   It is enough to break a son's heart to see it, I can tell you!

Gregers. And about when do you suppose the invention will be ready?

Hjalmar. Oh, good heavens!—you can't expect me to tell you to a day!   A man who has the inventive genius can't control it exactly as he wishes.   Its working depends in great measure on inspiration—on a momentary suggestion—and it is almost impossible to tell beforehand at what moment it will come.

Gregers. But I suppose it is making good progress?

Hjalmar. Certainly it is making progress.   Not a day passes without my turning it over in my mind.   It possesses me entirely. Every afternoon, after I have had my lunch, I lock myself in the sitting-room where I can ruminate in peace.   But it's no use trying to hurry me! that can't do any good—Relling says so, too.

Gregers. But don't you think all those arrangements in the attic there distract you and divert your attention too much?

Hjalmar. Not a bit, not a bit; quite the contrary.   You mustn't say that.   It is impossible for me to be perpetually poring over the same exhausting train of ideas.   I must have something as a secondary occupation, to fill in the blank hours when I am waiting for inspiration.   Nothing that I am doing can prevent the flash of inspiration coming when it has to come.

Gregers. My dear Hjalmar, I am beginning to think you have something of the wild duck in you.

Hjalmar. Something of the wild duck?   How do you mean?

Gregers. You have dived down and bitten yourself tight in the weeds.

Hjalmar. I suppose you refer to that all but fatal blow that crippled my father, and me as well?

Gregers. Not exactly that.   I won't say that you have been wounded, like the duck; but you have got into a poisonous marsh, Hjalmar; you have contracted an insidious disease and have dived down to the bottom to die in the dark.

Hjalmar. I?   Die in the dark?   Look here, Gregers, you really must stop talking such nonsense.

Gregers. Don't you worry, I shall find a way to get you up to the surface again. I have got an object in life too, now; I discovered it yesterday.

Hjalmar. Maybe, but you will have the goodness to leave me out of it. I can assure you that—apart, of course, from my very natural melancholy—I feel as well as any man could wish to be.

Gregers. That very fact is a result of the poison.

Hjalmar. Now, my dear Gregers, be good enough not to talk any more nonsense about diseases and poisons. I am not used to conversation of that sort; in my house no one ever speaks to me about ugly things.

Gregers. I can well believe it.

Hjalmar. Yes, that sort of thing doesn't suit me at all. And there *are* no marsh poisons, as you call them, here. The photographer's home is a humble one—that I know; and my means are small. But I am an inventor, let me tell you, and the bread-winner of a family. That raises me up above my humble circumstances.—Ah, here they come with the lunch!

(GINA *and* HEDVIG *bring in bottles of beer, a decanter of brandy, glasses, and so forth. At the same time* RELLING *and* MOLVIK *come in from the passage. They neither of them have hats or overcoats on;* MOLVIK *is dressed in black.*)

Gina (*arranging the table*). Ah, you have just come at the right moment.

Relling. Molvik thought he could smell herring-salad, and then there was no holding him. Good morning again, Ekdal.

Hjalmar. Gregers, let me introduce Mr Molvik, and Doctor—ah, of course you know Relling?

Gregers. Slightly, yes.

Relling. Mr Werle junior, isn't it? Yes, we have had one or two quarrels up at the Höidal works. Have you just moved in?

Gregers. I only moved in this morning.

Relling. Molvik and I live just below you; so you haven't far to go for a doctor or a parson, if you should need them!

Gregers. Thanks, it is quite possible I may; because yesterday we were thirteen at table.

Hjalmar. Oh, come—don't get on to ugly topics again!

Relling. You needn't worry, Ekdal; it isn't you that events point to.

Hjalmar. I hope not, for my family's sake. But now let us sit down, and eat, drink, and be merry.

Gregers. Shall we not wait for your father?

Hjalmar. No, he likes to have his lunch in his own room, later. Come along!

(*The men sit down at table, and eat and drink.* GINA *and* HEDVIG *move about, waiting on them.*)

Relling. Molvik was disgracefully drunk again yesterday, Mrs Ekdal.

Gina. What? Yesterday again?

Relling. Didn't you hear him when I came home with him last night?

Gina. No, I can't say I did.

Relling. It's just as well; Molvik was disgusting last night.

Gina. Is that true, Mr Molvik?

Molvik. Let us draw a veil over last night's doings. Such things have no connection with my better self.

Relling (*to* GREGERS). It comes over him like a spell; and then I have to go out on the spree with him. Mr Molvik is a demoniac, you see.

Gregers. A demoniac?

Relling. Molvik is a demoniac, yes.

Gregers. Hm!

Relling. And demoniacs are not capable of keeping to a perfectly straight line through life; they have to stray a little bit now and then.—Well, and so you can still stand it up at those disgustingly dirty works?

Gregers. I have stood it till now.

Relling. And has your 'demand,' that you used to go about presenting, been met?

Gregers. My demand? (*Understanding him.*) Oh, I see.

Hjalmar. What is this demand of yours, Gregers?

Gregers. He is talking nonsense.

Relling. It is perfectly true. He used to go round to all the cottagers' houses presenting what he called 'the demand of the ideal.'

Gregers. I was young then.

Relling. You are quite right, you were very young. And as for the 'demand of the ideal,' I never heard of your getting anyone to meet it while I was up there.

Gregers. Nor since, either.

Relling. Ah, I expect you have learnt enough to make you reduce the amount of your demand.

Gregers. Never when I am dealing with a man who *is* a man.

Hjalmar. That seems to me very reasonable. A little butter, Gina.

Relling. And a piece of pork for Molvik.

Molvik. Ugh! not pork!

(*Knocking is heard at the attic door.*)

Hjalmar. Open the door, Hedvig; father wants to come out.

(HEDVIG *opens the door a little.*   Old EKDAL *comes in, holding a fresh rabbit-skin.   He shuts the door after him.*)

Ekdal. Good morning, gentlemen.   I have had good sport; shot a big one.

Hjalmar. And you have skinned it without me——!

Ekdal. Yes, and salted it too.   Nice, tender meat, rabbit's meat; and sweet, too; tastes like sugar.   I hope you will enjoy your lunch, gentlemen!   (*Goes into his room.*)

Molvik (*getting up*). Excuse me—I can't—I must go downstairs at once——

Relling. Have some soda-water, you silly idiot!

Molvik (*hurrying away*). Ugh!—Ugh! (*Goes out by the outer door.*)

Relling (*to* HJALMAR*;*. Let us drink to the old sportsman's health.

Hjalmar (*clinking glasses with him*). To the old sportsman on the brink of the grave!—yes.

Relling. To the grey-haired—(*drinks*)—tell me, is it grey hair he has got, or white?

Hjalmar. As a matter of fact, it is between the two; but, as far as that goes, he hasn't much hair of any kind left.

Relling. Oh, well—a wig will take a man through the world. You are really very fortunate, you know, Ekdal.   You have got a splendid object in life to strive after——

Hjalmar. And you may be sure I *do* strive after it.

Relling. And you have got your clever wife, paddling about in her felt slippers, with that comfortable waddle of hers, making everything easy and cosy for you.

Hjalmar. Yes, Gina—(*nodding—to her*) you are an excellent companion to go through life with, my dear.

Gina. Oh, don't sit there making fun of me.

Relling. And then your little Hedvig, Ekdal!

Hjalmar (*with emotion*). My child, yes!   My child first and foremost.   Come to me, Hedvig.   (*Stroking her hair.*)   What day is to-morrow?

Hedvig (*shaking him*). No, you mustn't say anything about it, father.

Hjalmar. It makes my heart bleed to think what a meagre

affair it will be—just a little festive gathering in the attic there——

Hedvig. But that will be just lovely, father!

Relling. You wait till the great invention is finished, Hedvig!

Hjalmar. Yes, indeed—then you will see! Hedvig, I am determined to make your future safe. You shall live in comfort all your life. I shall demand something for you—something or other; and that shall be the poor inventor's only reward.

Hedvig (*throwing her arms round his neck*). Dear, dear father!

Relling (*to* GREGERS). Well, don't you find it very pleasant, for a change, to sit at a well-furnished table in the midst of a happy family circle?

Gregers. As far as I am concerned, I don't thrive in a poisonous atmosphere.

Relling. A poisonous atmosphere?

Hjalmar. Oh, don't begin that nonsense again!

Gina. Goodness knows there's no poisonous atmosphere here, Mr Werle; I air the place thoroughly every mortal day.

Gregers (*rising from table*). No airing will drive away the foulness I refer to.

Hjalmar. Foulness!

Gina. What do you think of that, Hjalmar!

Relling. Excuse me, but isn't it more likely that you yourself have brought the foulness with you from the mines up there?

Gregers. It is just like you to suggest that what I bring to a house is foulness.

Relling (*going up to him*). Listen to me, Mr Werle junior. I have a strong suspicion that you are going about still with the original unabridged 'demand of the ideal' in your pocket.

Gregers. I carry it in my heart.

Relling. Carry the damned thing where you like; but I advise you not to play at presenting demand notes here, as long as I am in the house.

Gregers. And suppose I do, in spite of that?

Relling. Then you will go downstairs head first. Now you know.

Hjalmar (*rising*). Really, Relling!

Gregers. Well, throw me out, then——

Gina (*interposing*). You mustn't do any such thing, Mr Relling. But this I will say, Mr Werle; it doesn't come well from you, who made all that filthy mess with your stove, to come in here and talk about foulness. (*A knock is heard at the outer door.*)

Hedvig. Somebody is knocking, mother.

Hjalmar. There now, I suppose we are going to be pestered with people!

Gina. Let me go and see.   (*She goes to the door and opens it, starts, shudders, and draws back.*)   Oh, my goodness!

(*The elder* WERLE, *wearing a fur coat, steps into the doorway.*)

Werle. Pardon me, but I fancy my son is living in this house.

Gina (breathlessly). Yes.

Hjalmar (coming up to them). Mr Werle, won't you be so good as to——

Werle. Thanks.   I only want to speak to my son.

Gregers. What do you want?   Here I am.

Werle. I want to speak to you in your own room.

Gregers. In my own room—very well.   (*Turns to go.*)

Gina. No, goodness knows it is not in a state for you to——

Werle. Well, outside in the passage, then.   I want to see you alone.

Hjalmar. You can do so here, Mr Werle.   Come into the sitting-room, Relling.

(HJALMAR *and* RELLING *go out to the right.* GINA *takes* HEDVIG *with her into the kitchen.*)

Gregers (after a short pause). Well, here we are, alone now.

Werle. You made use of certain expressions last night—and, seeing that now you have taken up your abode with the Ekdals, I am driven to suppose that you are meditating some scheme or other against me.

Gregers. I am meditating opening Hjalmar Ekdal's eyes.   He shall see his position as it really is; that is all.

Werle. Is this the object in life that you spoke of yesterday?

Gregers. Yes.   You have left me no other.

Werle. Is it I that have upset your mind, Gregers?

Gregers. You have upset my whole life.   I am not thinking of what we said about my mother—but it is you I have to thank for the fact that I am harried and tortured by a guilt-laden conscience.

Werle. Oh, it's your conscience that you are crazy about, is it?

Gregers. I ought to have taken a stand against you long ago, when the trap was laid for Lieutenant Ekdal.   I ought to have warned him, for I suspected then what the outcome of it would be.

Werle. Yes, you should have spoken then.

Gregers. I hadn't the courage to; I was so cowed and so scared of you.   I can't tell you how afraid I was of you, both then and long after.

Werle. You are not afraid of me now, apparently.

Gregers. No, fortunately.   The wrong that both I and—others have done to old Ekdal can never be undone; but I can set Hjalmar free from the falsehood and dissimulation that are dragging him down.

Werle. Do you imagine you will do any good by that?

Gregers. I am confident of it.

Werle. Do you really think Hjalmar Ekdal is the sort of man to thank you for such a service?

Gregers. Certainly.

Werle. Hm!—we shall see.

Gregers. And, besides, if I am to go on living, I must do something to cure my sick conscience.

Werle. You will never cure it.   Your conscience has been sickly from childhood.   It is an inheritance from your mother, Gregers—the only thing she did leave you.

Gregers (with a bitter smile). Haven't you managed to get over your mistaken calculation yet in thinking a fortune was coming to you with her?

Werle. Don't let us talk about irrelevant matters.   Are you determined on this course?—to set Hjalmar Ekdal on what you suppose to be the right scent?

Gregers. Yes, quite determined.

Werle. Well, in that case, I might have spared myself the trouble of coming here; because I suppose it isn't any use asking you to come home again.

Gregers. No.

Werle. And you won't come into the firm, either?

Gregers. No.

Werle. So be it.   But now that I propose to make a new marriage, the estate will be divided between us.

Gregers (quickly). No, I won't have that.

Werle. You won't have it?

Gregers. No, I won't have it.   My conscience forbids it.

Werle (after a short pause). Will you go up to the works again?

Gregers. No.   I don't consider myself in your service any longer.

Werle. But what are you going to do?

Gregers. Only attain the object of my life; nothing else.

Werle. Yes—but afterwards?   What will you live on?

Gregers. I have saved a little out of my pay.

Werle. That won't last you long.

Gregers. I think it will last out my time.

Werle. What do you mean?

Gregers. I shall answer no more questions.

Werle. Good-bye, then, Gregers.

Gregers. Good-bye. (WERLE *goes out.*)

Hjalmar (*peeping in*). Has he gone?

Gregers. Yes. (HJALMAR *and* RELLING *come in; at the same time* GINA *and* HEDVIG *come from the kitchen.*)

Relling. That lunch was a failure.

Gregers. Get your things on, Hjalmar; you must come for a long walk with me.

Hjalmar. With pleasure. What did your father want? Was it anything to do with me?

Gregers. Come along out; we must have a little talk. I will go and get my coat. (*Goes out.*)

Gina. You oughtn't to go out with him, Hjalmar.

Relling. No, don't. Stay where you are.

Hjalmar (*taking his hat and coat*). What do you mean! When an old friend feels impelled to open his mind to me in private——?

Relling. But, damn it, can't you see the fellow is mad, crazy, out of his senses!

Gina. It's quite true. His mother had fits of that kind from time to time.

Hjalmar. Then he has all the more need of a friend's watchful eye. (*To* GINA.) Be sure and see that dinner is ready in good time. Good-bye for now. (*Goes out by the outer door.*)

Relling. It's a great pity the fellow didn't go to hell in one of the mines at Höidal.

Gina. Good lord!—what makes you say that?

Relling (*muttering*). Oh, I have my own reasons.

Gina. Do you think he is really mad?

Relling. No, unfortunately. He is not madder than most people. But he has got a disease in his system, right enough.

Gina. What is the matter with him?

Relling. I will tell you, Mrs Ekdal. He is suffering from acute rectitudinal fever.

Gina. Rectitudinal fever?

Hedvig. Is that a kind of disease?

Relling. Indeed it is; it is a national disease; but it only crops up sporadically. (*Nods to* GINA.) Thanks for my lunch. (*Goes out by the outer door.*)

Gina (*walking about uneasily*). Ugh!—that Gregers Werle—he was always a horrid creature.

Hedvig (*standing at the table and looking searchingly at her*). It all seems to me very odd.

ACT IV

(THE SAME SCENE.—*A photograph has just been taken; the camera, with a cloth thrown over it, a stand, a couple of chairs, and a small table are in the middle of the floor. Afternoon light; the sun is on the point of setting; a little later it begins to grow dark. GINA is standing at the open door, with a small box and a wet glass plate in her hands, speaking to someone outside.*)

Gina. Yes, without fail. If I promise a thing, I keep my word. The first dozen will be ready by Monday. Good afternoon! (*Steps are heard going down the stairs. GINA shuts the door, puts the plate in the box and replaces the whole in the camera. HEDVIG comes in from the kitchen.*)

Hedvig. Are they gone?

Gina (*tidying the room*). Yes, thank goodness I have finished with them at last.

Hedvig. Can you imagine why father hasn't come home yet?

Gina. Are you sure he is not downstairs with Relling?

Hedvig. No, he isn't. I went down the back-stairs just now to see.

Gina. And there is the dinner standing and getting cold for him.

Hedvig. Think of father being so late! He is always so particular to come home in time for dinner.

Gina. Oh, he will come soon, no doubt.

Hedvig. I wish he would; it seems so odd here to-day, somehow.

Gina (*calls out*). Here he is! (HJALMAR *comes in from the passage.*)

Hedvig (*going to him*). Father, we have been waiting such a time for you!

Gina (glancing at him). What a long time you have been out, Hjalmar.

Hjalmar (without looking at her). I was rather long, yes. (*He takes off his overcoat.* GINA *and* HEDVIG *offer to help him, but he waves them aside.*)

Gina. Perhaps you have had your dinner with Mr Werle.

Hjalmar (hanging up his coat). No.

Gina (going towards the kitchen). I'll bring it in for you, then.

Hjalmar. No, leave it. I don't want anything to eat now.

Hedvig (going up to him). Aren't you well, father?

Hjalmar. Well? Oh, yes, I'm all right. Gregers and I had a very exhausting walk.

Gina. You shouldn't have done that, Hjalmar; you are not used to it.

Hjalmar. Ah!—one has to get used to a great many things in this world. (*Walks up and down.*) Has anyone been here while I was out?

Gina. No one but the engaged couple.

Hjalmar. No new orders?

Gina. No, not to-day.

Hedvig. Someone is sure to come to-morrow, father, you'll see.

Hjalmar. Let's hope so. To-morrow I intend to set to work as hard as I can.

Hedvig. To-morrow! But—have you forgotten what day to-morrow is?

Hjalmar. Ah, that's true. Well, the day after to-morrow then. In future I mean to do everything myself; I don't wish anyone to help me in the work at all.

Gina. But what's the good of that, Hjalmar? It will only make your life miserable. I can do the photographing all right, and you can give your time to the invention.

Hedvig. And to the wild duck, father—and all the hens and rabbits.

Hjalmar. Don't talk such nonsense! From to-morrow I am never going to set foot in the attic again.

Hedvig. But, father, you know you promised me that to-morrow we should have a little festivity——

Hjalmar. So I did. Well, from the day after to-morrow, then. As for that confounded wild duck, I should have great pleasure in wringing its neck!

Hedvig (with a scream). The wild duck!

Gina. Did you ever hear such a thing!

Hedvig (*pulling him by the arm*). Yes, but, father, it's my wild duck!

Hjalmar. That is why I won't do it. I haven't the heart— haven't the heart to do it, for your sake, Hedvig. But I feel at the bottom of my heart that I ought to do it. I ought not to tolerate under my roof a single creature that has been in that man's hands.

Gina. But, good heavens, as it was from that ass Pettersen that grandfather got it——

Hjalmar (*walking up and down*). But there are certain claims— what shall I call them?—let us say claims of the ideal—absolute demands on a man, that he cannot set aside without injuring his soul.

Hedvig (*following him about*). But think, father, the wild duck—the poor wild duck!

Hjalmar (*standing still*). Listen. I will spare it—for your sake. I won't hurt a hair of its head—well, as I said, I will spare it. There are greater difficulties than that to be tackled. Now you must go out for a little, as usual, Hedvig; it's dark enough now for you.

Hedvig. No, I don't want to go out now.

Hjalmar. Yes, you must go out. Your eyes seem to me to be watering. All these fumes in here are not good for you. There is a bad atmosphere in this house.

Hedvig. All right; I will run down the back-stairs and go for a little stroll. My cloak and hat——? Oh, they are in my room. Father—promise you won't do the wild duck any harm while I am out.

Hjalmar. It shall not lose a feather of its head. (*Drawing her to him.*) You and I, Hedvig—we two!—now run along, dear. .(HEDVIG *nods to her parents and goes out through the kitchen.* HJALMAR *walks up and down without raising his eyes.*) Gina!

Gina. Yes?

Hjalmar. From to-morrow—or let us say from the day after to-morrow—I should prefer to keep the household books myself.

Gina. You want to keep the household books too!

Hjalmar. Yes, or at any rate to keep account of what our income is.

Gina. Bless the man—that's simple enough!

Hjalmar. I am not sure; you seem to me to make what I give you go an astonishongly long way. (*Stands still and looks at her.*) How do you manage it?

Gina. Because Hedvig and I need so little.

Hjalmar. Is it true that father is so liberally paid for the copying he does for old Mr Werle?

Gina. I don't know about its being so liberal. I don't know what is usually paid for that kind of work.

Hjalmar. Well, roughly speaking, what does he make? Tell me.

Gina. It varies; roughly speaking, I should say it's about what he costs us and a little pocket-money over.

Hjalmar. What he costs us! And you have never told me that before?

Gina. No, I couldn't. You seemed so pleased to think that he had everything from you.

Hjalmar. And in reality he had it from old Werle!

Gina. Oh, well, Mr Werle has got plenty to spare.

Hjalmar. Light the lamp for me, please.

Gina (*lighting it*). Besides, we don't really know if it is Mr Werle himself; it might be Graaberg——

Hjalmar. Why do you want to shift it on to Graaberg?

Gina. I don't know anything about it; I only thought——

Hjalmar. Hm!

Gina. It wasn't me that got the copying for grandfather, remember. It was Bertha, when she came to the house.

Hjalmar. Your voice seems to me to be unsteady.

Gina (*putting the shade on the lamp*). Does it?

Hjalmar. And your hands are shaking, aren't they?

Gina (*firmly*). Tell me straight, Hjalmar, what nonsense has he been telling you about me?

Hjalmar. Is it true—can it possibly be true—that there was anything between you and old Mr Werle when you were in service there?

Gina. It's not true. Not then. Mr Werle was always after me, true enough. And his wife thought there was something in it; and then there was the devil's own fuss. Not a moment's peace did she give me, that woman—and so I threw up my job.

Hjalmar. But afterwards?

Gina. Well, then I went home. And my mother—she wasn't what you thought her, Hjalmar; she talked a lot of nonsense to me about this, that, and the other. Mr Werle was a widower by that time, you know.

Hjalmar. Well, and then?

Gina. It's best you should know it.   He never let me alone, till he had had his way.

Hjalmar (*clasping his hands*). And this is the mother of my child!   How could you conceal such a thing from me?

Gina. It was wrong of me, I know.   I ought to have told you about it long ago.

Hjalmar. You ought to have told me at the very first—then I should have known what sort of a woman you were.

Gina. But would you have married me, all the same?

Hjalmar. How can you imagine such a thing!

Gina. No; and that's why I didn't dare to tell you anything then.   I had got to love you so dearly, as you know.   And I couldn't make myself utterly wretched——

Hjalmar (*walking about*). And this is my Hedvig's mother! And to know that I owe everything I see here—(*kicks at a chair*) —my whole home—to a favoured predecessor!   Ah, that seducer, Werle!

Gina. Do you regret the fourteen—the fifteen years we have lived together?

Hjalmar (*standing in front of her*). Tell me this.   Haven't you regretted every day—every hour—this web of lies you have entangled me in?   Answer me!   Haven't you really suffered agonies of regret and remorse?

Gina. My dear Hjalmar, I have had plenty to do thinking about the housekeeping and all the work there was to do every day——

Hjalmar. Then you never wasted a thought on what your past had been!

Gina. No—God knows I had almost forgotten all about that old trouble.

Hjalmar. Oh, this callous, insensate content!   There is something so shocking about it, to me.   Just think of it!—not a moment's regret.

Gina. But you tell me this, Hjalmar—what would have become of you if you hadn't found a wife like me?

Hjalmar. A wife like you!

Gina. Yes; I have always been a better business man than you, so to speak.   Of course, it is true I am a year or two older than you.

Hjalmar. What would have become of me?

Gina. Yes, you had got into all sorts of bad ways when you first met me; you can't deny that.

Hjalmar. You talk about bad ways? You can't understand how a man feels when he is overcome with grief and despair—especially a man of my ardent temperament.

Gina. No, very likely not. And I oughtn't to say much about it anyway, because you made a real good husband as soon as you had a home of your own. And here we had got such a comfortable, cosy home, and Hedvig and I were just beginning to be able to spend a little bit on ourselves for food and clothes——

Hjalmar. In a swamp of deceit, yes.

Gina. If only that hateful chap hadn't poked his nose in here!

Hjalmar. I used to think, too, that I had a happy home. It was a delusion. Where am I to look now for the necessary incentive to bring my invention into existence? Perhaps it will die with me; and then it will be your past, Gina, that has killed it.

Gina (*on the brink of tears*). Don't talk about such things, Hjalmar. Me, who has all along only wanted what was best for you!

Hjalmar. I ask you—what has become of the dream of the bread-winner now? When I lay in there on the sofa, thinking over my invention, I used to have a presentiment that it would use up all my powers. I used to feel that when the great day came when I should hold my patent in my hands, that day would be the day of my—departure. And it was my dream, too, that you would be left as the well-to-do widow of the departed inventor.

Gina (*wiping away her tears*). You mustn't talk such nonsense, Hjalmar. I pray God I never may live to see the day when I am left a widow!

Hjalmar. Well, it's of no consequence now. It's all over now, anyway—all over now!

(GREGERS WERLE *opens the outer door cautiously and looks in.*)

Gregers. May I come in?

Hjalmar. Yes, come in.

Gregers (*advances with a beaming, happy face, and stretches out his hand to them*). Well, you dear people——! (*Looks alternately at one and the other, and whispers to* HJALMAR.) Haven't you done it yet?

Hjalmar (*aloud*). It is done.

Gregers. It is?

Hjalmar. I have passed through the bitterest moment of my life.

Gregers. But the most elevating too, I expect.

Hjalmar. Well, we have got it off our hands for the present, anyway.

Gina. God forgive you, Mr Werle.

Gregers (*greatly surprised*). But, I don't understand.

Hjalmar. What don't you understand?

Gregers. After such a momentous enlightenment—an enlightenment that is to be the starting-point of a completely new existence—a real companionship, founded on truth and purged of all falsehood——

Hjalmár. Yes, I know; I know.

Gregers. I certainly expected, when I came in, to be met by the light of transfiguration in the faces of you both. And yet I see nothing but gloomy, dull, miserable——

Gina (*taking off the lampshade*). Exactly.

Gregers. I dare say you won't understand me, Mrs Ekdal. Well, well—you will in time. But you, Hjalmar? You must feel consecrated afresh by this great enlightenment?

Hjalmar. Yes, of course I do. That's to say—in a sort of way. ·

Gregers. Because there is surely nothing in the world that can compare with the happiness of forgiveness and of lifting up a guilty sinner in the arms of love.

Hjalmar. Do you think it is so easy for a man to drink the bitter cup that I have just drained?

Gregers. No, not for an ordinary man, I dare say. But for a man like you——!

Hjalmar. Good heavens, I know that well enough. But you mustn't rush me, Gregers. It takes time, you know.

Gregers. You have a lot of the wild duck in you, Hjalmar.

(RELLING *has come in by the outer door.*)

Relling. Hallo! are you talking about the old wild duck again?

Hjalmar. Yes, the one old Mr Werle winged.

Relling. Old Mr Werle——? Is it him you are talking about?

Hjalmar. Him and—the rest of us.

Relling (*half aloud, to* GREGERS). Oh, damn you!

Hjalmar. What are you saying?

Relling. I was breathing an earnest wish that this quack doctor would take himself off home. If he stays here he is capable of being the death of both of you.

Gregers. No harm is coming to these two, Mr Relling. We needn't mention Hjalmar; we know him. And as for his wife,

I have little doubt that she, too, has the springs of trustworthiness and sincerity deep down in her heart.

Gina (*nearly crying*). Then you ought to have let me be as I was.

Relling (*to* GREGERS). Would it be indiscreet to ask precisely what you think you are doing here?

Gregers. I am trying to lay the foundation of a true marriage.

Relling. Then you don't think Ekdal's marriage is good enough as it is?

Gregers. Oh, it is as good a marriage as many others, I dare say. But a true marriage it has never yet been.

Hjalmar. You have never had your eyes opened to the demands of the ideal, Relling.

Relling. Rubbish, my dear chap!—But, excuse me, Mr Werle, how many 'true marriages,' roughly speaking, have you seen in your life?

Gregers. I hardly think I have seen a single one.

Relling. Nor me either.

Gregers. But I have seen such hundreds of marriages of the opposite kind, and I have had the opportunity of watching at close quarters the mischief such a marriage may do to both parties.

Hjalmar. A man's moral character may be completely sapped; that is the dreadful part of it.

Relling. Well, I have never exactly been married, so I can't lay down the law on the matter. But this I do know, that the child is part of the marriage too—and you must leave the child in peace.

Hjalmar. Ah—Hedvig! My poor little Hedvig!

Relling. Yes, you will have the goodness to keep Hedvig out of the matter. You two are grown people; goodness knows, you may play ducks and drakes with your own happiness, for all I care. But you must walk warily with Hedvig, believe me; otherwise it may end in your doing her a great harm.

Hjalmar. A great harm?

Relling. Yes, or it may end in her doing a great harm to herself—and perhaps to others too.

Gina. But how can you know anything about it, Mr Relling?

Hjalmar. There is no imminent danger for her eyes, is there?

Relling. What I mean has nothing to do with her eyes at all. But Hedvig is at a critical age. She may take all sorts of strange fancies into her head.

Gina. There!—and my goodness she is doing that already! She has begun to be very fond of meddling with the fire, out in the kitchen. She calls it playing at houses-on-fire. Often and often I have been afraid she *would* set the house on fire.

Relling. There you are. I knew it.

Gregers (*to* RELLING). But how do you explain such a thing?

Relling (*sulkily*) She is becoming a woman, my friend.

Hjalmar. So long as the child has me——! So long as my life lasts——! (*A knock is heard at the door.*)

Gina. Hush, Hjalmar; there is someone outside. (*Calls out.*) Come in! (Mrs SÖRBY, *dressed in outdoor clothes, comes in.*)

Mrs Sörby. Good evening!

Gina (*going to her*). Bertha!—is it you!

Mrs Sörby. Certainly it's me! But perhaps I have come at an inconvenient time?

Hjalmar. Not at all; a messenger from *that* house——

Mrs Sörby (*to* GINA). To tell you the truth, I rather hoped I shouldn't find your menfolk at home just now; I just ran up to have a little chat with you and say good-bye.

Gina. Oh? Are you going away?

Mrs Sörby. Early to-morrow morning, yes—up to Höidal. Mr Werle went this afternoon. (*Meaningly,* to GREGERS.) He asked to be remembered to you.

Gina. Just fancy——!

Hjalmar. So Mr Werle has gone away?—and now you are going to join him?

Mrs Sörby. Yes, what do you say to that, Mr Ekdal?

Hjalmar. Be careful what you are doing, I say.

Gregers. I can explain. My father and Mrs Sörby are going to be married!

Hjalmar. Going to be married!

Gina. Oh, Bertha! Has it come to that?

Relling (*his voice faltering a little*). Is this really true?

Mrs Sörby. Yes, my dear Relling, it is perfectly true.

Relling. Are you going to marry again?

Mrs Sörby. Yes, that's what it has come to. Mr Werle has got a special licence, and we are going to get married very quietly up at the works.

Gregers. Then I suppose I must wish you happiness, like a good stepson.

Mrs Sörby. Many thanks—if you mean it. And I am sure I hope it will mean happiness, both for Mr Werle and for me.

Relling. You can confidently hope that. Mr Werle never gets drunk—so far as I know; and I don't imagine he is in the habit of ill-treating his wives, either, as the late lamented horse-doctor used to do.

Mrs Sörby. Sörby is dead; let him alone. And even he had his good points.

Relling. Mr Werle has points that are better, I expect.

Mrs Sörby. At any rate he hasn't wasted all that was best in him. A man who does that must take the consequences.

Relling. To-night I shall go out with Molvik.

Mrs Sörby. That is wrong of you. Don't do that—for my sake, don't.

Relling. There is nothing else for it. (*To* Hjalmar.) You can come too, if you like.

Gina. No, thank you. Hjalmar is not going with you to places of *that* kind.

Hjalmar (*half aloud in an irritated voice*). Oh, do hold your tongue!

Relling. Good-bye, Mrs—Werle. (*Goes out at the outer door.*)

Gregers (*to* Mrs Sörby). You and Doctor Relling seem to know each other pretty well.

Mrs Sörby. Yes, we have known each other many years. At one time it looked as if our friendship were going to ripen into something warmer.

Gregers. But, luckily for you, I suppose, it didn't.

Mrs Sörby. You may well say that. But I have always been chary of giving way to impulse. A woman mustn't absolutely throw herself away, either.

Gregers. Aren't you in the least afraid of my letting my father get a hint of this old acquaintance?

Mrs Sörby. I have told him about it myself, of course.

Gregers. Indeed?

Mrs Sörby. Your father knows every single thing with a grain of truth in it that anyone could find to tell him about me. I have told him absolutely everything; it was the first thing I did when he made it evident what his intentions were.

Gregers. Then you have been more frank than is usually the case, I expect.

Mrs Sörby. I always have been frank. It's the best way for us women.

Hjalmar. What do you say to that, Gina?

Gina. Oh, women are all so different.   Some are built that way; some aren't.

Mrs Sörby. Well, Gina, I believe now that the wisest line to take is the one I have taken.   And Mr Werle hasn't concealed anything on his side, either.   It is that, you see, that knits us so closely together.   Now he can sit and talk to me as fearlessly as a child.   That's something he has never had a chance of doing yet.   All his young days, and for the best years of his life, when he was a healthy and vigorous man, he had to sit and listen to nothing but sermons on his sins.   And very often the point of the sermons turned on the most imaginary offences—at least, so it seems to me.

Gina. Yes, that's quite certainly true.

Gregers. If you ladies are going into those subjects, I had better go.

Mrs Sörby. Oh, you can stay, for that matter.   I won't say a word more.   But I wanted you to understand that I have done nothing deceitful or in the least degree underhand.   Very likely you think I am coming in for a big slice of luck; and so I am, in a way.   But, all the same, I don't believe I shall be taking more than I shall be giving.   At any rate I shall never forsake him; and what I *can* do is to look after him and care for him as no one else can, now that he will soon be helpless.

Hjalmar. Soon be helpless?

Gregers (*to* Mrs Sörby). Don't mention that here.

Mrs Sörby. It's no good concealing it any longer, however much he would like to.   He is going blind.

Hjalmar (*with a start*). Going blind?   That is extraordinary. Is he going blind too?

Gina. A great many people do.

Mrs Sörby. And you can well imagine what that means to a business man.   Well, I shall try to use my eyes for him as well as I can.   But I mustn't stay any longer; I am frightfully busy just now.—Oh, I was to tell you this, Mr Ekdal, that if there were anything in which Mr Werle could be of service to you, you were just to go to Graaberg about it.

Gregers. A message that I should think Hjalmar Ekdal would be *very* grateful for!

Mrs Sörby. Really?   I rather think there was a time when——

Gina. He's quite right, Bertha.   Hjalmar doesn't need to take anything from Mr Werle now.

Hjalmar (*slowly and weightily*). Will you give my kind regards to your future husband, and say that I mean as soon as possible to call on Graaberg——

Gregers. What! Do you really mean to do that?

Hjalmar. To call on Graaberg, I say, and ask for an account of the sum I owe his employer. I will pay that debt of honour—ha! ha! debt of honour is a good name for it!—but enough of that. I will pay the whole sum, with five per cent interest.

Gina. But, my dear Hjalmar, we have no money to do that with, Heaven knows!

Hjalmar. Will you tell your fiancé that I am working busily at my invention. Will you tell him that what keeps up my strength for this exhausting task is the desire to be quit of a painful burden of debt. That is why I am working at this invention. The whole proceeds of it shall be devoted to freeing myself from the obligation under which your future husband's pecuniary advances have laid me.

Mrs Sörby. Something or other has happened in this house.

Hjalmar. You are quite right.

Mrs Sörby. Well—good-bye, then. I had something I wanted to talk over with you, Gina; but that must wait till another time. Good-bye! (HJALMAR *and* GREGERS *bow silently;* GINA *follows her to the door.*)

Hjalmar. Not farther than the door, Gina! (Mrs SÖRBY *goes out;* GINA *shuts the door after her.*) There, Gregers. Now I have got that load of debt off my hands.

Gregers. Soon you will, anyway.

Hjalmar. I think my attitude may be called correct.

Gregers. You are the man I always took you for.

Hjalmar. In certain cases it is impossible to overlook the claim of the ideal. As breadwinner of the family, I have to writhe and smart under this. I can tell you it is by no means a joke for a man, who is not well off, to get free from a debt of many years' standing, over which the dust of oblivion, so to speak, has collected. But that makes no difference; the manhood in me demands its rights too.

Gregers (*putting his hands on his shoulders*). Dear Hjalmar, wasn't it a good thing I came?

Hjalmar. Yes.

Gregers. Hasn't it been a good thing that you have got a clear knowledge of the whole situation?

Hjalmar (*a little impatiently*). Of course it's a good thing.

But there is one thing that goes against my sense of what is right.

Gregers. What is that?

Hjalmar. It is this.   I—well, I don't know whether I ought to speak so freely about your father?

Gregers. Don't think of me in the matter at all.

Hjalmar. Very well. It seems to me a very aggravating thought that now it isn't I, but he, who will realize the true marriage.

Gregers. How can you say such a thing?

Hjalmar. It certainly is so.   Your father and Mrs Sörby are entering upon a marriage which is based upon complete confidence, based upon an entire and unrestricted frankness on both sides; they conceal nothing from each other; there is no dissimulation at the back of things; they have proclaimed, if I may so express myself, a mutual forgiveness of sins.

Gregers. Well, what if they have?

Hjalmar. Well, surely that is the whole thing.   That is all that this difficult position needs, to lay the foundations of a true marriage—you said so yourself.

Gregers. But this is a different thing altogether, Hjalmar. Surely you are not going to compare either you or your wife with these two—well, you know what I mean?

Hjalmar. Still I can't help feeling that in all this there is something that sorely injures my sense of justice.   It looks for all the world as though there were no such thing as a just Providence at all.

Gina. Gracious, Hjalmar!—for heaven's sake don't say such a thing.

Gregers. Ahem!—I think we had better not enter into that question.

Hjalmar. But, on the other hand, I certainly seem to see the directing finger of destiny in it, all the same.   He is going blind.

Gina. Perhaps it isn't quite certain that he is.

Hjalmar. There's no doubt he is.   We ought not to doubt that he will, anyway; for it is that very fact that constitutes the just retribution.   He himself, in his time, has blinded the eyes of a credulous fellow creature.

Gregers. I'm afraid he has done that to a good many!

Hjalmar. And now comes the inexorable, mysterious power, and demands this man's own eyes.

Gina. Hjalmar, how can you dare say such dreadful things! You make me all of a tremble.

Hjalmar. It is good for one sometimes to plunge down into the dark side of life. (HEDVIG, *in her hat and coat, comes in at the outer door, breathless and looking happy.*)

Gina. Are you back again?

Hedvig. Yes, I didn't want to stay out any longer; and it was lucky I didn't, because I have just met someone at the door.

Hjalmar. Mrs Sörby, I suppose.

Hedvig. Yes.

Hjalmar (*walking up and down*). I hope you have seen her for the last time. (*A pause.* HEDVIG, *obviously disheartened, looks first at one and then at the other of them, as if to try and read their thoughts.*)

Hedvig (*going up to her father coaxingly*). Father!

Hjalmar. Well, what is it, Hedvig?

Hedvig. Mrs Sörby had something with her for me.

Hjalmar (*standing still*). For you?

Hedvig. Yes, it's something for to-morrow.

Gina. Bertha has always sent some little thing for her birthday.

Hjalmar. What is it?

Hedvig. You mustn't know anything about it yet. Mother is to give it to me in bed first thing to-morrow morning.

Hjalmar. All this mystery!—and I am to be kept in the dark, I suppose.

Hedvig (*quickly*). No, you can see it if you like. It's a big letter. (*Takes a letter out of the pocket of her coat.*)

Hjalmar. A letter, too?

Hedvig. She only gave me the letter. The rest of it is coming afterwards, I suppose. Just fancy—a letter! I have never had a letter before. And there is 'Miss' on the envelope. (*Reads.*) 'Miss Hedvig Ekdal.' Think of it—that's me!

Hjalmar. Let me see the letter.

Hedvig (*giving it to him*). There you are.

Hjalmar. It is old Mr Werle's writing.

Gina. Are you sure, Hjalmar?

Hjalmar. See for yourself.

Gina. Do you suppose I know anything about such things?

Hjalmar. Hedvig, may I open the letter—and read it?

Gina. Not to-night, Hjalmar. It is for to-morrow, you know.

Hedvig (*softly*). Oh, can't you let him read it! It's sure to be something nice, and then father will be happy and things will get pleasant again.

Hjalmar. Then I have permission to open it?

Hedvig. Yes, please, father. It will be such fun to see what it is.

Hjalmar. Very well. (*He opens the letter, takes out a paper that is in it, and reads it through with evident astonishment.*) What on earth is this?

Gina. What does it say?

Hedvig. Yes, father—do tell us.

Hjalmar. Be quiet. (*Reads it through again; he has turned pale, but collects himself.*) It is a deed of gift, Hedvig.

Hedvig. Really? What am I getting?

Hjalmar. Read it for yourself. (HEDVIG *goes to the lamp and reads.* HJALMAR *clasps his hands and says half aloud.*) The eyes! The eyes!—and then this letter.

Hedvig (*who stops reading*). Yes, but it seems to me it is grandfather who is getting it.

Hjalmar (*taking the letter from her*). Gina—can you understand this?

Gina. I know nothing whatever about it. Tell me what it is.

Hjalmar. Old Mr Werle writes to Hedvig that her old grandfather need not bother himself with copying work any longer, but that for the future he will be entitled to five pounds a month paid from the office——

Gregers. Aha!

Hedvig. Five pounds, mother!—I read that.

Gince. How nice for grandfather!

Hjalmar. Five pounds a month, as long as he needs it; that means, naturally, till his death.

Gina. Well, then, he is provided for, poor old man.

Hjalmar. But that is not all. You didn't read the rest, Hedvig. Afterwards the gift is to be transferred to you.

Hedvig. To me! All that?

Hjalmar. You are assured the same amount for the whole of your life, it says. Do you hear that, Gina?

Gina. Yes, yes, I hear.

Hedvig. Just think of it—I am to get all that money. (*Shakes him.*) Father, father, aren't you glad?

Hjalmar (*moving away from her*). Glad! (*Walks up and down.*) What a future—what a picture it calls up to my eyes! It is Hedvig for whom he provides so liberally—Hedvig!

Gina. Yes, it's Hedvig's birthday——

Hedvig. You shall have it all the same, father! Of course I shall give all the money to you and mother.

Hjalmar. To your mother, yes!—that's just the point.

Gregers. Hjalmar, this is a trap he is laying for you.

Hjalmar. Do you think this is another trap?

Gregers. When he was here this morning, he said: 'Hjalmar Ekdal is not the man you imagine he is.'

Hjalmar. Not the man——!

Gregers. 'You will see,' he said.

Hjalmar. You will see whether I allow myself to be put off with a bribe——

Hedvig. Mother, what does it all mean?

Gina. Go away and take your things off. (HEDVIG *goes out by the kitchen door, half in tears.*).

Gregers. Yes, Hjalmar—now we shall see who is right, he or I.

Hjalmar (*tears the paper slowly across, and lays the two pieces on the table*). That is my answer.

Gregers. That is what I expected.

Hjalmar (*goes over to* GINA, *who is standing by the stove, and speaks to her in a low voice*). No more lies, now. If everything was over between you and him when you—when you began to love me, as you call it, why was it that he put us in a position to marry?

Gina. I suppose he thought he would get a footing in the house.

Hjalmar. Only that? Wasn't he afraid of a certain possibility?

Gina. I don't understand what you mean.

Hjalmar. I want to know, whether—whether your child has the right to live under my roof.

Gina (*drawing herself up, with eyes flashing*). How dare you ask that!

Hjalmar. You shall answer this question. Does Hedvig belong to me—or to——? Well?

Gina (*looking at him with cold bravado*). I don't know.

Hjalmar (*in a trembling voice*). You don't know?

Gina. How should I know? A woman like me——

Hjalmar (*quietly, as he turns away from her*). Then I have no longer any part in this house.

Gregers. Think well what you are doing, Hjalmar!

Hjalmar (*putting on his overcoat*). There is nothing here for a man like me to think about.

Gregers. Indeed there is a tremendous lot here for you to

think about. You three must be together, if you are going to reach the goal of self-sacrificing forgiveness.

Hjalmar. I have no desire for that. Never! Never! My hat! (*Takes his hat.*) My home has fallen into ruins round me. (*Bursts into tears.*) Gregers, I have no child now!

Hedvig (*who has opened the kitchen door*). What are you saying! (*Goes to him.*) Father! Father!

Gina. Now, what's going to happen!

Hjalmar. Don't come near me, Hedvig! Go away—go away! I can't bear to see you. Ah—the eyes! Good-bye. (*Goes towards the door.*)

Hedvig (*clings to him, screaming*). No, no! Don't turn away from me.

Gina (*crying out*). Look at the child, Hjalmar! Look at the child!

Hjalmar. I won't! I can't! I must get out of here—away from all this! (*He tears himself away from* HEDVIG *and goes out by the outer door.*)

Hedvig (*with despair in her eyes*). He is going away from us, mother! He is going away! He will never come back!

Gina. Don't cry, Hedvig. Father will come back.

Hedvig (*throws herself on the sofa, sobbing*). No, no—he will never come back any more.

Gregers. Will you believe that I meant it all for the best, Mrs Ekdal?

Gina. I almost believe you did; but, God forgive you, all the same.

Hedvig (*lying on the sofa*). I think this will kill me! What have I done to him? Mother, you *must* get him home again!

Gina. Yes, yes; just be quiet, and I will go out and look for him. (*Puts on her coat.*) Perhaps he has gone down to Relling. But, if I go, you mustn't lie there crying. Will you promise me that?

Hedvig (*sobbing convulsively*). Yes, I won't cry—if only father comes back.

Gregers (*to* GINA, *as she goes out*). Wouldn't it be better, anyway, to let him first fight his bitter fight to the end?

Gina. He can do that afterwards. First and foremost we must get the child quiet. (*Goes out.*)

Hedvig (*sitting upright and wiping away her tears*). Now you must tell me what is the matter. Why won't father have anything to do with me any more?

Gregers. You mustn't ask that until you are a big girl and grown up.

Hedvig (*gulping down her tears*). But I can't go on being so utterly miserable till I am a big girl and grown up.   I believe I know what it is—perhaps I am not really father's child.

Gregers (*uneasily*). How on earth could that be?

Hedvig. Mother might have found me.   And now perhaps father has found that out; I have read about that kind of thing.

Gregers. Well, even if it were so——

Hedvig. Yes, it seems to me he might love me just as much in spite of that—even more.   We had the wild duck sent us as a present, too, but all the same I love it very much.

Gregers (*to divert her thoughts*). The wild duck—that's true! Let's talk about the wild duck a little, Hedvig.

Hedvig. The poor wild duck!—he can't bear to look at it any more, either.   Imagine, he wanted to wring its neck.

Gregers. Oh, he won't do that.

Hedvig. No, but he said so.   And I think it was so unkind of him to say so, because I say a prayer every night for the wild duck, and pray that it may be saved from death and anything that will harm it.

Gregers (*looking at her*). Do you say your prayers at night?

Hedvig. Of course.

Gregers. Who taught you?

Hedvig. I taught myself.   It was once when father was very ill and had leeches on his neck, and said he was at death's door.

Gregers. Really?

Hedvig. So I said a prayer for him when I had got into bed—and since then I have gone on doing it.

Gregers. And now you pray for the wild duck too?

Hedvig. I thought it would be best to put the wild duck in the prayer too, because it was so sickly at first.

Gregers. Do you say prayers in the morning, too?

Hedvig. No, of course I don't.

Gregers. Why don't you say them in the morning as well?

Hedvig. Because in the morning it's light, and there's nothing more to be afraid of.

Gregers. And your father wanted to wring the neck of the wild duck that you love so much?

Hedvig. No, he said it would give him great pleasure to do it, but that he would spare it for my sake; and I think that was very nice of father.

Gregers (coming nearer to her). But now, suppose you sacrificed the wild duck, of your own free will, for his sake?

Hedvig (getting up). The wild duck?

Gregers. Suppose now you gave up for him, as a free-will offering, the dearest possession you have in the world?

Hedvig. Do you think it would help?

Gregers. Try it, Hedvig.

Hedvig (gently, with glistening eyes). Yes, I will try it.

Gregers. Have you really the strength of mind to do it, do you think?

Hedvig. I will ask grandfather to shoot the wild duck for me.

Gregers. Yes, do. But not a word about anything of the kind to your mother.

Hedvig. Why not?

Gregers. She doesn't understand us.

Hedvig. The wild duck! I will try it first thing to-morrow morning. (GINA *comes in by the outer door.* HEDVIG *goes to her.*) Did you find him, mother?

Gina. No, but I heard he had gone out and taken Relling with him.

Gregers. Are you certain?

Gina. Yes, the porter's wife said so. Molvik has gone with them too, she said.

Gregers. And this, when his mind is so badly in need of fighting in solitude——!

Gina (taking off her things). Oh, you never know what men are going to do. Heaven knows where Relling has taken him off to! I ran over to Mrs Eriksen's, but they weren't there.

Hedvig (struggling with her tears). Oh, suppose he never comes back any more!

Gregers. He'll come back. I have a message to give him in the morning, and you will see how he will come home. You can go to sleep quite hopefully about that, Hedvig. Good night. (*Goes out.*)

Hedvig (throws herself into GINA's *arms, sobbing).* Mother! Mother!

Gina (patting her on the back and sighing). Yes, yes—Relling was right. This is what happens when mad folk come presenting these demands that no one can make head or tail of.

ACT V

(THE SAME SCENE.—*The cold grey light of morning is shining in; wet snow is lying on the large panes of the skylight.* GINA *comes in from the kitchen wearing a high apron and carrying a broom and a duster, and goes towards the sitting-room door. At the same moment* HEDVIG *comes hurriedly in from the passage.*)

Gina (*stopping*). Well?

Hedvig. Mother, I believe he is downstairs with Relling——

Gina. Well, would you believe it!

Hedvig. Because the porter's wife said she heard two people come in with Relling when he came home last night.

Gina. That's just what I thought.

Hedvig. But that is no good if he won't come up to us.

Gina. At any rate I shall be able to go down and have a talk with him.

(*Old* EKDAL *comes in from his room, in dressing-gown and slippers and smoking his pipe.*)

Ekdal. Look here, Hjalmar—— Isn't Hjalmar at home?

Gina. No, he has gone out.

Ekdal. So early? and in such a heavy snowstorm? Well, well; that's his affair. I can take my morning stroll by myself. (*He opens the attic door;* HEDVIG *helps him. He goes in, and she shuts the door after him.*)

Hedvig (*in an undertone*). Just think, mother—when poor grandfather hears that father wants to go away from us!

Gina. Nonsense—grandfather mustn't hear anything about it. Thank God he wasn't here yesterday when all that rumpus was going on.

Hedvig. Yes, but——

(GREGERS *comes in by the outer door.*)

Gregers. Well? Have you any trace of him yet?

Gina. He is most likely downstairs with Relling, I am told.

Gregers. With Relling! Can he really have been out with that fellow?

Gina. Evidently he has.

Gregers. Yes, but he—who so urgently needed solitude to collect himself seriously together——!

Gina. You may well say that.

(RELLING *comes in from the passage.*)

Hedvig (*going up to him*). Is father in your rooms?

Gina (*at the same time*). Is he there?

Relling. Of course he is.

Hedvig. And you never told us!

Relling. Yes, I know I'm a beast. But first of all I had the other beast to keep in order—our demoniac gentleman, I mean—and after that I fell so dead asleep that——

Gina. What does Hjalmar say to-day?

Relling. He doesn't say anything at all.

Hedvig. Hasn't he talked to you at all?

Relling. Not a blessed word.

Gregers. Of course not; I can understand that very well.

Gina. But what is he doing with himself, then?

Relling. He is lying on the sofa, snoring.

Gina. Is he? Hjalmar's a good hand at snoring.

Hedvig. Is he asleep? Can he sleep?

Relling. Well, it looks like it.

Gregers. It is easy to understand that; after the conflict of soul that has torn him——

Gina. Besides, he has never been used to wandering out at night.

Hedvig. I dare say it is a good thing he is getting some sleep, mother.

Gina. I think so, too; and it would be a pity to wake him up too soon. Many thanks, Mr Relling. Now first of all I must get the house cleaned up and tidied a bit, and then—— Come and help me, Hedvig. (*She goes with* HEDVIG *into the sitting-room.*)

Gregers (*turning to* RELLING). What do you think of the spiritual upheaval that is going on in Hjalmar Ekdal?

Relling. As far as I am concerned, I haven't noticed any spiritual upheaval going on in him at all.

Gregers. What! After such a crisis, when the whole of his life has been shifted on to a new basis? How can you imagine that a personality like Hjalmar's——

Relling. Personality!—he? Even if he ever had any tendency to any such abnormality as you call 'personality,' it has been absolutely rooted out of him and destroyed when he was a boy. I can assure you of that.

Gregers. It would certainly be very strange if that were true, in the case of a man brought up with such loving care as he was.

Relling. By those two crazy hysterical maiden aunts of his, do you mean?

Gregers. Let me tell you that they were women who were never oblivious to the demands of the ideal—but if I say that, you will only begin making fun of me again.

Relling. No, I am in no humour for that. Besides, I know all about them. He has delivered himself to me of any amount of rhetoric about these two 'soul-mothers' of his. But I don't think he has much to thank them for. Ekdal's misfortune is that all his life he has been looked upon as a shining light in his own circle——

Gregers. And isn't that what he is?—in profundity of mind, I mean?

Relling. I have never noticed anything of the sort. His father believed it, I dare say; the poor old lieutenant has been a simpleton all his days.

Gregers. He has been a man with a childlike mind all his days; that is a thing you can't understand.

Relling. All right! But when our dear sweet Hjalmar became a student of sorts, he was at once accepted amongst his fellow students as the great light of the future. Good-looking he was, too, the ninny—pink and white—just what common girls like for a lover; and with his susceptible disposition and that sympathetic voice of his, and the facility with which he declaimed other people's verses and other people's thoughts——

Gregers (*indignantly*). Is it Hjalmar Ekdal that you are speaking of like this?

Relling. Yes, with your permission; for that is the real man, instead of the idol you have been falling on your knees to.

Gregers. I venture to think I was not so blind as all that.

Relling. Well, it's not far from the truth, anyway. You are a sick man too, you see.

Gregers. You are right there.

Relling. Exactly. You are suffering from a complicated complaint. First of all there is that debilitating rectitudinal fever of yours; and then, what's worse, you are always in a raving delirium of hero-worship—you must always have some object of admiration outside your own affairs.

Gregers. I can certainly only find that by looking outside my own concerns.

Relling. But you are so monstrously mistaken as to these miraculous beings you think you find around you. This is just another case of your coming to a workman's cottage to present your 'demands of the ideal'; but the people in this house are all insolvent.

Gregers. If you haven't any higher opinion of Hjalmar Ekdal than that, how can you find any pleasure in being always hand-in-glove with him?

Relling. Bless your heart—I am supposed to be a kind of doctor, though you mightn't think it; and it is only my duty to pay some attention to the poor invalids I live in the house with.

Gregers. Really! Is Hjalmar Ekdal a sick man too, then?

Relling. All the world is sick, pretty nearly—that's the worst of it.

Gregers. And what treatment are you using for Hjalmar?

Relling. My usual one. I am trying to keep up the make-believe of life in him.

Gregers. The make-believe? I don't think I heard you correctly?

Relling. Yes, I said make-believe. That is the stimulating principle of life, you know.

Gregers. May I ask what sort of a make-believe enters into the scheme of Hjalmar's life?

Relling. No, you mayn't. I never disclose secrets like that to quacks. You were making an even worse mess of his case than I. My method has stood the test of trial. I have applied it in Molvik's case too. I have made a 'demoniac' of him. That is the blister I have put on *his* neck.

Gregers. Isn't he a demoniac, then?

Relling. What in heaven's name do you mean by 'being a demoniac'? That is only a bit of make-believe I invented to keep the life in him. If I hadn't done that, the poor honest wretch would have given way to self-contempt and despair years ago. And the same with the old lieutenant there! But he has happened to hit upon the cure by himself.

Gregers. Lieutenant Ekdal? what about him?

Relling. Well, what do you make of an old bear-stalker, like him, going into that dark attic there to shoot rabbits? There isn't a happier sportsman in the world than that poor old man playing about in there in that scrap-heap. The four or five withered Christmas-trees that he has kept are the same to him as the great tall live trees in the Höidal forests; the cocks and hens are the wildfowl in the tree-tops; and the rabbits, that lop about all over the attic floor, are the big game this famous backwoodsman used to pit himself against.

Gregers. Poor old man! Yes, he has indeed had to endure the quenching of all his youthful ideals.

Relling. And, while I think of it, Mr Werle junior—don't use that outlandish word 'ideals.' There is a good home-grown word—'lies.'

Gregers. Do you really think the two things are the same?

Relling. Just as nearly as typhus and putrid fever are.

Gregers. Doctor Relling, I won't give in till I have rescued Hjalmar from your clutches.

Relling. So much the worse for him. If you take away make-believe from the average man, you take away his happiness as well. (*To* HEDVIG, *who has come in from the sitting-room.*) Well, little wild-duck mother, I am going down now to see whether your daddy is still lying pondering over the wonderful invention. (*Goes out by the outer door.*)

Gregers (*going up to* HEDVIG). I can see by your face that the deed isn't done yet.

Hedvig. What deed? Oh, the wild duck. No.

Gregers. Your courage failed you when the time came to do it, I suppose?

Hedvig. No, it's not that. But when I woke up early this morning and remembered all we said, it all seemed so strange to me.

Gregers. Strange?

Hedvig. Yes, I don't know—— Last night, when we were talking about it, it seemed such a wonderful idea; but, after my sleep, when I thought about it again, it all seemed different.

Gregers. I see; I suppose it was impossible for you to grow up here without something being injured in you.

Hedvig. I don't care anything about that; if only father would come up, then——

Gregers. Ah, if only your eyes had been opened to what makes life worth living—if you possessed the true, happy, courageous spirit of self-sacrifice—you would see how you would be able to bring him up to you. But I have faith in you still, Hedvig. (*Goes out by the outer door.* HEDVIG *walks up and down; she is just going into the kitchen, but at the same moment a knock is heard on the attic door; she goes and opens it a little, and old* EKDAL *comes out, after which she shuts the door again.*)

Ekdal. Hm! There's not much pleasure in taking one's morning walk alone.

Hedvig. Didn't you feel like any shooting, grandfather?

Ekdal. It isn't the weather for shooting to-day. Too dark in there, you can hardly see a hand before you.

Hedvig. Haven't you ever felt you wanted to shoot anything else but the rabbits?

Ekdal. Why? Aren't the rabbits good enough sport?

Hedvig. Yes, but the wild duck?

Ekdal. Ho! ho!—are you afraid I shall shoot your wild duck for you? Never in the world: I would never do that.

Hedvig. No, I suppose you couldn't; wild duck must be very hard to shoot.

Ekdal. Couldn't! I should jolly well think I could.

Hedvig. How would you manage it, grandfather?—not my wild duck, I mean, but with others?

Ekdal. I would see that I shot them in the breast, you know, because that is the surest place. And you must shoot against the lie of the feathers, do you understand—not with the lie of the feathers.

Hedvig. Do they die then, grandfather?

Ekdal. Certainly they do, if you shoot properly. Well, I must go in and make myself tidy. Hm!—you understand— hm! (*Goes into his room.* HEDVIG *waits a little; glances at the door, then goes to the bookcase, stands on tiptoe, and takes the pistol down from the shelf and looks at it.* GINA *comes in from the sitting-room, with her broom and duster.* HEDVIG *hastily puts down the pistol unnoticed.*)

Gina. Don't go rummaging among your father's things, Hedvig.

Hedvig (*moving away from the bookcase*). I only wanted to put things straight a little.

Gina. You had much better go into the kitchen and see if the coffee is keeping hot; I will take his tray with me, when I go down to him.

(HEDVIG *goes out.* GINA *begins to sweep and clean the studio. After a while the outer door is opened slowly, and* HJALMAR *looks in. He is wearing his overcoat, but is hatless; he is unwashed and his hair is ruffled and untidy; his eyes are dull and heavy.* GINA *stands still with the broom in her hand and looks at him.*)

Gina. Well there you are, Hjalmar!—have you come after all?

Hjalmar (*walks in and answers in a dull voice*). I have come— but only to go away again at once.

Gina. Yes, yes—I suppose so. But, goodness me, what a sight you are!

Hjalmar. What a sight?

Gina. And your good overcoat too! It *has* had a doing!

Hedvig (from the kitchen doorway). Mother, shall I——? (*Sees* HJALMAR, *screams with joy and runs to him.*) Father! father!

Hjalmar (turning away and waving her back). Go away, go away! (*To* GINA.) Make her go away from me, I tell you!

Gina (in an undertone). Go into the sitting-room, Hedvig. (HEDVIG *goes in silently.*)

Hjalmar (pulling out the table-drawer, with a show of being busy). I must have my books with me. Where are my books?

Gina. What books?

Hjalmar. My scientific works, of course—the technical journals I use for my invention.

Gina (looking in the bookcase). Are they these unbound ones?

Hjalmar. Of course they are.

Gina (laying a pile of magazines on the table). Shan't I get Hedvig to cut them for you?

Hjalmar. I don't need to have them cut. (*Short silence.*)

Gina. Is it settled that you are leaving us, then, Hjalmar?

Hjalmar (rummaging among the books). I should think that was evident.

Gina. Yes, yes.

Hjalmar (vehemently). I can't come here and get a knife into my heart every hour of the day!

Gina. God forgive you, for saying such hard things about me.

Hjalmar. Prove to me——

Gina. I think it is you should prove to me.

Hjalmar. After a past like yours? There are certain demands —one might almost call them demands of the ideal——

Gina. But what about grandfather? What is to become of him, poor old man?

Hjalmar. I know my duty; the helpless old man will go with me. I shall go into the town and make my arrangements.—Hm —(*hesitatingly*)—has anyone found my hat on the stairs?

Gina. No. Have you lost your hat?

Hjalmar. I know I must have had it when I came in last night, there's no doubt about that; but this morning I couldn't find it.

Gina. Good Lord!—wherever did you go with those two rowdies?

Hjalmar. Don't ask silly questions. Do you think I am in a condition to remember details?

Gina. I only hope you haven't caught cold, Hjalmar. (*Goes into the kitchen.*)

Hjalmar (*talks to himself in an angry undertone while he empties the table drawer*). You are a scoundrel, Relling! You are a blackguard!—a shameless seducer!—I should like to murder you! (*He puts some old letters on one side, comes upon the torn paper of the day before, takes it up and looks at the pieces, but puts it down hastily as* GINA *comes in.*)

Gina (*putting down a breakfast tray on the table*). Here is a drop of something hot, if you could fancy it. And some bread and butter and a little salt meat with it.

Hjalmar (*glancing at the tray*). Salt meat? Never under this roof!—It's true I haven't tasted a bit of food for twenty-four hours, but that makes no difference.—My notes! The beginning of my memoirs! Where on earth are my diary and my important papers? (*Opens the sitting-room door, but draws back.*) There she is again!

Gina. Good gracious, the child must be somewhere!

Hjalmar. Come out. (*Stands aside, and* HEDVIG *comes out into the studio, looking frightened.* HJALMAR *stands with his hand on the door-handle.*) In these last moments I am spending in my former home, I wish to be protected from those who have no business here. (*Goes into the room.*)

Hedvig (*goes with a bound towards her mother and speaks in a low trembling voice*). Does he mean me?

Gina. Stay in the kitchen, Hedvig; or, no—better go into your own room. (*Talks to* HJALMAR, *as she goes in to him.*) Wait a minute, Hjalmar; don't turn all the drawers upside down; I know where all the things are.

Hedvig (*stands motionless for a moment frightened and irresolute, biting her lips to keep back the tears. Then she clenches her hands convulsively and says softly.*) The wild duck! (*She creeps over and takes the pistol from the shelf, opens the attic door a little, slips in, and shuts the door after her.* HJALMAR *and* GINA *are heard wrangling in the sitting-room.* HJALMAR *comes out carrying some note-books and old loose papers which he lays on the table.*)

Hjalmar. That portmanteau won't nearly hold them? There are a hundred and one things I must take with me.

Gina (*following him with the portmanteau*). Well, let the rest wait. Just take a shirt and a pair of pants with you.

Hjalmar. Poof!—these exhausting preparations——! (*Takes off his overcoat and throws it on the sofa.*)

Gina. And there is the coffee getting all cold, too.

Hjalmar. Hm! (*Drinks a mouthful absently and then another.*)

Gina (*dusting the backs of the chairs*). You will have a job to find another big attic like this for the rabbits.

Hjalmar. What! Have I got to take all the rabbits with me too?

Gina. Yes, grandfather can't live without his rabbits, I'm sure.

Hjalmar. He will have to get used to it. I have got to give up something of far more vital importance than rabbits.

Gina (*dusting the bookcase*). Shall I put your flute in the portmanteau for you?

Hjalmar. No. No flute for me. But give me the pistol.

Gina. Are you going to take that there gun with you?

Hjalmar. Yes. My loaded pistol.

Gina (*looking for it*). It isn't here. He must have taken it in with him.

Hjalmar. Is he in the attic?

Gina. No doubt he is.

Hjalmar. Hm—poor lonely old fellow. (*Takes a piece of bread and butter, eats it, and drinks up his cup of coffee.*)

Gina. If only we hadn't let our other room, you might have moved in there.

Hjalmar. I should be living under the same roof with——! Never—never!

Gina. But couldn't you put up for a day or two in the sitting-room? You could have it all to yourself.

Hjalmar. Never within these walls.

Gina. Well, then, downstairs, with Relling and Molvik?

Hjalmar. Don't mention those fellows' names! The very thought of them almost takes my appetite away. No, no—I must go out into the storm and snow—go from house to house seeking shelter for my father and myself.

Gina. But you have no hat, Hjalmar! You know you have lost your hat.

Hjalmar. Oh, those scum of the earth, steeped in every vice!—I must get a hat as I go. (*Takes another piece of bread and butter.*) I must make the necessary arrangements. I am not going to endanger my life. (*Searches for something on the tray.*)

Gina. What are you looking for?

Hjalmar. Butter.

Gina. I'll get some in a moment.   (*Goes into the kitchen.*)

Hjalmar (*calling after her*). Oh, it doesn't matter.   Dry bread will do just as well for me.

Gina (*bringing in a butter-dish*). Look, this is fresh churned.   (*She pours out another cup of coffee for him; he sits down on the sofa, puts more butter on his bread, and eats and drinks for a little while in silence.*)

Hjalmar. If I decided to do so, could I—without being exposed to intrusion on anyone's part—put up for a day or two in the sitting-room there?

Gina. Of course you could, if only you would.

Hjalmar. Because I don't see there is any possibility of getting all father's things out in a hurry.

Gina. And, besides that, you have got to tell him first that you don't mean to live here with us any longer.

Hjalmar (*pushing his cup away*). Yes, that's another thing; I have got to open up all this complicated question again—I must consider the situation; I must have time to breathe; I cannot sustain all these burdens in a single day.

Gina. No, and in such vile weather as this, too.

Hjalmar (*turning over Mr* WERLE'S *letter*). I see this paper is still lying here.

Gina. Yes, I haven't touched it.

Hjalmar. The rubbish is no concern of mine——

Gina. Well, I am sure *I* had no idea of doing anything with it.

Hjalmar. But it might be as well not to let it get out of sight altogether.   In all the upset of my moving, it might so easily——

Gina. I'll take care of it, Hjalmar.

Hjalmar. The deed of gift, after all, belongs first and foremost to my father, and it is his affair whether he chooses to make any use of it.

Gina (*sighing*). Yes, poor old father.

Hjalmar. Just for the sake of safety—where can I find some paste?

Gina (*going to the book-shelf*). Here is the paste-pot.

Hjalmar. And a brush.

Gina. Here's a brush too.   (*Brings them to him.*)

Hjalmar (*taking up a pair of scissors*). Just a strip of paper along the back—— (*Cuts and pastes.*)   Far be it from me to

want to do anything wrong with other people's property—
least of all with what belongs to a poor old man—and, indeed,
to someone else as well. There we are! Let it lie there for a
while. And when it's dry, take it away. I don't wish ever to
set eyes on the paper again. Never!

(GREGERS WERLE *comes in from the passage.*)

Gregers (*slightly astonished*). What—are you sitting here,
Hjalmar?

Hjalmar (*getting up hurriedly*). I had sunk down from
exhaustion.

Gregers. You have been having some breakfast, I see.

Hjalmar. The body makes its claims felt sometimes, too.

Gregers. What have you decided to do?

Hjalmar. For a man like me, there is only one thing to be
done. I am just engaged in putting my most important things
together. But it takes time, as you can imagine.

Gina (*a little impatiently*). Well, am I to get the room ready
for you, or pack your portmanteau?

Hjalmar (*with a glance of irritation towards* GREGERS). Pack—
and get the room ready as well!

Gregers (*after a short pause*). I should never have thought this
would be the end of it. Is there really any necessity for you to
leave house and home?

Hjalmar (*walking about uneasily*). What do you want me to do,
then?—I am not fit to stand unhappiness, Gregers. I need a
sense of security and peace about me.

Gregers. But can't you have that here? Just make the trial.
It seems to me that now you have firm ground to build upon—
and to begin afresh. Remember, too, you have your invention
to live for.

Hjalmar. Oh, don't talk to me about my invention. I
shouldn't wonder if that were a very long way off.

Gregers. Really?

Hjalmar. Good heavens! Yes. Just tell me what you
suppose I am going to invent? Other people have invented
most things already. It becomes harder every day——

Gregers. But you, who have worked so hard at it——

Hjalmar. It was that scoundrel Relling who set me on to it.

Gregers. Relling?

Hjalmar. Yes, it was he that first called my attention to my
talent for making some remarkable discovery in photography.

Gregers. Aha!—it was Relling!

Hjalmar. I got so much happiness out of it, Gregers.   Not so much for the sake of the invention itself, as because Hedvig believed in it—believed in it with a child's wholehearted enthusiasm.   Perhaps I should say that I have been fool enough to go and imagine she believed in it.

Gregers. Can you really think that Hedvig has not been genuine about it?

Hjalmar. I can think anything now.   It is Hedvig who stands in my way.   She has taken all the sunshine out of my life.

Gregers. Hedvig?   How can you say that about Hedvig? How can she have done anything of the sort?

Hjalmar (without answering him). How overwhelmingly I have loved that child!   How overwhelmingly happy I have felt every time I came home into my poor room, and she ran to meet me with her sweet little half-closed eyes!—Credulous fool! I loved her so overwhelmingly that I deluded myself with the dream that she loved me just as much.

Gregers. Do you say that was a delusion?

Hjalmar. How can I tell?   I can get nothing whatever out of Gina, and she is so utterly lacking in any sense of the ideal side of all these complications.   But to you I feel forced to open my mind, Gregers.   There is that terrible doubt—perhaps Hedvig has never really honestly loved me.

Gregers. It is possible you may have proof of that.   (*Listens.*) What's that?   I thought I heard the wild duck cry.

Hjalmar. It's the wild duck quacking.   Father is in the attic.

Gregers. Is he?   (*A look of happiness lights up his face.*)   I tell you, you may have proof yet that your poor misunderstood Hedvig loves you.

Hjalmar. What proof can she give me?   I daren't believe in any assurances from that quarter.

Gregers. There is not an atom of deceitfulness in Hedvig.

Hjalmar. Ah, Gregers, that is just what I am not so certain about.   Who knows what Gina and that Mrs Sörby may have sat here whispering and gossiping about?   And Hedvig is usually all ears, I can tell you.   Perhaps the deed of gift did not come so unexpectedly, after all.   In fact, I thought I noticed something.

Gregers. What sort of spirit is this that has taken hold of you?

Hjalmar. I have had my eyes opened.   Just you wait.   You will see the deed of gift is only a beginning.   Mrs Sörby has been very thick with Hedvig all along, and now she has it in her power to do whatever she pleases for the child.   They can take her from me whenever they like.

Gregers. Hedvig will never leave you.

Hjalmar. Don't be so sure of that.   If they come beckoning to her with their hands full of presents——   And I have loved her so overwhelmingly!   I, who would have thought it my greatest joy to take her carefully by the hand and lead her through life—just as one leads a child, who is frightened of the dark, through a great empty room!   Now I feel such a gnawing certainty that the poor photographer, up in his garret here, has never really and truly been anything to her.   She has only been cunningly careful to keep on a good footing with me till the time came.

Gregers. You don't really believe that, Hjalmar?

Hjalmar. That is just the cruellest part of it—that I don't know what to believe—and that I never shall know.   But can you really doubt that it is as I say?   Ha! ha!   You rely far too much on your 'demands of the ideal,' my good Gregers!   If the others were to come, with their hands full, and call to the child: 'Come away from him: you will learn what life is with us——'

Gregers (*hastily*). Well, what then, do you suppose?

Hjalmar. If I asked her then: 'Hedvig, are you willing to give up this life they offer you, for my sake?' (*Laughs derisively.*)   Thank you!—you would just hear what answer I should get.

(*A pistol shot is heard from within the attic.*)

Gregers (*with a happy shout*). Hjalmar!

Hjalmar. Listen to that.   He must needs go shooting too.

Gina (*coming in*). Hjalmar, I think grandfather is blundering about in the attic by himself.

Hjalmar. I will look in——

Gregers (*quickly and with emotion*). Wait a moment!   Do you know what that was?

Hjalmar. Of course I know.

Gregers. No, but you don't.   I know.   That was the proof you wanted!

Hjalmar. What proof?

Gregers. That was a child's act of sacrifice.   She has got your father to shoot the wild duck.

Hjalmar. Shoot the wild duck!

Gina. Fancy that, now!

Hjalmar. What for?

Gregers. She wanted to sacrifice, for your sake, what she prized most in the world; because she believed it would make you love her again.

Hjalmar (*tenderly, with emotion*). Poor child!

Gina. What things she thinks of!

Gregers. She only wanted your love again, Hjalmar; she did not feel as if she could live without it.

Gina (*struggling with her tears*). There you are, Hjalmar!

Hjalmar. Gina, where is she?

Gina (*sniffing*). Poor thing, she is sitting out in the kitchen, I expect.

Hjalmar (*crosses the room and opens the kitchen door*). Hedvig— come here! Come here to me! (*Looks around.*) No, she is not there.

Gina. Then she must be in her own little room.

Hjalmar (*who has gone out to look*). No, she is not here either. (*Comes in.*) She must have gone out.

Gina. Yes, you wouldn't have her anywhere in the house.

Hjalmar. If only she would come home soon, so that I could let her know—— Everything will be all right now, Gregers; now I believe we can begin life over again.

Gregers (*quietly*). I knew it was through the child that everything would be made right.

(*Old* EKDAL *comes to the door of his room; he is in full uniform, and is occupied in trying to buckle on his sword.*)

Hjalmar (*in astonishment*). Father! are you there!

Gina. Was it in your own room that you fired?

Ekdal (*indignantly as he approaches*). So you go shooting alone, do you, Hjalmar?

Hjalmar (*anxious and perplexed*). Wasn't it you, then, that was shooting in the attic?

Ekdal. I shooting? Hm!

Gregers (*calls to* HJALMAR). She has shot the wild duck herself, don't you see?

Hjalmar. What can it mean! (*Hurries to the attic door, tears it aside, looks in, and gives a loud scream.*) Hedvig!

Gina (*running to the door*). Heavens! what is it?

Hjalmar (*going in*). She is lying on the floor!

Gregers. Hedvig on the floor! (*Goes in to* HJALMAR.)

Gina (*at the same time*). Hedvig! (*From within the garret.*) Oh, no! no! no!

Ekdal. Ho! ho! does she go out shooting too!

(HJALMAR, GINA, *and* GREGERS *carry* HEDVIG *into the studio; the pistol is clasped tight in the fingers of her right hand, which is hanging down.*)

Hjalmar (distractedly). The pistol has gone off—and she has been shot. Call for help! Help!

Gina (runs into the passage and calls out). Relling! Relling! Doctor Relling! come up as quickly as you can! (HJALMAR *and* GREGERS *lay* HEDVIG *on the sofa.*)

Ekdal (quietly). The forests avenge themselves.

Hjalmar (on his knees beside HEDVIG). She is coming to now. She is coming to—yes, yes, yes.

Gina (who has come in again). Where has she been shot? I can't see anything. (RELLING *comes in hurriedly with* MOLVIK *at his heels; the latter is without waistcoat or necktie, and with his coat flying open.*)

Relling. What is the matter?

Gina. They say Hedvig has shot herself.

Hjalmar. Come here and help!

Relling. Shot herself! (*Pushes the table aside and begins to examine her.*)

Hjalmar (looking anxiously up at him). It can't be dangerous, Relling? What? She's hardly bleeding at all. It can't be dangerous?

Relling. How did it happen?

Hjalmar. I can't imagine——!

Gina. She wanted to shoot the wild duck.

Relling. The wild duck?

Hjalmar. The pistol must have gone off.

Relling. Hm! Yes, of course.

Ekdal. The forests avenge themselves. But I am not afraid, anyway. (*Goes into the attic and shuts the door after him.*)

Hjalmar. Well, Relling—why don't you say something?

Relling. The bullet has entered her chest.

Hjalmar. Yes—but she's coming to!

Gina (bursting into tears). My child, my child!

Gregers (in a choked voice). In the ocean's depths——

Hjalmar (springing up). Yes, yes, she *must* live! Oh, for God's sake, Relling—just for a moment—just long enough for me to let her know how overwhelmingly I have loved her all the time!

Relling. The heart has been hit. Internal haemorrhage. She died on the spot.

Hjalmar. And I hunted her away from me! And she crept like a frightened animal into the attic and died for love of me. (*Sobbing.*) I can never make it right now! I can never tell her——! (*Clenches his fists and cries up to heaven.*) Thou who art there above us—if indeed Thou *art* there! Why hast Thou done this to me!

Gina. Hush, hush! you mustn't take on in that terrible way. We had no right to keep her, I suppose.

Molvik. The child is not dead, but sleepeth.

Relling. Rubbish!

Hjalmar (*goes more calmly over to the sofa and, folding his arms, looks down at* HEDVIG). There she lies, so stiff and still.

Relling (*trying to take the pistol from her fingers*). She holds so tight, so tight.

Gina. No, no, Relling, don't hurt her fingers; let the thing alone.

Hjalmar. She shall take it with her.

Gina. Yes, let her. But the child mustn't lie out here for a show. She shall go into her own little room, she shall. Carry her with me, Hjalmar. (*She and* HJALMAR *take her up.*)

Hjalmar (*as they carry her out*). Oh, Gina, Gina—can you ever get over this?

Gina. We must help one another. Now, I think, we each have a share in her.

Molvik (*stretches out his arms and babbles*). Blessed be the Lord! Earth to earth, dust to dust——

Relling (*whispering*). Shut up, you fool—you're drunk.

(HJALMAR *and* GINA *carry the body out through the kitchen.* RELLING *stands looking after them.* MOLVIK *sneaks out into the passage.*)

Relling (*going over to* GREGERS). No one will ever persuade me this was an accident.

Gregers (*who has stood terror-stricken, his face twitching convulsively*). No one can tell how the dreadful thing happened.

Relling. The flame has scorched her dress. She must have held the pistol to her chest and fired.

Gregers. Hedvig has not died in vain. You saw how his grief called out all the best that was in him.

Relling. Most people show their best side in the presence of death. But how long do you suppose this turn for the better will last in his case?

Gregers. Surely it will last and increase as long as he lives!

Relling. In eight or nine months little Hedvig will be no more to him than a beautiful theme to declaim upon.

Gregers. How can you dare to say that of Hjalmar Ekdal?

Relling. We will talk of it again as soon as the grass has grown over her grave. Then you will hear him pumping up his fine phrases about 'the child torn prematurely from her father's loving heart'; you will see him wallowing in emotional fits of self-admiration and self-compassion. Just you wait and see!

Gregers. If you are right, and I am wrong, life is no longer worth living.

Relling. Oh, life would be all right if we could only be rid of these infernal fools who come to poor people's doors presenting their 'demands of the ideal.'

Gregers (*looking in front of him*). If that is so, I am glad my destiny is what it is.

Relling. Excuse me, but—what *is* your destiny?

Gregers (*turning to go*). To be the thirteenth at table.

Relling. So I should imagine!

THE LADY FROM THE SEA

DRAMATIS PERSONAE

Doctor Wangel.

Ellida Wangel, his second wife.

Bolette
Hilde (not yet grown up) } his daughters by his first wife.

Arnholm, a schoolmaster.

Lyngstrand.

Ballested.

A Stranger.

Young People of the Town.

Tourists.

Visitors.

*(The action takes place in a small fiord town,
Northern Norway.)*

THE LADY FROM THE SEA

ACT I

(SCENE.—DOCTOR WANGEL's *house, with a large veranda to the left. Garden in front of and around the house. Under the veranda a flagstaff. In the garden an arbour, with table and chairs. Hedge, with small gate at the back. Beyond, a road along the seashore. An avenue of trees along the road. Between the trees are seen the fiord, high mountain ranges and peaks. A warm and brilliantly clear summer morning.*

BALLESTED, *middle aged, wearing an old velvet jacket and a broad-brimmed artist's hat, stands under the flagstaff, arranging the lines. The flag is lying on the ground. A little way from him an easel, with an outspread canvas. By the easel on a camp-stool, brushes, a palette, and box of colours.*

BOLETTE WANGEL *comes from the room opening on the veranda. She carries a large vase of flowers, which she puts down on the table.*)

Bolette. Well, Ballested, is it working smoothly now?

Ballested. Oh yes, Miss Bolette, it's all right now. May I ask—do you expect any visitors to-day?

Bolette. Yes, we're expecting Mr Arnholm this morning. He arrived in town during the night.

Ballested. Arnholm? Wait a minute—wasn't Arnholm the man who was tutor here several years ago?

Bolette. Yes, that's the man.

Ballested. Oh, really! Is he over this way again?

Bolette. That's why we want to have the flag up.

Ballested. Yes, that's quite understandable.

(BOLETTE *goes into the room again. A little later* LYNGSTRAND *enters from the road and stands still, interested by the easel and painting gear. He is a slender youth, poorly but carefully dressed, and looks delicate.*)

Lyngstrand (*on the other side of the hedge*). Good morning.

Ballested (*turning round*). Hallo! Good morning. (*Hoists up the flag.*) That's it! Up goes the balloon. (*Fastens the lines,*

167

and then busies himself about the easel.)   Good morning, my dear sir.   I really don't think I've the pleasure of——

Lyngstrand. I'm sure you're a painter.

Ballested. Of course I am.   Why shouldn't I be?

Lyngstrand. Yes, I can see you are.   May I take the liberty of coming in a moment?

Ballested. Would you like to come in and have a look round?

Lyngstrand. I should like to immensely.

Ballested. Oh, there's nothing much to see yet.   But come in.   Come a little closer.

Lyngstrand. Thank you so much.   (*Comes in through the garden gate.*)

Ballested (*painting*). I'm working at the fiord there between the islands.

Lyngstrand. So I see.

Ballested. But the figure is still lacking.   There's not a model to be had in this town.

Lyngstrand. Is there going to be a figure, too?

Ballested. Yes.   Here by the rocks in the foreground I shall have a mermaid lying, half dead.

Lyngstrand. Why half dead?

Ballested. She has wandered here from the sea, and can't find her way out again.   And so she lies there dying in the brackish water.

Lyngstrand. Ah, I see.

Ballested. The lady of the house put it into my head to do something of the kind.

Lyngstrand. What will you call the picture when it's finished?

Ballested. I think of calling it 'The Mermaid's End.'

Lyngstrand. That's excellent!   You're sure to make a good job of it.

Ballested (*looking at him*). In the profession too, perhaps?

Lyngstrand. Do you mean a painter?

Ballested. Yes.

Lyngstrand. No, I'm not that; but I'm going to be a sculptor. My name is Hans Lyngstrand.

Ballested. So you're going to be a sculptor?   Oh well, sculpture is quite a nice sort of art in its way.   I fancy I've seen you in the street once or twice.   Have you been staying here long?

Lyngstrand. No; I've only been here a fortnight.   But I shall try to stay on till the end of the summer.

Ballested. For the bathing?

Lyngstrand. Yes; I wanted to see if I could get a little stronger.

Ballested. You're not delicate, surely?

Lyngstrand. Well, yes, I am a little delicate; but it's nothing dangerous. Just a little tightness on the chest.

Ballested. Oh, that's nothing! You should consult a good doctor.

Lyngstrand. Yes, I thought of speaking to Doctor Wangel one of these days.

Ballested. You should. (*Looks out to the left.*) There's another steamer, crowded with passengers. It's really marvellous how travelling has increased here these last few years.

Lyngstrand. Yes, there's a good deal of traffic here, I think.

Ballested. And lots of summer visitors come here too. I'm afraid our good town will lose its individuality with all these trippers around.

Lyngstrand. Were you born in the town?

Ballested. No, but I have accla—acclimatized myself. I feel bound to the place by the ties of time and habit.

Lyngstrand. Then you've lived here a long time?

Ballested. Well—about seventeen or eighteen years. I came here with Skive's Dramatic Company. But then we got into difficulties, and so the company broke up and dispersed in all directions.

Lyngstrand. But you yourself remained here?

Ballested. I remained, and I've done very well. I have been working chiefly as an interior decorator as a matter of fact.

(BOLETTE *comes out with a rocking-chair, which she places on the veranda.*)

Bolette (*speaking into the room*). Hilde, see if you can find the embroidered footstool for father.

Lyngstrand (*going up to the veranda, bows*). Good morning, Miss Wangel.

Bolette (*by the balustrade*). What! Is it you, Mr Lyngstrand? Good morning. Excuse me one moment, I'm only—— (*Goes into the room.*)

Ballested. Do you know the family?

Lyngstrand. No, not well. I've only met the young ladies now and again socially; and I had a chat with Mrs Wangel the last time we had music up at the Prospect. She said I might come and see them.

Ballested. You know, you ought to get to know them better.

Lyngstrand. Yes; I'd been thinking of paying them a visit. Just a sort of casual call. If only I could find some excuse——

Ballested. Excuse! Nonsense! (*Looking out to the left.*) Damn it! (*Gathering his things.*) The steamer's by the pier already. I must get off to the hotel. Some of the new arrivals might want me. I'm a hairdresser, too, you see.

Lyngstrand. You are certainly a man of many parts.

Ballested. In small towns one has to try to acclam—acclimatize oneself in various branches. If you should require anything in the hair line—a little hair-cream or such like—you've only to ask for Ballested the Dancing-master.

Lyngstrand. Dancing-master!

Ballested. President of the Brass Band Society, if you prefer it. We've a concert on this evening up at the Prospect. Good-bye, good-bye!

(*He goes out with his painting gear through the garden gate.* HILDE *comes out with the footstool.* BOLETTE *brings more flowers.* LYNGSTRAND *greets* HILDE *from the garden below.*)

Hilde (*by the balustrade, not returning his greeting*). Bolette said you had ventured in to-day.

Lyngstrand. Yes, I took the liberty of coming in for a moment.

Hilde. Have you been out for a morning walk?

Lyngstrand. Oh, no! the walk didn't materialize this morning.

Hilde. Have you been bathing, then?

Lyngstrand. Yes; I've had a short dip. I saw your mother down there. She was going into her bathing-cabin.

Hilde. Who was?

Lyngstrand. Your mother.

Hilde. Oh! I see. (*She puts the stool in front of the rocking-chair.*)

Bolette (*interrupting*). Didn't you see anything of father's boat out on the fiord?

Lyngstrand. Well, I thought I saw a sailing-boat that was heading up the fiord.

Bolette. I'm sure that was father. He's been to visit patients on the islands. (*She is arranging things on the table.*)

Lyngstrand (*taking a step up the stairs to the veranda*). My goodness, everything's decorated here with flowers!

Bolette. Yes, doesn't it look nice?

Lyngstrand. It looks lovely! It looks as if there is something special going on here to-day.

Hilde. That's exactly what there is.

Lyngstrand. I might have guessed it! I'm sure it's your father's birthday.

Bolette (*warningly to* HILDE). Hm—hm!

Hilde (*taking no notice of her*). No, mother's.

Lyngstrand. Oh! your mother's!

Bolette (*in a low voice, angrily*). Really, Hilde!

Hilde (*the same*). Let me be! (*To* LYNGSTRAND.) I suppose you're going home to lunch now?

Lyngstrand (*going down steps*). Yes, I suppose I must go and get something to eat.

Hilde. You probably find the accommodation very good at the hotel!

Lyngstrand. I'm not staying at the hotel now. It was too expensive for me.

Hilde. Where are you staying, then?

Lyngstrand. I'm staying up at Mrs Jensen's.

Hilde. Which Mrs Jensen's?

Lyngstrand. The midwife.

Hilde. Excuse me, Mr Lyngstrand, but I really have other matters to attend to——

Lyngstrand. Oh! I'm sure I ought not to have said that.

Hilde. Said what?

Lyngstrand. What I said just now.

Hilde (*looking contemptuously at him*). I don't understand you in the least.

Lyngstrand. Oh well—— But I must say good-bye for the present.

Bolette (*comes forward to the steps*). Good-bye, good-bye, Mr Lyngstrand. You must excuse us now. But another day— when you've plenty of time—and would like to—you really must come in and see father and the rest of us.

Lyngstrand. Yes, thank you, very much. I should love to.

(*Bows, and goes out through the garden gate. As he goes along the road he bows again towards the veranda.*)

Hilde (*in a low voice*). Adieu, monsieur! Please remember me to Mother Jensen.

Bolette (*in a low voice, shaking her arm*). Hilde! You naughty girl. Are you quite crazy? He might have heard you.

Hilde. Pooh! Do you think I care about *that*?

Bolette (*looking out to the right*). Here's father!

(WANGEL, *in outdoor clothes and carrying a small bag, comes from the footpath.*)

Wangel. Look! I'm back again, children! (*He enters through the garden gate.*)

Bolette (*going towards him at the bottom of the garden*). Oh! We're so pleased you've come!

Hilde (*also going up to him*). Have you got off for the whole day now, father?

Wangel. Oh, no! I must go down to the surgery for a little while presently. Tell me—do you know if Arnholm has come?

Bolette. Yes, he arrived in the night. We sent to the hotel to inquire.

Wangel. Then you've not seen him yet?

Bolette. No, but he's sure to come here this morning.

Wangel. Yes, he's sure to do that.

Hilde (*pulling him*). Father, now you must look round.

Wangel (*looking towards the veranda*). Yes, I see it all, child. It's quite gay.

Bolette. But don't you think we've arranged it nicely?

Wangel. Yes, I must say you have. Are—are we alone at home now?

Hilde. Yes, she's gone to——

Bolette (*interrupting quickly*). Mother has gone to bathe.

Wangel (*looks lovingly at* BOLETTE, *and pats her head. Then he says, hesitating*). Look here, my dears, do you really want to keep this up all day? And the flag hoisted, too?

Hilde. Surely you understand, don't you, father?

Wangel. Hm! Yes. But you see——

Bolette (*looks at him and nods*). Surely you know we've been doing all this in honour of Mr Arnholm. When such a good friend comes to see you for the first time——

Hilde (*smiling, and shaking him*). Think! the man who used to be Bolette's tutor, father!

Wangel (*with a half-smile*). You're a pair of sly minxes. Well—good heavens—after all, it's only natural we should remember the one who is no longer with us. But all the same—— Here, Hilde (*Gives her his bag*), take that down to the surgery. No, girls. I don't like all this—the way it's done, I mean. This habit of every year—well—what can I say? But still, I suppose it can't be managed any other way.

Hilde (*about to go out of the garden, and with the bag, stops short, turns, and points*). Look at that man coming up here, I'm sure it's your tutor.

Bolette (*looks in that direction*). Who, him? (*Laughs.*) I like that! Do you think that middle-aged fellow is Arnholm?

Wangel. Wait a moment, child. Why, by Jove, I do believe it is. Yes, it certainly is.

Bolette (*staring at him in quite amazement*). Yes, my goodness, I almost think——

(ARNHOLM, *in elegant morning dress, with gold spectacles and a thin cane, comes along the road. He looks overworked. He looks in at the garden, nods in friendly fashion and enters by the garden gate.*)

Wangel (*going to meet him*). Welcome, my dear Arnholm! Heartily welcome back to your old quarters again!

Arnholm. Thank you, Doctor Wangel. Thank you, indeed. (*They shake hands and walk up the garden together.*) And there are the children! (*Holds out his hands and looks at them.*) I should hardly have known these two again.

Wangel. No, I quite believe you.

Arnholm. And yet—perhaps Bolette—yes, I should have known Bolette.

Wangel. Hardly, I think. Why, it is eight—nine years since you saw her. Ah, yes! Many things have changed here in that time.

Arnholm (*looking round*). I really can't see that it has, except that the trees have grown remarkably, and that you've made that arbour.

Wangel. Oh, no—not outwardly.

Arnholm (*smiling*). And then, of course, you've two grown-up daughters here now.

Wangel. Grown up! Well, there's only one grown up.

Hilde (*aside*). Oh, listen to father!

Wangel. But now let's sit down up there on the veranda, shall we? It's cooler than here.

Arnholm. Thank you so much, my dear doctor.

(*They go up.* WANGEL *motions him to the rocking-chair.*)

Wangel. That's right! Now make yourself comfortable, and rest, you seem rather tired after your journey.

Arnholm. Oh, that's nothing. Here, in these surround-ings——

Bolette (*to* WANGEL). Hadn't we better have some soda and fruit squash in the sitting-room? It's sure to be too hot out here soon.

Wangel. Yes, girls. Let's have some soda and fruit squash, and perhaps a drop of brandy, too.

Bolette. Brandy, too!

Wangel. Just a little, in case anyone should like some.

Bolette. All right. Hilde, take the bag down to the surgery.

(BOLETTE *goes into the room, and closes the door after her.* HILDE *takes the bag, and goes through the garden to the back of the house.*)

Arnholm (*who has followed* BOLETTE *with his eyes*). What a delightful—— They are both delightful girls, who've grown up here for you.

Wangel (*sitting down*). Yes, so you think so, too?

Arnholm. Why, it's simply . amazing, how Bolette!—and Hilde, too—— But now, you yourself, my dear doctor. Are you thinking of staying here all your life?

Wangel. Yes, I expect so. Why, I've been born and bred here, so to speak. I lived here so very happily with—her who left us so early—she whom you knew when you were here before, Arnholm.

Arnholm. Oh yes!

Wangel. And now I live here so happily with the one who has taken her place. Ah! On the whole, fate has been very kind to me.

Arnholm. You have no children by your second marriage?

Wangel. We had a little boy, two—two and a half years ago. But he didn't stay long. He died when he was four or five months old.

Arnholm. Isn't your wife at home to-day?

Wangel. Oh yes. She's sure to be here soon. She's down there bathing. She does so every single day whatever the weather.

Arnholm. Is she ill, then?

Wangel. Not exactly ill, although she has been strangely nervy for the last few years—that is to say, she is now and then. I can't make out what is really the matter. But a plunge into the sea is sheer delight to her.

Arnholm. Yes, I remember that of old.

Wangel (*with an almost imperceptible smile*). Of course! You knew Ellida when you were teacher out there at Skjoldviken.

Arnholm. I did indeed. She often used to visit the parsonage. But I mostly met her when I went to the lighthouse to see her father.

Wangel. Those times out there, believe me, have set their

mark upon her.   The people in the town here can't understand
her at all.   They call her the 'Lady from the Sea.'

Arnholm. Do they?

Wangel. Yes.   And so—now, talk to her about the old days,
my dear Arnholm, it will do her good.

Arnholm (*looks at him in doubt*). Have you any reason for
thinking so?

Wangel. I have indeed.

Ellida (*her voice is heard outside the garden*). Are you there,
Wangel?

Wangel (*rising*). Yes, dear.

(Mrs ELLIDA WANGEL, *in a large, light wrap, and with wet hair
     hanging loose over her shoulders, comes from between the trees
     by the arbour.   ARNHOLM rises.*)

Wangel (*smiling, and holding out his hands to her*). Ah!   Here
comes our Mermaid!

Ellida (*goes quickly up the veranda, and seizes his hands*).
Thank God that you are back!   When did you come?

Wangel. Just now, a little while ago.   (*Pointing to* ARNHOLM.)
But won't you say hallo to an old acquaintance?

Ellida (*holding out her hand to* ARNHOLM). So here you are!
Welcome!   And forgive me for not being at home——

Arnholm. Don't mention it—don't stand on any ceremony.

Wangel. Was the water nice and fresh to-day?

Ellida. Fresh!   Heavens!   The water here is never fresh.
It is so tepid and lifeless.   Ugh!   The fiord water here is sick.

Arnholm. Sick?

Ellida. Yes, sick.   And I believe it makes people sick, too.

Wangel (*smiling*). You're giving our bathing resort a good
name!

Arnholm. I rather think, Mrs Wangel, that you have a peculiar
relation to the sea, and to everything that belongs to it.

Ellida. That may be.   Yes, I almost think I have myself.
But do you see how gaily the girls have arranged everything in
your honour?

Wangel (*embarrassed*). Hm!   (*Looks at his watch.*)   Well,
I suppose I must be quick and——

Arnholm. Is it really for me?

Ellida. Yes.   We don't decorate like this every day, you may
be sure.   Ugh!   How suffocatingly hot it is under this roof.
(*Goes down into the garden.*)   Come over here.   Here at least
there is a little air.   (*Sits down in the arbour.*)

Arnholm (*going there*). I think the air is quite fresh here.

Ellida. Yes, but you are used to the stifling air of the city! It's terrible there in the summer, I hear.

Wangel (*who has also gone into the garden*). Hm, Ellida dear, you must entertain our friend alone for a little while now.

Ellida. Are you busy, then?

Wangel. Yes, I must go down to the surgery. And then I must change. But I won't be long.

Arnholm (*sitting down in the arbour*). Now, don't hurry, my dear doctor. Your wife and I will manage to kill the time.

Wangel (*nodding*). Oh yes! I'm sure you will. Well, good-bye for the present. (*He goes out through the garden.*)

Ellida (*after a short pause*). Don't you think it's pleasant sitting out here?

Arnholm. Yes, I think it's pleasant now.

Ellida. They call this *my* arbour, because I had it fitted up, or rather Wangel did for me.

Arnholm. And you usually sit here?

Ellida. Yes, I spend most of the day here.

Arnholm. With the girls, I suppose?

Ellida. No, the girls—they usually sit on the veranda.

Arnholm. And Wangel himself?

Ellida. Oh! Wangel wanders between the two—sometimes he's with me and sometimes he's with his children.

Arnholm. And is it you who want it like this?

Ellida. I think all parties feel more comfortable with this arrangement. You see we can talk across to one another—if we happen to find there is anything to say.

Arnholm (*after thinking a while*). When I last crossed your path—out at Skjoldviken, I mean—Hm! That's a long time ago now.

Ellida. It's quite ten years since you were there with us.

Arnholm. Yes, I suppose it is about that. But when I think of you out there in the lighthouse! The heathen, as the old parson used to call you, because he said your father had named you after an old ship, and hadn't given you a name fit for a Christian.

Ellida. Well, what of it?

Arnholm. The last thing I should have believed then was that I should see you again down here as the wife of Wangel.

Ellida. No, at that time Wangel wasn't—at that time the girls' first mother was still alive. Their real mother, so——

Arnholm. Yes, of course, of course!   But even if that hadn't been so—even if he had been free—I could never have believed this would have come about.

Ellida. Nor I.   Never for a moment—then.

Arnholm. Wangel is such a nice chap.   So honourable.   So thoroughly kind and considerate to everyone.

Ellida (*warmly and heartily*). Yes, he is indeed.

Arnholm. But I have a feeling he must be so completely different from you.

Ellida. Yes, you are absolutely right there.   He is.

Arnholm. Well, but how did it all happen?

Ellida. Ah! my dear Arnholm, you mustn't ask me about that. I couldn't explain it to you, and even if I could you would never be able to understand in the least.

Arnholm. Hm!   (*In a lower tone.*)   Have you ever confided anything about me to your husband?   I mean, of course, about the futile step—I let myself take.

Ellida. No.   Don't worry about that.   I haven't said a word to him about—about anything that happened then.

Arnholm. Oh, I am glad.   I felt rather awkward at the thought that——

Ellida. There was no need.   I have only told him what is true—that I liked you very much, and that you were the best and closest friend I had out there.

Arnholm. Thank you for that.   But tell me—why did you never write to me after I had gone away?

Ellida. I thought that perhaps it might hurt you to hear from someone who—who could not respond as you wanted.   It seemed like reopening a painful subject.

Arnholm. Hm.   Oh, well, perhaps you were right.

Ellida. But why didn't you write?

Arnholm (*looks at her and smiles half reproachfully*).   I make the first move?   Perhaps lay myself open to the suspicion of wanting to begin all over again?   After such a rebuff as I had had?

Ellida. Oh no!   I do understand that.   Have you never thought since then of forming any other tie?

Arnholm. Never!   I have been faithful to my first memories.

Ellida (*half jestingly*). Nonsense!   Forget the sad old memories.   You'd far better think of becoming a happy husband, I should say.

Arnholm. I should have to be quick about it, then, Mrs

Wangel. Remember, I'm already—I'm ashamed to say—past thirty-seven.

Ellida. Well, all the more reason for being quick. (*She is silent for a moment, and then says, earnestly, in a low voice.*) But listen, Arnholm dear; now I am going to tell you something that I could not have told you then to save my life.

Arnholm. What is that?

Ellida. When you took the—the futile step you were just speaking of—I could not answer you in any other way than I did.

Arnholm. I know that you had nothing but friendship to give me; I know that well enough.

Ellida. But you do not know that my whole mind and soul then were centred elsewhere.

Arnholm. Then!

Ellida. Yes.

Arnholm. But that's impossible. You are mistaken about the time. You scarcely knew Wangel then.

Ellida. I'm not speaking about Wangel.

Arnholm. Not Wangel? But at that time, out there at Skjoldviken—I can't remember a single person whom I can possibly imagine your caring for.

Ellida. No, I can quite believe that. It was all such bewildering madness—all of it.

Arnholm. But tell me more about it.

Ellida. Oh! It's enough if you know I wasn't free; and you know it now.

Arnholm. And if you had been free?

Ellida. Well?

Arnholm. Would your answer to my letter have been different?

Ellida. How can I tell? When Wangel came the answer was different.

Arnholm. What is your object, then, in telling me that you weren't free?

Ellida (*getting up, as if in fear and unrest*). Because I must have someone to confide in. No, no, sit still!

Arnholm. Then your husband knows nothing about this?

Ellida. I confessed to him from the first that my thoughts had once been elsewhere. Ne never asked to know more, and we have never touched upon it since. Besides, at bottom it was sheer madness. And then it was over so soon—that is, in a way.

Arnholm (*rising*). Only in a way? Not quite?

Ellida. Yes, yes, it is! Oh, good heavens! Dear Arnholm, it isn't what you think. It is something so absolutely incomprehensible, I don't know how I could tell you. You would only think I was ill, or quite mad.

Arnholm. My dearest Mrs Wangel! Now you must and shall tell me all about it.

Ellida. All right, then, I'll try to. How would you, as a sensible man, explain to yourself that—— (*Looks round, and breaks off.*) Wait a moment. Here's a visitor.

(LYNGSTRAND *comes along the road, and enters the garden. He has a flower in his buttonhole, and carries a large, handsome bouquet done up in paper and silk ribbons. He stands somewhat hesitatingly and undecidedly by the veranda.*)

Ellida (*from the arbour*). Have you come to see the girls, Mr Lyngstrand?

Lyngstrand (*turning round*). Ah, Mrs Wangel, are you there? (*Bows, and comes nearer.*) No, it's not that. It's not the girls. It's you yourself, Mrs Wangel. You know you said I might come and see you——

Ellida. Of course I did. You are always welcome here.

Lyngstrand. Thank you, and as luck would have it it's a celebration here to-day——

Ellida. Oh! Do you know about that?

Lyngstrand. Rather! And so I should like to take the liberty of presenting this to Mrs Wangel. (*Bows, and offers her the bouquet.*)

Ellida (*smiling*). But, my dear Mr Lyngstrand, oughtn't you to give these lovely flowers to Mr Arnholm himself? For you know it's really he——

Lyngstrand (*looking uncertainly at both of them*). I'm so sorry, but I don't know this gentleman. It's only—I've only come because of the birthday, Mrs Wangel.

Ellida. Birthday? You've made a mistake, Mr Lyngstrand. It's no one's birthday here to-day.

Lyngstrand (*smiling slyly*). Oh! I know all about that! But I didn't think it was to be kept so dark.

Ellida. What do you know?

Lyngstrand. That it is your birthday.

Ellida. Mine?

Arnholm (*looks questioningly at her*). To-day? Surely not.

Ellida (*to* LYNGSTRAND). Whatever made you think that?

Lyngstrand. It was Miss Hilde who let it out. I just looked in here a little while ago, and I asked the young ladies why they were decorating the place like this, with flowers and flags.

Ellida. Well?

Lyngstrand. And so Miss Hilde said, 'Why, to-day is mother's birthday.'

Ellida. Mother's!—I see.

Arnholm. Oh! (*He and* ELLIDA *exchange a meaning look.*) Well, now that the young man knows about it——

Ellida (*to* LYNGSTRAND). Well, now that you know——

Lyngstrand (*offering her the bouquet again*). May I wish you many happy returns.

Ellida (*taking the flowers*). Very many thanks. Won't you sit down a moment, Mr Lyngstrand? (ELLIDA, ARNHOLM, *and* LYNGSTRAND *sit down in the arbour.*) This—birthday business —was to have been kept secret, Mr Arnholm.

Arnholm. So I see. It wasn't for us uninitiated folk!

Ellida (*putting down the bouquet*). No, indeed. Not for the uninitiated.

Lyngstrand. I won't tell a living soul about it, I really won't.

Ellida. Oh, it wasn't meant like that. But how are you getting on? I think you look better than you did.

Lyngstrand. Oh, I think I'm getting on famously. And by next year, if I can go south——

Ellida. And you are going south, the girls tell me.

Lyngstrand. Yes, I've a patron and friend at Bergen, who looks after me, and has promised to help me next year.

Ellida. How did you find such a friend?

Lyngstrand. Well, it all happened very luckily I once went to sea in one of his ships.

Ellida. Did you? So you wanted to go to sea?

Lyngstrand. No, not in the least. But when mother died, father wouldn't have me knocking about at home any longer, and so he sent me to sea. Then we were wrecked in the English Channel on our way home; and that was very fortunate for me.

Arnholm. How do you make that out?

Lyngstrand. Well, it was in the shipwreck that I got this little weakness—of my chest. I was so long in the ice-cold water before they picked me up; and so I had to give up the sea. And that was very fortunate.

Arnholm. Oh? Why do you think so?

Lyngstrand. Well, you see the weakness isn't dangerous, and now I can be a sculptor, as I so badly want to be.   Just think what it's like to model in that delicious clay, that yields so exquisitely under your fingers!

Ellida. And what are you going to model?   Will it be mermen and mermaids?   Or will it be old Vikings?

Lyngstrand. No, nothing like that.   As soon as I can set about it, I am going to try my hand at a great work—a group, as they call it.

Ellida. Yes.   But what's the group to be?

Lyngstrand. Oh! something I've experienced myself.

Arnholm. Yes, I think it's best to stick to that.

Ellida. But what's it to be?

Lyngstrand. Well, I thought it should be a young woman—a sailor's wife, who lies sleeping in strange unrest, and she is dreaming.   I believe I shall manage to do it so that anyone will be able to see she is dreaming.

Arnholm. Will there be anything else?

Lyngstrand. Yes, there will be another figure—a sort of apparition, as they say.   It's her husband, she has been unfaithful while he was away, and he has been drowned at sea.

Arnholm. What?

Ellida. Drowned?

Lyngstrand. Yes, he was drowned on a sea voyage.   But that's the wonderful part of it—he comes home all the same. It is night.   And he is standing by her bed looking at her. He is to stand there dripping wet, like one drawn from the sea.

Ellida (leaning back in her chair). What an extraordinary idea! *(Shutting her eyes.)*   Oh!   I can see it all so vividly, before my very eyes!

Arnholm. But how on earth, Mr—Mr—I thought you said it was something you had experienced.

Lyngstrand. Yes.   I did experience that—that is to say, in a way.

Arnholm. You saw a dead man?

Lyngstrand. Well, I don't mean I've actually seen this— experienced it in the flesh.   But still——

Ellida (quickly, intently). Do tell me all you can about it!   I must know about all this.

Arnholm (smiling). Yes, that'll be quite in your line.   Something to do with sea fantasies.

Ellida. What happened, Mr Lyngstrand?

Lyngstrand. Well, it was like this.   Just when we were about to sail home in the brig from a town they called Halifax, we had to leave the bos'n behind in hospital.   So we had to sign on an American instead.   This new bos'n——

Ellida. The American?

Lyngstrand. Yes, one day he got the captain to lend him a lot of old newspapers.   After that he was always reading them. He said he wanted to teach himself Norwegian.

Ellida. Well, and then what happened?

Lyngstrand. It was one evening in rough weather.   All hands were on deck—except the bos'n and myself.   He had sprained his ankle and couldn't walk, and I was feeling rather low, and was lying in my bunk.   Well, he was sitting there in the fo'c'sle, reading one of those old papers again——

Ellida. Yes, what happened?

Lyngstrand. Well, just as he was sitting there quietly reading, I heard him utter a sort of yell.   And when I looked at him, I saw his face was as white as chalk.   And then he began to crush and crumple the paper, and to tear it into a thousand shreds. But he did it so quietly, so very quietly.

Ellida. Didn't he say anything?   Didn't he speak?

Lyngstrand. Not at first, but a little while after he said, as if to himself: 'Married—to another man.   While I was away.'

Ellida (closes her eyes, and says, half to herself). Did he say that?

Lyngstrand. Yes.   And furthermore—he said, it in perfect Norwegian.   That man must have learnt foreign languages very easily——

Ellida. And what then?   What else happened?

Lyngstrand. Well, now comes the extraordinary part—which I shall never forget as long as I live.   For he added, and that quite quietly, too: 'But she is mine, and she shall remain mine. And she shall follow me, if I should return home and fetch her, like a drowned man from the dark sea.'

Ellida (pouring herself out a glass of water.   Her hand trembles). Oh!   How close it is here to-day.

Lyngstrand. And he said this with such conviction that I thought he would certainly be the man to do it.

Ellida. Don't you know anything about—what became of the man?

Lyngstrand. Oh!   Mrs Wangel, he's certainly not alive now.

Ellida (quickly). Why do you think that?

Lyngstrand. Why? Because we were shipwrecked afterwards in the Channel. I had got into the longboat with the captain and five others. The mate got into the stern-boat; and the American was in that too, and another man.

Ellida. And nothing has been heard of them since?

Lyngstrand. Not a word. The friend who looks after me said so quite recently in a letter. But it's just because of this I was so anxious to make it into a work of art. I can see the faithless sailor's wife so lifelike before me, and the avenger who is drowned, but who nevertheless comes home from the sea. I can see them both so distinctly.

Ellida. I, too. (*Rises.*) Come, let's go in—or, rather, let's go down to Wangel. I think it is so suffocatingly hot. (*She goes out of the arbour.*)

Lyngstrand (*who has also risen*). I, for my part, must ask you to excuse me. This was only to be a short visit because of the birthday.

Ellida. As you wish. (*Holds out her hand to him.*) Goodbye, and thank you for the flowers.

(LYNGSTRAND *bows, and goes off through the garden gate.*)

Arnholm (*rises, and goes up to* ELLIDA). I can see that you have taken this to heart, my dear Mrs Wangel.

Ellida. Yes, you may well say so. Although——

Arnholm. But still—after all, it's no more than you were bound to expect.

Ellida (*looks at him surprised*). Expect!

Arnholm. Well, so it seems to me.

Ellida. Expect that anyone should come back again!—come to life again like that!

Arnholm. But what on earth!—is it that mad sculptor's fisherman's tale, then?

Ellida. Oh, dear Arnholm, perhaps he isn't so mad after all!

Arnholm. Is it that nonsense about the dead man that has moved you so? And I was thinking that——

Ellida. What were you thinking?

Arnholm. I was naturally thinking that was only a make-believe of yours. And that you were sitting here grieving because you had found out a family celebration was being kept secret; because your husband and his children live a life of memories which you can't share in.

Ellida. Oh! no, no! Let that be as it may. I have no right to claim my husband wholly and solely for myself.

Arnholm. I should have thought you had.

Ellida. Yes.   But the truth is, I have not.   Why, I, too, live in something from which they are shut out.

Arnholm. You!   (*In lower tone.*)   Do you mean?—you, you do not really love your husband!

Ellida. Oh! yes, yes!   I have learnt to love him with all my heart!   And that's why it's so terrible—so inexplicable—so absolutely inconceivable!

Arnholm. Now you must and shall confide all your troubles in me.   Won't you, Mrs Wangel?

Ellida. I cannot, dear friend.   Not now, in any case.   Later, perhaps.

(BOLETTE *comes out on to the veranda, and goes down into the garden.*)

Bolette. Father's coming up from the surgery.   Hadn't we better all of us go into the sitting-room?

Ellida. Yes, let us.

(WANGEL, *in other clothes, comes with* HILDE *from behind the house.*)

Wangel. Well, here I am at your service.   And now how about a nice glass of something cool.

Ellida. Wait a moment.   (*She goes into the arbour and fetches the bouquet.*)

Hilde. I say!   All those lovely flowers!   Where did you get them?

Ellida. From the sculptor, Lyngstrand, my dear Hilde.

Hilde (*starts*). From Lyngstrand?

Bolette (*uneasily*). Has Lyngstrand been here again?

Ellida (*with a half-smile*). Yes.   He came here with these. Because of the birthday, you see.

Bolette (*looks at* HILDE). Oh!

Hilde (*mutters*). The idiot!

Wangel (*in painful confusion, to* ELLIDA). Hm!—yes, well you see—I must tell you, my dearest Ellida——

Ellida (*interrupting*). Come, girls!   Let's go and put my flowers in water with the others.   (*Goes up to the veranda.*)

Bolette (*to* HILDE). She really is good after all, you see.

Hilde (*in a low tone, with an angry look*). Fiddlesticks!   She only does it to take in father.

Wangel (*on the veranda, presses* ELLIDA'S *hand*). Thank you— thank you!   My heartfelt thanks for that, dear Ellida.

Ellida (*arranging the flowers*). Nonsense! Shouldn't I be in it, too, and take part in—in mother's birthday?

Arnholm. Hm!

(*He goes up to* WANGEL, *and* ELLIDA, BOLETTE, *and* HILDE *remain in the garden below.*)

ACT II

(SCENE.—*At the Prospect, a shrub-covered hill behind the town. A little in the background a beacon and a weather vane. Big stones arranged as seats around the beacon, and in the foreground. Farther back is seen the outer fiord, with islands and outstanding headlands. The open sea is not visible. It is a summer's evening, and twilight. A golden-red shimmer in the air and over the mountain-tops in the far distance. A quartet is faintly heard singing below in the background. Young townsfolk, men and women, come up in pairs, from the right, and, talking familiarly, pass out beyond the beacon. A little later,* BALLESTED *enters, as guide to a party of foreign tourists with their womenfolk. He is laden with shawls and travelling bags.*)

Ballested (*pointing upwards with a stick*). Sehen Sie, meine Herrschaften, dort, out there, liegt eine andere mountain. That wollen wir also besteigen, and so herunter——   (*He goes on with the conversation in French, and leads the party off to the left.* HILDE *comes quickly along the uphill path, stands still, and looks back. Soon after* BOLETTE *comes up the same way.*)

Bolette. But, my dear Hilde, why should we run away from Lyngstrand?

Hilde. Because I can't bear going uphill so slowly. Look —look at him crawling up!

Bolette. Yes! But you know how delicate he is.

Hilde. Do you think it's very—dangerous?

Bolette. I certainly do.

Hilde. He went to consult father this afternoon. I should like to know what father thinks about him.

Bolette. Father told me it was a thickening of the lungs, or something of the sort. He won't last very long, father says.

Hilde. No! Did he say that? Fancy—that's exactly what I thought.

Bolette. For heaven's sake don't show it!

Hilde. How could you think such a thing? (*In an undertone.*) Look, here comes Hans crawling up. Don't you think you can see by the look of him that he's called Hans?

Bolette (*whispering*). Now do behave! You really must.

(LYNGSTRAND *comes in from the right, a sunshade in his hand.*)

Lyngstrand. I hope the young ladies will excuse me for not getting along as quickly as they did.

Hilde. Have you got a sunshade too, now?

Lyngstrand. It's your mother's. She said I was to use it as a stick. I hadn't mine with me.

Bolette. Are they down there still—father and the others?

Lyngstrand. Yes, your father looked in at the restaurant for a moment, and the others are sitting out there listening to the music. But they were coming up here presently, your mother said.

Hilde (*stands looking at him*). I suppose you're thoroughly tired out now?

Lyngstrand. Yes, I think perhaps I am a little tired now. I really believe I shall have to sit down a moment. (*He sits on one of the stones in the foreground.*)

Hilde (*standing in front of him*). Do you know there's going to be dancing down there on the parade?

Lyngstrand. Yes, I heard there was some talk about it.

Hilde. You think dancing's great fun, don't you?

Bolette (*who begins gathering wild flowers among the heather*). Oh, Hilde! Now do let Mr Lyngstrand get his breath.

Lyngstrand (*to* HILDE). Yes, Miss Hilde; I should very much like to dance—if only I could.

Hilde. Oh, I see! Haven't you ever learnt?

Lyngstrand. No, I've not. But it wasn't *that* I meant. I meant I couldn't because of my chest.

Hilde. Because of that weakness you said you suffered from?

Lyngstrand. Yes, because of that.

Hilde. Aren't you very sorry you've got that—weakness?

Lyngstrand. Oh no! I can't say I am (*smiling*), because I think it's because of it that everyone is so nice and friendly, and kind to me.

Hilde. Yes. And then, besides, it's not dangerous.

Lyngstrand. No, it's not at all dangerous. So I gathered from what your father said to me.

Hilde. And then it will get better as soon as ever you begin travelling.

Lyngstrand. Of course it will get better.

Bolette (with flowers). Look, Mr Lyngstrand, you must put this in your buttonhole.

Lyngstrand. Oh! thank you, Miss Wangel. It's most kind of you.

Hilde (looking down the path). There they are, coming along the road.

Bolette (also looking down). I hope they know where to turn off. No, now they're going wrong.

Lyngstrand (rising). I'll run down to the turning and call to them.

Hilde. You'll have to call pretty loud.

Bolette. No, it's not worth it. You'll only tire yourself again.

Lyngstrand. Oh, but it's so easy going downhill. (*Goes off to the right.*

Hilde. Downhill—yes. (*Looking after him.*) Why, he's actually jumping! But he forgets he'll have to come up again.

Bolette. Poor chap.

Hilde. If Lyngstrand were to propose, would you marry him?

Bolette. Heavens, are you quite mad?

Hilde. Of course, I mean if he weren't troubled with that 'weakness.' And if he weren't going to die so soon, would you marry him *then*?

Bolette. I think you'd better marry him yourself!

Hilde. No jolly fear! Why, he hasn't a penny. He hasn't enough to keep himself even.

Bolette. Then why are you always going about with him?

Hilde. Oh, I only do that because of his weakness.

Bolette. I've never noticed that you pity him in the least for it!

Hilde. No, I don't. But I think it's most interesting.

Bolette. What is?

Hilde. To look at him and make him tell you it isn't dangerous; and that he's going abroad, and is going to be an artist. He really believes it all, and is so thoroughly happy about it. And yet nothing will ever come of it; nothing whatever. Because he won't live long enough. I find that's terribly thrilling to think of.

Bolette. Thrilling!

Hilde. Yes, I think it's terribly thrilling. I must call it that.

Bolette. Hilde, you really are a dreadful child!

Hilde. That's just what I want to be—out of spite. (*Looking down.*) At last! I bet Arnholm hates coming uphill. (*Turns round*.)   By the way, do you know what I noticed about Arnholm at dinner?

Bolette. No?

Hilde. Imagine—his hair's beginning to come off—right on the top of his head.

Bolette. Don't be silly.   I'm sure that's not true.

Hilde. It is!   And he has wrinkles round both his eyes too. Good gracious, Bolette, how could you be so much in love with him when he used to be your tutor?

Bolette (*smiling*). Yes.   Can you believe it?   I remember I once shed bitter tears because he thought Bolette was an ugly name.

Hilde. Yes, think of it.   (*Looking down*.)   I say, do just look down here!   There's 'The Lady from the Sea' walking along and chatting with him.   Not with father.   I wonder if those two aren't sweet on each other.

Bolette. You ought to be ashamed of yourself!   How can you stand there and say such a thing about her?   Now, when everything was beginning to be so pleasant between us.

Hilde. Don't try and kid yourself about that, my girl!   Oh no!   We shall never get on well with her.   She doesn't belong to us.   And we don't belong to her either.   Goodness knows what father dragged her home for!   I shouldn't wonder if some fine day she went mad under our very eyes.

Bolette. Mad!   Whatever makes you say that?

Hilde. Oh! it wouldn't be so extraordinary.   Her mother went mad, too.   She died mad—that I know.

Bolette. Yes, heaven only knows what you don't poke your nose into.   But now don't go chattering about this.   Do be good—for father's sake.   Do you year, Hilde?

(WANGEL, ELLIDA, ARNHOLM, *and* LYNGSTRAND *come up from the right*.)

Ellida (*pointing to the background*). It lies out there.

Arnholm. You're right.   It must be in that direction.

Ellida. Out there is the sea.

Bolette (*to* ARNHOLM). Don't you think it's pretty up here?

Arnholm. It's magnificent, I think.   Glorious view!

Wangel. I suppose you have never been up here before?

Arnholm. No, never.   In my time I don't think it was accessible.   There wasn't any path even.

Wangel. And not laid out either.   All this has been done during the last few years.

Bolette. Over there, at the Pilot's Mount, it's even grander than here.

Wangel. Shall we go there, Ellida?

Ellida (sitting down on one of the stones). No thanks, I won't go, but you others can.   I'll sit here meanwhile.

Wangel. Then I'll stay with you.   The girls can show Arnholm around.

Bolette. Would you like to go with us, Mr Arnholm?

Arnholm. I should like to, very much.   Does a path lead up there too?

Bolette. Oh yes.   There's a nice broad path.

Hilde. The path is so broad that two people can walk along it comfortably, arm-in-arm.

Arnholm (jestingly). Is that really so, little missie?   *(To* BOLETTE.)   Shall we two see if she is right?

Bolette (suppressing a smile). Very well, let's go.   *(They go out to the left, arm-in-arm.)*

Hilde (to LYNGSTRAND).* Shall we go too?

Lyngstrand. Arm-in-arm?

Hilde. Oh, why not?   For all I care!

Lyngstrand (taking her arm, laughing contentedly). This is great fun.

Hilde. Great fun?

Lyngstrand. Yes, because it looks exactly as if we were engaged.

Hilde. I'm sure you've never walked out arm-in-arm with a lady before, Mr Lyngstrand.   *(They go off.)*

Wangel (who is standing beside the beacon). Dear Ellida, now we have a moment to ourselves.

Ellida. Yes, come and sit down here, by me.

Wangel (sitting down). It's so peaceful and quiet here.   Now we can have a little talk together.

Ellida. What about?

Wangel. About yourself, and about our relationship to each other.   Ellida, I see quite well that it can't go on like this.

Ellida. What do you propose instead?

Wangel. Perfect confidence, my dear.   A true life together— as we used to have.

Ellida. Oh, if that could only be!   But it is so absolutely impossible.

Wangel. I think I understand you, from certain things you have let fall now and again.

Ellida (passionately). Oh, you do not! Don't say you understand!

Wangel. Oh yes. You have an honest nature, Ellida—you have a loyal heart.

Ellida. Yes, I have.

Wangel. Any position in which you could feel safe and happy must be a completely true and real one.

Ellida (looking eagerly at him). Well, and then?

Wangel. You are not suited to be a man's second wife.

Ellida. What makes you think that?

Wangel. It has often flashed across me like a foreboding. To-day it was made clear to me. The children's memorial celebration—you saw in me a kind of accomplice. Well, yes; a man's memories, after all, cannot be wiped out—not mine, anyhow. It isn't in me.

Ellida. I know that. Oh, I know that so well!

Wangel. But you are mistaken all the same. To you it is almost as if the children's mother were still living—as if she were still here invisible amongst us. You think my heart is equally divided between you and her. It is this thought that shocks you. You see something immoral in our relationship, and that is why you no longer can or will live with me as my wife.

Ellida (rising). Have you seen all that, Wangel—seen into all this?

Wangel. Yes. To-day I have at last seen into the very heart of it—to its utmost depths.

Ellida. To its very heart, you say? Oh, I don't believe it.

Wangel (rising). I know very well that there is more than this, my dear Ellida.

Ellida (anxiously). You know there is more?

Wangel. Yes. You cannot bear your surroundings here. The mountains oppress you, and weigh upon your mind. Nothing is open enough for you here. The heavens above you are not spacious enough. The air is not strong and bracing enough.

Ellida. You are right there. Night and day, winter and summer, it weighs upon me—this irresistible home-sickness for the sea.

Wangel. I know that very well, Ellida dear *(laying his hands upon her head).* And that is why the poor sick child shall go home to her own again.

Ellida. What do you mean?

Wangel. Something quite simple.   We are moving.

Ellida. Moving?

Wangel. Yes.   To somewhere by the open sea—a place where you can find a home after your own heart.

Ellida. Oh, my dear, you mustn't think of it!   That is quite impossible.   You could never live happily anywhere on earth but here!

Wangel. Be that as it may.   And, besides, do you think I can live happily here—without you?

Ellida. But I am here.   And I will stay here.   You have me.

Wangel. Have I, Ellida?

Ellida. Oh! don't let's talk about it.   Why, here you have all that you love and work for.   Your life's work lies here.

Wangel. Be that as it may, I tell you.   We are going away from here—moving somewhere—out there.   That is quite settled now, dear Ellida.

Ellida. What do you think we should gain by that?

Wangel. You would regain your health and peace of mind.

Ellida. I doubt it.   And what about you.   Think of yourself, too!   What would happen to you?

Wangel. I would win you back again, my dearest.

Ellida. But you can't do that!   No, no, you can't do that, Wangel!   That is the terrible part of it—heart-breaking to think of.

Wangel. That remains to be seen.   If that is what you think, then there is really no other cure for you but to go away.   And the sooner the better.   Now this is absolutely settled, do you hear?

Ellida. No!   Then in heaven's name I had better tell you everything straight out.   Everything just as it is.

Wangel. Yes, yes, do!

Ellida. You can't ruin your happiness for my sake, especially as it won't help us in any way.

Wangel. You have promised to tell me everything just as it is.

Ellida. I'll tell you everything as well as I can, and as far as I understand it.   Come here and sit by me.   (*They sit down on the stones.*)

Wangel. Well, Ellida, so——

Ellida. That day when you came out there and asked me if I would be your wife, you spoke so frankly and honestly to me about your first marriage.   It had been so happy, you said.

Wangel. And so it was.

Ellida. Yes, yes, I am sure of that, dear! But that isn't why I am referring to it now. I only want to remind you that I, on my side, was frank with you. I told you quite openly that once in my life I had cared for someone else. That there had been a—a kind of engagement between us.

Wangel. A kind of——

Ellida. Yes, something of the sort. Well, it only lasted such a very short time. He went away, and after that I broke it off. I told you all that.

Wangel. But my dear Ellida, why rake up all this now? It really didn't concern me, nor have I once asked you who he was.

Ellida. No, you haven't. You are always so considerate as far as I'm concerned.

Wangel (*smiling*). Well, in this case I could guess the name easily enough for myself.

Ellida. The name?

Wangel. Out in Skjoldviken and thereabouts there weren't many to choose from, or, rather, there was only one man.

Ellida. I suppose you think it was Arnholm!

Wangel. Well, wasn't it?

Ellida. No!

Wangel. Not Arnholm? Then I certainly don't understand.

Ellida. Can you remember that late in the autumn a big American ship once put into Skjoldviken for repairs?

Wangel. Yes, I remember it very well. It was on board that ship that the captain was found one morning in his cabin—murdered. I myself went out to make the post-mortem.

Ellida. Yes, you did.

Wangel. It was the second mate who had murdered him.

Ellida. No one can say that. It was never proved.

Wangel. There was enough evidence against him anyhow, or why should he have drowned himself as he did?

Ellida. He didn't drown himself. He escaped in a ship sailing north.

Wangel (*startled*). How do you know?

Ellida (*with an effort*). Well, Wangel—it was this second mate I was—engaged to.

Wangel (*springing up*). What! Is it possible!

Ellida. Yes, it is so. It was to him!

Wangel. But how on earth, Ellida! How did you come to get engaged to such a man? To an absolute stranger! What was his name?

Ellida. At that time he called himself Friman.   Later, in his letters, he signed himself Alfred Johnston.

Wangel. And where did he come from?

Ellida. From Finmark, he said.   But he was born in Finland, had come to Norway as a child with his father, I think.

Wangel. A Finn, then?

Ellida. Yes, I think so.

Wangel. What else do you know about him?

Ellida. Only that he went to sea very young.   And that he had been on long voyages.

Wangel. Nothing else?

Ellida. No.   We never talked about that sort of thing.

Wangel. What did you talk about, then?

Ellida. We talked mostly about the sea.

Wangel. Oh!   About the sea——

Ellida. About storms and about calm.   About dark nights at sea.   And about the sea in the glittering sunshiny days.   But we talked most about the whales, and the dolphins, and the seals who lie out there on the rocks in the midday sun.   And then we talked about the gulls, and the eagles, and all the other sea birds. I think—isn't it wonderful?—when we talked about those things it seemed to me as if both the sea beasts and the sea birds were one with him.

Wangel. And with you?

Ellida. Yes, I almost thought I belonged to them all, too.

Wangel. Well, well!   And that was how you became engaged to him?

Ellida. Yes.   He said I had to.

Wangel. You had to?   Hadn't you any will of your own, then?

Ellida. Not when he was near.   Oh, afterwards I thought it utterly inexplicable.

Wangel. Were you often together?

Ellida. No, not very often.   One day he came out to our place, and looked over the lighthouse.   After that I got to know him, and we met now and again.   But then all that happened about the captain, and he had to go away.

Wangel. Yes.   Tell me more about that.

Ellida. It was just daybreak when I had a note from him.   He said in it I was to go out to him at Bratthammer.   You know the headland there between the lighthouse and Skjoldviken?

Wangel. I know, I know!

Ellida. I was to go out there at once, he wrote, because he wanted to speak to me.

Wangel. And you went?

Ellida. Yes. I couldn't do otherwise. Well, then he told me he had stabbed the captain in the night.

Wangel. He said that himself! Actually said so in so many words?

Ellida. Yes. But he said he had only acted rightly and justly.

Wangel. Rightly and justly! Why did he stab him then?

Ellida. He wouldn't tell me that. He said it was not fit for me to hear.

Wangel. And you took his word for it?

Ellida. Yes. It never occurred to me to do otherwise. Well, anyhow, he had to go away. But then, when he was going to say good-bye—— No, you never could imagine what he thought of——

Wangel. Well? Tell me.

Ellida. He took a key-ring from his pocket—and drew a ring that he always wore from his finger, and he took a small ring that I had. These two he put on the key-ring. And then he said we two together should be wedded to the sea.

Wangel. Wedded——?

Ellida. Yes, so he said. And with that he threw the key-ring, and our rings, with all his might, as far as he could into the deep water.

Wangel. And you, Ellida, you did all this?

Ellida. Yes—just imagine—it seemed to me then that everything was as it should be. But, thank God!—he went away.

Wangel. And when he was gone?

Ellida. Oh! You may be sure I soon came to my senses again —I saw how absolutely mad and meaningless it had all been.

Wangel. But you spoke just now of letters. So you have heard from him since?

Ellida. Yes, I have heard from him. First I had a few short lines from Archangel. He only wrote he was going to America. And then he told me where to send an answer.

Wangel. And did you?

Ellida. At once. I wrote him, of course, that it must be all finished between us; and that he must no longer think of me, just as I should no longer think of him.

Wangel. But did he write again?

Ellida. Yes, he wrote again.

Wangel. And what did he reply to what you had told him?

Ellida. He took no notice of it. It was exactly as if I had never broken with him. He wrote back and quite calmly told me that I must wait for him. When he was ready for me he would let me know, and then I was to go to him at once.

Wangel. So he would not release you?

Ellida. No. Then I wrote again, almost word for word as I had before, or perhaps more firmly.

Wangel. And he gave in then?

Ellida. Oh no! Not for a moment! He wrote calmly, as before—not a word of my having broken with him. Then I knew it was useless, and so I never wrote to him again.

Wangel. And you never heard from him?

Ellida. Oh yes! I have had three letters since then. Once he wrote to me from California, and a second time from China. The last letter I had from him was from Australia. He wrote that he was going to the gold-mines. But since then he has made no sign.

Wangel. This man has had a strange power over you, Ellida.

Ellida. Oh yes, indeed! A terrible man!

Wangel. But you mustn't think of that any more. Never again—never! Promise me that, my dear, beloved Ellida. Now we must try another treatment for you. Fresher air than here in the fiords. The salt, fresh air of the sea! What do you say to that?

Ellida. Oh! don't talk about that! Don't even think of it! It won't help me. I feel that so strongly. I can't shake it off—not even there.

Wangel. Shake what off, dear?—What do you mean?

Ellida. I mean the terror of it all, this incomprehensible power over my mind.

Wangel. But you have shaken it off—long ago—when you broke with him. Why, all this was over long ago.

Ellida (springing up). No, that it is not—it is not!

Wangel. Not over?

Ellida. No, Wangel, it is not over; and I'm afraid it never will be—never, in all this life.

Wangel (in a pained voice). Do you mean to say that in your innermost heart you have never been able to forget this strange man?

Ellida. I had forgotten him, but then it was as if he had suddenly come back again.

Wangel. How long ago is that?

Ellida. It's about three years ago, now, or a little longer.   It was just when I expected the baby.

Wangel. Ah! then, was it?   Yes, Ellida—now I am beginning to understand many things.

Ellida. You are mistaken, dear.   What has come over me? Oh! I don't believe anything on earth will ever make it clear.

Wangel (*looking sadly at her*). Just to think that all these three years you have loved another man.   Loved someone else.   Not me—but another man.

Ellida. Oh, you are absolutely mistaken!   I love no one but you.

Wangel (*in a subdued voice*). Then why have you refused to live with me as my wife all these years?

Ellida. Because of the dread of the strange man.

Wangel. The dread?

Ellida. Yes, the dread.   A dread so terrible—such as only the sea could hold.   I'll tell you about it now, Wangel.

(*The young townsfolk come back, nod, and pass out to the right.*
    With them come ARNHOLM, BOLETTE, HILDE, *and* LYNG-
    · STRAND.)

Bolette (*as she passes by*). Well, are you still wandering about up here?

Ellida. Yes, it is so cool and pleasant up here on the heights.

Arnholm. Well, we are going down for a dance.

Wangel. All right.   We'll soon come down as well.

Hilde. Good-bye for the present then.

Ellida. Mr Lyngstrand, will you wait one moment? (LYNG-
STRAND *stops.* ARNHOLM, BOLETTE, *and* HILDE *go out. To*
LYNGSTRAND.) Are you going to dance too?

Lyngstrand. No, Mrs Wangel.   I don't think I dare.

Ellida. No, you should be careful, you know—your chest. You're not quite well yet, you know.

Lyngstrand. No, not quite.

Ellida (*with some hesitation*). How long is it now since you went on that voyage?

Lyngstrand. That time when I contracted this weakness?

Ellida. Yes, the voyage you were telling me about this morning?

Lyngstrand. Oh! it's about—wait a moment—yes, it's a good three years now.

Ellida. Three years, then.

Lyngstrand. Perhaps a little more. We left America in February, and we were wrecked in March. We came in for the equinoctial gales.

Ellida (looking at WANGEL). So it was then——

Wangel. But, my dear Ellida——

Ellida. Well, don't let me hinder you, Mr Lyngstrand. Now go down, but don't dance.

Lyngstrand. No, I'll only look on. (*He goes out.*)

Wangel. Ellida dear, why did you ask him about that voyage?

Ellida. Johnston was on board too, I am quite certain of it.

Wangel. What makes you think so?

Ellida (without answering). It was on board he discovered that I had married someone else while he was away. And then at that very moment this came over me.

Wangel. What, the dread?

Ellida. Yes, all of a sudden I see him alive right in front of me, or, rather a little in profile. He never looks at me. He just is there.

Wangel. What do you think he looks like?

Ellida. Exactly as when I saw him last.

Wangel. Ten years ago?

Ellida. Yes, out there at Bratthammer. Most distinctly of all I see his scarf-pin, with a large bluish-white pearl in it. The pearl is like a dead fish's eye, and it seems to glare at me.

Wangel. Good God! You are more ill than I thought. More ill than you yourself know, Ellida.

Ellida. Yes, yes! Please help me if you can, I feel it is closing in on me more and more.

Wangel. And you have gone about in this state for three whole years, keeping this secret suffering to yourself, without confiding in me.

Ellida. But I couldn't, not until now when it became necessary for your own sake. If I had confided in you I should also have had to confide to you the unspeakable.

Wangel. Unspeakable?

Ellida. No, no, no! Don't ask. Only one thing, nothing more. Wangel, when shall we understand that mystery of the boy's eyes?

Wangel. My dear love, Ellida, I assure you it was only your own fancy. The child had exactly the same eyes as other normal children have.

Ellida. No, he had not. And you could not see it! The

child's eyes changed colour with the sea.   When the fiord lay bathed in sunshine, so were his eyes.   And the same in a storm. Oh, I saw it, if you didn't!

Wangel (*humouring her*). Maybe.   But even if it were true, what then?

Ellida (*in lower voice, and coming nearer*). I have seen eyes like that before.

Wangel. Have you?   Where?

Ellida. Out at Bratthammer, ten years ago.

Wangel (*stepping back*). What does that——

Ellida (*whispers, trembling*). The child had the strange man's eyes.

Wangel (*cries out reluctantly*). Ellida!

Ellida (*clasps her hands despairingly about her head*). Now you understand why I would not, why I dared not, live with you as your wife.   (*She turns suddenly and rushes off over the heights.*)

Wangel (*hurrying after her and calling*). Ellida, Ellida!   My poor unhappy Ellida!

ACT III

(SCENE.—*A more remote part of* DOCTOR WANGEL'*s garden. It is boggy and overshadowed by large old trees.   To the right is seen the edge of a dank pond.   A low, open fence separates the garden from the footpath and the fiord in the background.   Beyond is the range of mountains, with its peaks.   It is afternoon, almost evening.   BOLETTE sits on a stone seat, and on the seat lie some books and a work-basket.   HILDE and LYNGSTRAND, both with fishing-tackle, walk along the edge of the pond.*)

Hilde (*making a sign to* LYNGSTRAND). Wait!   I can see a large one.

Lyngstrand (*looking*). Where?

Hilde (*pointing*). Can't you see?   He's down there.   Good gracious!   There's another!   (*Looks through the trees.*)   Out there.   Now he's coming to frighten him away!

Bolette (*looking up*). Who's coming?

Hilde. Your tutor, Madam!

Bolette. Mine?

Hilde. Yes.   Goodness knows he was never mine.

(ARNHOLM *enters from between the trees.*)

Arnholm. Are there fish in the pond now?

Hilde. There are some very ancient carp.

Arnholm. No! D'you mean to say the old carp are still alive?

Hilde. Yes, they're pretty tough. But now we're going to try and get rid of some of them.

Arnholm. You'd better try out there in the fiord.

Lyngstrand. No, the pond is—well—let's say—more mysterious.

Hilde. Yes, it's fascinating here. Have you been in the sea?

Arnholm. Yes, I've come straight from the baths.

Hilde. I suppose you kept in the swimming pool?

Arnholm. Yes, I'm not much of a swimmer.

Hilde. Can you swim on your back?

Arnholm. No.

Hilde. I can. (*To* LYNGSTRAND.) Let's try out there on the other side. (*They go off along the pond.*)

Arnholm (*coming closer to* BOLETTE). Are you sitting all alone here, Bolette?

Bolette. Yes, I generally do.

Arnholm. Isn't your mother down here in the garden?

Bolette. No—she's sure to be out with father.

Arnholm. How is she this afternoon?

Bolette. I don't really know. I forgot to ask.

Arnholm. What books have you got there?

Bolette. Oh, one's something about botany, and the other's a geography.

Arnholm. Do you usually read that sort of thing?

Bolette. Yes, when I can find time for it. But housekeeping has first claim on my time.

Arnholm. Doesn't your mother help you—your stepmother—doesn't she help with that?

Bolette. No, that's my job. After all, I had to do it during the two years father was alone. And so I've continued ever since.

Arnholm. But you're as fond as ever of reading.

Bolette. Yes, I read all the instructive books I can get hold of. One wants to know something about the world. For here we live so completely outside all that's going on—or almost.

Arnholm. Now don't say that, Bolette dear.

Bolette. Oh yes! I think we live very much like the carp down there in the pond do. They have the fiord so near them, where the shoals of wild fishes pass in and out. But the poor, tame domestic fishes know nothing, and they can never join in.

Arnholm. I don't think they would fare very well if they could get out there.

Bolette. Well, that's not everything, is it?

Arnholm. Moreover, you can't say that you are so completely out of the world here—not in the summer anyhow. Why, nowadays this is quite a rendezvous for the busy world—almost a junction for the time being.

Bolette. Ah, yes, but you are only here for the time being— it's easy for you to make fun of us.

Arnholm. I make fun? How can you think that?

Bolette. Well, all that about this being a rendezvous, and a junction for the busy world—that's something you've heard the townsfolk here saying. Yes—they often say that sort of thing.

Arnholm. Well, frankly, I've noticed that, too.

Bolette. But there's really not an atom of truth in it. Not for us who always live here. What good is it to us that the great strange world comes here for a time on its way north to see the midnight sun? We ourselves have no part in that. There's no midnight sun for us. No! We've got to be good, and live our lives here in our carp pond.

Arnholm (*sitting down by her*). Now tell me, Bolette dear, isn't there something or other—something definite you are longing for?

Bolette. Well, yes actually. Perhaps there is.

Arnholm. What is it? What is it you are longing for?

Bolette. Chiefly to get away.

Arnholm. That above all, then?

Bolette. Yes, and then to learn more. To really know something about everything.

Arnholm. When I used to teach you, your father often said he would let you go to college.

Bolette. Yes, poor father! He says so many things. But when it comes to the point he—there's no real initiative in father.

Arnholm. No, unfortunately you're right there. He hasn't initiative exactly. But have you ever spoken to him about it— spoken really seriously?

Bolette. No, I haven't really done that.

Arnholm. But you ought to, you know. Before it is too late. Bolette, why don't you?

Bolette. Oh! I suppose it's because there's no real initiative in me either. I certainly take after father in that.

Arnholm. Hm—don't you think you're unjust to yourself there?

Bolette. No, unfortunately. Besides, father has so little time for thinking about me and my future, and not much desire to either. He prefers to shelve things like that whenever he can. He is so completely taken up with Ellida——

Arnholm. With whom? How?

Bolette. I mean that he and my stepmother—— (*Breaks off.*) Father and mother are sufficient unto themselves, as you see.

Arnholm. Well, so much the better if you were to get away from here.

Bolette. Yes, but I don't think I've a right to—not to leave father.

Arnholm. But, dear Bolette, you'll have to do that some time, anyhow. So it seems to me the sooner the better.

Bolette. I suppose there is nothing else for it. After all, I must think of myself, too. I must try and get a job of some sort. When once father's gone, I have no one to depend on. But, poor father! I dread leaving him.

Arnholm. Dread?

Bolette. Yes, for father's sake.

Arnholm. But, good heavens! Your stepmother? She is with him.

Bolette. That's true. But she's incapable of doing everything that mother did so well. There is so much she doesn't see, or that she won't see, or doesn't trouble about. I don't know which it is.

Arnholm. Hm, I think I understand what you mean.

Bolette. Poor father! He is weak in some things. Perhaps you've noticed that yourself? He hasn't enough to do, either, to fill up his time. And then she is so thoroughly incapable of helping him; however, that's to some extent his own fault.

Arnholm. In what way?

Bolette. Oh! father always likes to see cheerful faces around. There must be sunshine and joy in the house, he says. And so I'm afraid he often gives her medicine which will do her little good in the long run.

Arnholm. Do you really think that?

Bolette. Yes, I can't get rid of the thought. She is so odd at times. (*Passionately.*) But isn't it unfair that I should have to stay at home here? It's really no earthly use to father. Besides, I have a duty towards myself, too, I think.

Arnholm. Do you know what, Bolette? We two must talk these matters over more carefully.

Bolette. Oh! That won't be much use. I suppose I was born to live here in the carp pond.

Arnholm. Not a bit of it. It depends entirely upon yourself.

Bolette (*quickly*). Do you think so?

Arnholm. Yes, believe me, it lies wholly and solely in your own hands.

Bolette. If only that were true! Perhaps you would put in a good word for me with father?

Arnholm. Certainly. But first of all I must speak frankly and freely with you yourself, my dear—— (*Looks out to the left.*) Hush, don't let them notice anything. We'll talk about this later.

(ELLIDA *enters from the left. She has no hat on, but a large shawl is thrown over her head and shoulders.*)

Ellida (*with restless animation*). How lovely it is here! How delightful it all is!

Arnholm (*rising*). Have you been for a walk?

Ellida. Yes, a long, long, lovely walk up there with Wangel. And now we're going for a sail.

Bolette. Won't you sit down?

Ellida. No, thanks, I won't sit down.

Bolette (*making room on the seat*). There's room here.

Ellida (*walking about*). No, no, no! I don't want to sit down —I don't want to!

Arnholm. I'm sure your walk has done you good. You look quite refreshed.

Ellida. Oh, I feel so thoroughly well—I feel so unspeakably happy. So safe, so safe! (*Looking out to the left.*) What big steamer is that coming along there?

Bolette (*rising, and also looking out*). It must be the big English one.

Arnholm. It's tying up. Does it usually stop here?

Bolette. Only for half an hour. It goes farther up the fiord.

Ellida. And then sails away again to-morrow—away over the great open sea—right over the sea. Just think of being with them. If one could. If only one could!

Arnholm. Have you never been on any long sea voyage, Mrs Wangel?

Ellida. Never. Only those little trips in the fiord here.

Bolette (*with a sigh*). Ah, well! I suppose we must put up with the dry land.

Arnholm. Well, after all, that really is our home.

Ellida. No, I don't think it is.

Arnholm. Not the land?

Ellida. No, I don't believe so. I think that if only men had accustomed themselves from the beginning to live on the sea, or *in* the sea perhaps, we should be more perfect than we are—both better and happier.

Arnholm. You really think that?

Ellida. Yes. I wonder if we wouldn't. I've often spoken to Wangel about it.

Arnholm. And what does he think?

Ellida. He thinks it might be so.

Arnholm (*jestingly*). Well, perhaps! But it can't be helped. We've once and for all taken the wrong turning, and have become land beasts instead of sea beasts. Anyhow, I suppose it's too late to make good the mistake now.

Ellida. Yes, you've spoken a sad truth. And I think men instinctively feel something of this themselves. They carry it about with them like a secret regret and sorrow. Believe me— here lies the deepest cause of the sadness of men. Believe me, it is so.

Arnholm. But, my dearest Mrs Wangel, I have not noticed that men are so extremely sad. On the contrary, it seems to me that most of them take life easily and pleasantly—and with a great, quiet, unconscious joy.

Ellida. Oh no! that's not so. The joy is, I suppose, something like our joy at the long pleasant summer days—it has the presentiment of the dark days coming. And it is this presentiment that casts its shadows over the joy of men, just as the driving clouds cast their shadow over the fiords. It lies there so bright and blue—and all of a sudden——

Bolette. You shouldn't give way to such sad thoughts. Just now you were so happy and so bright.

Ellida. Why, yes, perhaps I was. Oh, this—this is so stupid of me. (*Looking about her uneasily.*) If only Wangel would come! He promised me so faithfully he would. And yet he doesn't come. He must have forgotten. Dear Mr Arnholm, won't you try and find him for me?

Arnholm. Yes. Gladly——

Ellida. Tell him he must come here immediately. For now I can't see him——

Arnholm. Not see him?

Ellida. Oh, you don't understand. When he isn't with me I often can't remember what he looks like. And then it is as if I had lost him entirely. That is so terribly painful. But do go, please. (*She paces round the pond.*)

Bolette (*to* ARNHOLM). I'll go with you—you don't know——

Arnholm. Nonsense, I shall be all right.

Bolette (*softly*). No, no, I am anxious. I'm afraid he is on board the steamer.

Arnholm. Afraid?

Bolette. Yes. He usually goes to see if there are any acquaintances of his. And there's a restaurant on board——

Arnholm. Ah, I see. Come on then.

(*He and* BOLETTE *go off.* ELLIDA *stands still a while, staring down at the pond. Now and again she talks to herself in a low voice, and breaks off. Along the footpath beyond the garden fence a* STRANGER *in travelling clothes comes from the left. His hair and beard are bushy and red. He has a Scotch cap on, and a travelling bag on a strap over his shoulder.*)

The Stranger (*goes slowly along by the fence and peeps into the garden. When he catches sight of* ELLIDA *he stands still, looks at her fixedly and searchingly, and speaks in a low voice*). Good evening, Ellida.

Ellida (*turns round with a cry*). Oh, my dear, have you come at last!

The Stranger. Yes, at last.

Ellida (*looking at him astonished and frightened*). Who are you? Do you want anyone here?

The Stranger. You surely know that well enough, Ellida.

Ellida (*starting*). What is this? Why do you address me like that? Who are you looking for?

The Stranger. Well, I suppose I'm looking for you.

Ellida (*shuddering*). Oh! (*She stares at him, totters back, uttering a half-suffocated cry.*) The eyes!—the eyes!

The Stranger. Are you beginning to recognize me at last? I knew you at once, Ellida.

Ellida. The eyes! Don't look at me like that! I shall shout for help!

The Stranger. Hush, hush! Don't be afraid. I shan't hurt you.

Ellida (*covering her eyes with her hands*). Don't look at me like that, I say!

The Stranger (leaning with his arms on the garden fence). I came on the English steamer.

Ellida (stealing a frightened look at him). What do you want with me?

The Stranger. I promised you to come as soon as I could——

Ellida. Go—go away! Never, never come here again! I wrote to you that everything must be over between us—everything! Oh, you know that!

The Stranger (imperturbably, and not answering her). I would like to have come to you sooner; but I could not. Now, at last, I am able to. And so here I am, Ellida.

Ellida. What is it you want? What do you mean? Why have you come here?

The Stranger. Surely you know I've come to fetch you.

Ellida (recoils in terror). To fetch me! Is that what you mean?

The Stranger. Of course.

Ellida. But surely you know that I am married.

The Stranger. Yes, I know.

Ellida. And yet—and yet you have come to—to fetch me!

The Stranger. I most certainly have.

Ellida (seizing her head with both her hands). Oh, this is ghastly—this terror, this terror!

The Stranger. Perhaps you don't want to come?

Ellida (bewildered). Don't look at me like that.

The Stranger. I was asking you if you didn't want to come.

Ellida. No, no, no! I will not. Never in all eternity! I will not, I tell you. I neither can nor will. *(In a lower tone.)* I dare not, either.

The Stranger (climbs over the fence, and comes into the garden). Well then, Ellida, let me tell you one thing before I go.

Ellida (wants to fly, but cannot. She stands like one paralysed with terror, and leans for support against the trunk of a tree by the pond). Don't touch me! Don't come near me! No nearer! Don't touch me, I say!

The Stranger (cautiously coming a few steps nearer). You need not be so afraid of me, Ellida.

Ellida (covering her eyes with her hands). Don't look at me like that.

The Stranger. Don't be afraid—not afraid.

(WANGEL *comes through the garden, from the left.*)

Wangel (still half-way between the trees). Well, you've had to wait for me a long while.

Ellida (*rushes towards him, clings fast to his arm, and cries out*). Oh! Wangel! Save me! *You* save me—if you can!

Wangel. Ellida! What in heaven's name——

Ellida. Save me, Wangel! Don't you see him there? Why, he is standing there!

Wangel (*looking at him*). *That* man? (*Coming nearer.*) May I ask you who you are, and what you have come into this garden for?

The Stranger (*motions with a nod towards* ELLIDA). I want to talk to her.

Wangel. Oh! Indeed. So I suppose it was you. (*To* ELLIDA.) I hear a stranger has been to the house and asked for you?

The Stranger. Yes, it was me.

Wangel. And what do you want with my wife? (*Turning round.*) Do you know him, Ellida?

Ellida (*in a low voice, and wringing her hands*). Do I know him! Yes, yes, yes!

Wangel (*quickly*). Well!

Ellida. Why, it is him, Wangel!—he himself! The man who you know——

Wangel. What! What are you saying? (*Turning.*) Are you the Johnston who once——

The Stranger. You can call me Johnston for all I care! But that's not my name.

Wangel. It's not?

The Stranger. Not now. No.

Wangel. And what do you want with my wife? I suppose you know the lighthouse-keeper's daughter has been married a long time, and you also know of course who she married.

The Stranger. I've known it over three years.

Ellida (*eagerly*). How did you get to know it?

The Stranger. I was on my way home to you, Ellida. I came across an old newspaper. It was a paper from this district, and in it was the notice of your wedding.

Ellida (*looking straight in front of her*). The wedding! So that was it!

The Stranger. It all seemed so strange to me. For the rings—why that, too, was a wedding, Ellida.

Ellida (*covering her face with her hands*). Oh!——

Wangel. How dare you?

The Stranger. Have you forgotten that?

Ellida (feeling his look, suddenly cries out). Don't stand there looking at me like that!

Wangel (goes up to him). You will please deal with me now, and not with her. In short—now that you know the circumstances —what is it you really want here? Why have you come here to find my wife?

The Stranger. I promised Ellida to come to her as soon as I could.

Wangel. Ellida—again!——

The Stranger. And Ellida promised faithfully she would wait for me until I came.

Wangel. I notice you call my wife by her first name. We are not used to that kind of familiarity here.

The Stranger. I know that perfectly well. But as she first and foremost belongs to me——

Wangel. To you, still——

Ellida (draws back behind WANGEL). Oh! he will never release me!

Wangel. To you? You say she belongs to you?

The Stranger. Has she told you anything about the two rings —my ring and Ellida's?

Wangel. Certainly. But what about it? She put an end to that long ago. You have had her letters, so you know that yourself.

The Stranger. Both Ellida and I agreed that what we did should have all the strength and authority of a real and true marriage.

Ellida. But you hear, I will not! Never on this earth do I want to have anything more to do with you. Don't look at me like that. I will not, I tell you!

Wangel. You must be mad to think you can come here and base any claim upon such childish nonsense.

The Stranger. That's true. In your sense, I certainly haven't any claim.

Wangel. What do you propose to do, then? You surely don't imagine you can take her from me by force, against her own will?

The Stranger. No. What would be the good of that? If Ellida wishes to be with me she must come of her own free will.

Ellida (starts, crying out). Of my own free will!

Wangel. And you actually believe that——

Ellida (to herself). Of my own free will!

Wangel. You must have taken leave of your senses! Clear off! We have nothing more to do with you.

The Stranger (*looking at his watch*). It's almost time for me to go on board again. (*Coming nearer.*) Very well, Ellida, now I have done my duty. (*Coming still nearer.*) I have kept my word I gave you.

Ellida (*beseechingly, drawing away*). Oh, don't touch me!

The Stranger. And so now you must think it over till to-morrow night——

Wangel. There is nothing further to think over. Get out of our sight!

The Stranger (*still to* ELLIDA). I'm going now on the steamer up the fiord. To-morrow night I shall be back again, and then I shall look for you here. You must wait for me here in the garden, because I prefer settling the matter with you alone. You understand?

Ellida (*in a low, trembling tones*). Oh, do you hear that, Wangel?

Wangel. Just keep calm. We shall know how to prevent this visit.

The Stranger. Good-bye for the present, Ellida. Until to-morrow night——

Ellida (*imploringly*). Oh, no, no! Do not come to-morrow night! Never come here again!

The Stranger. And should you then decide to come with me over the seas——

Ellida. Oh, don't look at me like that!

The Stranger. I only mean that you must then be ready to set out.

Wangel. Go up to the house, Ellida.

Ellida. I cannot! Oh, help me! Save me, Wangel!

The Stranger. For you must remember that if you don't come with me to-morrow it will be the end.

Ellida (*looks tremblingly at him*). The end? For ever?

The Stranger (*nodding*). Nothing can change it then, Ellida. I shall never come back to this country. You will never see me again, nor hear from me either. Then I shall be as though dead and gone from you for ever.

Ellida (*breathing with difficulty*). Oh!

The Stranger. So think over carefully what you do. Good-bye! (*He goes to the fence and climbs over it, stands still, and says.*) Yes, Ellida. Be ready for the journey to-morrow night. For then I shall come and fetch you. (*He goes slowly and calmly down the footpath to the right.*)

Ellida (*looking after him for a time*). Of my own free will, he said. Imagine, he said that I must go with him of my own free will!

Wangel. Just keep calm. Why, he's gone now, and you'll never see him again.

Ellida. Oh! how can you say that? He's coming again to-morrow night!

Wangel. Let him come. He shall not meet you again in any case.

Ellida (*shaking her head*). Ah, Wangel! you mustn't believe you can prevent him.

Wangel. I can, dearest; if you'll only trust me.

Ellida (*pondering, and not listening to him*). When he's been here to-morrow night—and then when he has gone overseas in the steamer——

Wangel. Yes, what then?

Ellida. I should like to know if he will really never, never come back again.

Wangel. No, dearest Ellida. You can be quite sure of that. What should he do here after this? Now that he has learnt from your own lips that you will have nothing more to do with him. With that the whole thing is over.

Ellida (*to herself*). To-morrow, then, or never!

Wangel. And should it ever occur to him to come here again——

Ellida. Well?

Wangel. Why, then we have it in our power to make him harmless.

Ellida. Oh, don't believe that!

Wangel. It is in our power, I tell you. If you can get rid of him in no other way, he must be made to answer for the murder of the captain.

Ellida (*passionately*). No, no, no! Never that! We know absolutely nothing about the murder of the captain! Absolutely nothing whatever!

Wangel. Know nothing? Why, he himself confessed it to you!

Ellida. No, nothing about that. If you say anything at all about it I shall deny it. He shall not be imprisoned. He belongs out there—to the open sea. He belongs out there!

Wangel (*looks at her and says slowly*). Oh! Ellida—Ellida!

Ellida (*clinging passionately to him*). Oh, dear, faithful one—save me from this man!

Wangel (*disengaging himself gently*). Come, come with me!

(LYNGSTRAND *and* HILDE, *both with fishing tackle, come in from the right, along the pond.*)

Lyngstrand (*going quickly up to* ELLIDA). Mrs Wangel, I've got something really wonderful to tell you.

Wangel. What is it?

Lyngstrand. Fancy! We've seen the American!

Wangel. The American?

Hilde. Yes, I saw him, too.

Lyngstrand. He went round the back of the garden, and then on board the big English steamer.

Wangel. How do you know the man?

Lyngstrand. Why, I went to sea with him once. I felt so certain he'd been drowned—and now he's very much alive!

Wangel. Do you know anything more about him?

Lyngstrand. No. But I'm sure he's come to be revenged upon his faithless sailor's wife.

Wangel. What do you mean?

Hilde. Lyngstrand's going to use him for a work of art.

Wangel. I don't understand one word——

Ellida. You shall hear about it afterwards.

(ARNHOLM *and* BOLETTE *come from the left along the footpath outside the garden.*)

Bolette (*to those in the garden*). Do come and see! The big English steamer's just going up the fiord.

(*A large steamer glides slowly past in the distance.*)

Lyngstrand (*to* HILDE *behind the garden fence*). To-night he's sure to come to her.

Hilde (*nods*). To the faithless sailor's wife—yes.

Lyngstrand. At midnight!

Hilde. How thrilling!

Ellida (*looking after the ship*). To-morrow, then!

Wangel. And then never again.

Ellida (*in a low, imploring tone*). Oh, Wangel, save me from myself!

Wangel (*looks anxiously at her*). Ellida—I feel there is something behind this——

Ellida. There is—the temptation!

Wangel. Temptation?

Ellida. That man is like the sea!

(*She goes slowly and thoughtfully through the garden, and out to the left.* WANGEL *walks uneasily by her side, watching her closely.*)

ACT IV

(SCENE.—DOCTOR WANGEL's *garden-room. Doors right and left. In the background, between the windows, an open glass door, leading out on to the veranda. Below this a portion of the garden is visible. A sofa and table down left. To the right a piano, and farther back a large flower-stand. In the middle of the room a round table, with chairs. On the table is a rose-tree in bloom, and other plants round it. Morning.*

In the room, by the table, BOLETTE *is sitting on the sofa, busy with some embroidery.* LYNGSTRAND *is seated on a chair at the upper end of the table. In the garden below* BALLESTED *sits painting.* HILDE *stands by watching him.*)

Lyngstrand (*with his arms on the table, sits silent a while, looking at* BOLETTE's *work*). It must be awfully difficult to do a border like that, Miss Wangel?

Bolette. Oh no!   It's not very difficult, if only you are careful to count right.

Lyngstrand. To count?   Must you count, too?

Bolette. Yes, the stitches.   Look!

Lyngstrand. So you do!   Fancy that!   Why, it's almost a kind of art.   Can you draw, too?

Bolette. Oh yes!   When I've a design in front of me.

Lyngstrand. Not otherwise?

Bolette. No, not otherwise.

Lyngstrand. Oh, well, then it's not a real art after all.

Bolette. No, it's really only a sort of—handicraft.

Lyngstrand. But still, I think that perhaps you could learn art.

Bolette. When I haven't any talent?

Lyngstrand. Even so, if you could always be with a really true artist——

Bolette. Do you think, then, I could learn it from him?

Lyngstrand. Not exactly learn in the ordinary sense; but I think it would grow upon you little by little—by a kind of miracle as it were, Miss Wangel.

Bolette. That's strange.

Lyngstrand (*after a pause*). Have you ever thought about—I mean, have you ever thought deeply and seriously about marriage, Miss Wangel?

Bolette (*looking quickly at him*). About—no!

Lyngstrand. I have.

Bolette. Really? Have you?

Lyngstrand. Oh yes! I often think about things of that sort, especially about marriage; and besides, I've read several books about it. I think marriage must be counted a sort of miracle— that a woman should gradually change till she is like her husband.

Bolette. You mean have his interests?

Lyngstrand. Yes, that's it.

Bolette. Well, but his abilities—his talents—and his skill?

Lyngstrand. Hm—well—I wonder whether all that too wouldn't——

Bolette. Then, perhaps, you also believe that everything a man has read for himself, or thought out for himself, that this, too, can pass over to his wife?

Lyngstrand. Yes, I think it can. Little by little—like a sort of miracle. But, of course, I know such things can only happen in a marriage that is true, and loving, and really happy.

Bolette. Has it never occurred to you that a man, too, might, perhaps, be drawn over to his wife in this way? Grow like her, I mean.

Lyngstrand. A man? No, I never thought of that.

Bolette. But why not one as well as the other?

Lyngstrand. No, because a man has a calling that he lives for; and *that*'s what makes a man so strong and firm, Miss Wangel. He has a calling in life.

Bolette. Has every man?

Lyngstrand. Oh no! I am thinking more especially of artists.

Bolette. Do you think it right for an artist to get married?

Lyngstrand. Yes, I think so. If he can find someone he can truly love, I——

Bolette. But, even so, I think he should live for his art alone.

Lyngstrand. Of course he must do that. But he can do that just as well, even if he marries.

Bolette. But how about her then?

Lyngstrand. Her? Who do you mean?

Bolette. The woman he marries. What is she to live for?

Lyngstrand. She, too, must live for his art. It seems to me a woman must feel so thoroughly happy in *that*.

Bolette. Hm, I don't really know——

Lyngstrand. Yes, Miss Wangel, you can be sure of that. It's not merely all the honour and respect she enjoys through him;

that seems almost the least important to me.   The important thing is—that she can help him to create, that she can lighten his work for him, be around and see to his comfort, look after him well, and make his life thoroughly pleasant.   I should think that must be perfectly wonderful for a woman.

Bolette. Oh, you don't know how selfish you really are!

Lyngstrand. I, selfish! Good heavens! Oh, if only you knew me a little better than you do! (*Bending closer to her.*) Miss Wangel, when once I am gone—and that will be very soon now——

Bolette (*looks pityingly at him*). Oh, don't think of anything so sad!

Lyngstrand. But, I don't really think it is so very sad.

Bolette. What do you mean?

Lyngstrand. Well, you know that I set out in a month's time. First from here, and then, of course, I'm going south.

Bolette. Oh, I see! Of course.

Lyngstrand. Will you think of me sometimes, then, Miss Wangel?

Bolette. Yes, of course I will.

Lyngstrand (*pleased*). No, promise!

Bolette. I promise.

Lyngstrand. By all that is sacred, Miss Bolette?

Bolette. By all that is sacred. (*In a changed manner.*) Oh, but what can come of it all?   Nothing can possibly come of it!

Lyngstrand. How can you say that!   It would be so wonderful for me to know you were at home here thinking of me!

Bolette. Well, and what else?

Lyngstrand. I don't exactly know of anything else.

Bolette. No, neither do I.   There are so many things in the way.   Everything stands in the way, I think.

Lyngstrand. Oh, another miracle might happen.   A lucky change in my fortunes, or something of the sort.   I really believe luck is on my side now.

Bolette (*eagerly*). Really?   You do believe that?

Lyngstrand. Yes, I believe it absolutely.   And so—after a few years—when I come home again as a celebrated sculptor, and well off, and in perfect health——

Bolette. Yes, yes!   Of course, we will hope so.

Lyngstrand. You may be perfectly certain about it.   If only you will think faithfully and kindly of me when I am down there in the south.   And now I have your word for it that you will.

Bolette. You have (*shaking her head*). But, all the same, nothing can surely come of it.

Lyngstrand. Oh yes, Miss Bolette.   At least this will come of it.   I shall get on so much more easily and quickly with my art.

Bolette. Do you really believe that?

Lyngstrand. I am convinced of it.   And I also think it will be so cheering for you, too—here in this out-of-the-way place—to know within yourself that you are, so to speak, helping me to create.

Bolette (*looking at him*). Well, but you on your side?

Lyngstrand. Me?

Bolette (*looking out into the garden*). Hush!   Let's talk about something else.   Here's Mr Arnholm.

(ARNHOLM *is seen in the garden below.   He stops and talks to* HILDE *and* BALLESTED.)

Lyngstrand. Are you fond of your old tutor, Miss Bolette?

Bolette. Am I fond of him?

Lyngstrand. Yes, I mean do you like him?

Bolette. Yes, indeed I do, for he is a real friend—and adviser, too—and then he is always so ready to help when he can.

Lyngstrand. Isn't it extraordinary that he hasn't married!

Bolette. Do you think it is extraordinary?

Lyngstrand. Yes, since they say he's well to do.

Bolette. He is certainly said to be.   But probably it wasn't so easy to find anyone who'd have him.

Lyngstrand. Why?

Bolette. Oh!   He's been the tutor of nearly all the young girls that he knows.   He says that himself.

Lyngstrand. But what does that matter?

Bolette. Why, good heavens!   You don't marry a man who's been your tutor!

Lyngstrand. Don't you think a young girl could love her tutor?

Bolette. Not after she's really grown up.

Lyngstrand. No—fancy that!

Bolette (*cautioning him*). Sh!   Sh!

(*Meanwhile* BALLESTED *has been gathering together his things, and carries them out from the garden to the right.* HILDE *helps him.* ARNHOLM *goes up the veranda, and comes into the room.*)

Arnholm. Good morning, my dear Bolette.   Good morning, Mr—Mr—hm——

(*He looks displeased, and nods coldly to* LYNGSTRAND, *who rises and bows.*)

Bolette (*rising and going up to* ARNHOLM). Good morning,
Mr Arnholm.

Arnholm. Everything all right here to-day?

Bolette. Yes, thank you, quite.

Arnholm. Has your stepmother gone to bathe again to-day?

Bolette. No. She is upstairs in her room.

Arnholm. Not very bright?

Bolette. I don't know, because she has locked herself in.

Arnholm. Hm—has she?

Lyngstrand. I suppose Mrs Wangel was very much frightened
about that American yesterday?

Arnholm. What do *you* know about that?

Lyngstrand. I told Mrs Wangel that I had seen him in the
flesh going round behind the garden.

Arnholm. Oh! I see.

Bolette (*to* ARNHOLM). You and father probably sat up very
late last night, didn't you?

Arnholm. Yes, rather late. We were talking over important
matters.

Bolette. Did you put in a word for me, and my affairs, too?

Arnholm. No, my dear Bolette, I couldn't manage it. He was
so completely taken up with something else

Bolette (*sighs*). Ah, yes, he always is.

Arnholm (*looks at her meaningly*). But later on to-day we'll
talk more fully about—the subject. Where's your father now?
Not at home?

Bolette. Yes, he is. He must be down in the surgery. I'll
fetch him.

Arnholm. No, thank you, don't do that. I'd rather go down
to him myself.

Bolette (*listening*). Wait one moment, Mr Arnholm. I believe
that's father on the stairs. Yes, he's probably been up to look
after her.

(WANGEL *comes in from the door on the left.*)

Wangel (*shaking* ARNHOLM'S *hand*). What, dear friend, are
you here already? It was good of you to come so early, because
I should like to talk a little more with you.

Bolette (*to* LYNGSTRAND). Hadn't we better go down to Hilde
in the garden?

Lyngstrand. I shall be delighted, Miss Wangel.

(*He and* BOLETTE *go down into the garden, and out between the
    trees in the background.*)

Arnholm (following them with his eyes, turns to WANGEL). Do you know anything about that young man?

Wangel. No, nothing at all.

Arnholm. But do you think it right he should be around so much with the girls?

Wangel. Is he? I really hadn't noticed it.

Arnholm. You ought to keep an eye on it, I think.

Wangel. Yes, probably you're right. But, good Lord! what's a man to do? The girls are so used to looking after themselves now. They won't listen to me, nor to Ellida.

Arnholm. Not to her either?

Wangel. No, and besides I really can't expect Ellida to trouble about such things. She's not fit for that—— (*Breaking off*). But it wasn't *that* which we were going to talk about. Now tell me, have you thought everything over—everything that I told you about?

Arnholm. I have thought of nothing else ever since we parted last night.

Wangel. And what do you think should be done?

Arnholm. My dear doctor, I think you, as a medical man, must know that better than I do.

Wangel. Oh, if you only knew how difficult it is for a doctor to judge rightly about a patient who is so dear to him! Besides, this is no ordinary illness. No ordinary doctor and no ordinary medicines can help her.

Arnholm. How is she to-day?

Wangel. I was upstairs with her just now, and then she seemed to me quite calm. But behind all her moods something lies hidden which it is impossible for me to fathom. And then she is so changeable, so capricious—she varies so suddenly.

Arnholm. No doubt that is the result of her morbid state of mind.

Wangel. Not altogether. When you get down to rock bottom it was born in her. Ellida belongs to the sea-folk. That is the trouble.

Arnholm. What do you mean exactly, my dear doctor?

Wangel. Haven't you noticed that the people from out there by the open sea are, in a way, a people apart? It is almost as if they themselves lived the life of the sea. There is the rush of waves, and an ebb and flow too, in their thoughts and in their feelings, and so they can never bear transplanting. Oh, I ought to have remembered that. It was a veritable sin against Ellida to take her away from the sea and bring her here.

Arnholm. You have come to that opinion?

Wangel. Yes, more and more. But I ought to have told myself this beforehand. Oh, I knew it well enough deep down. But I wouldn't face up to it. You see, I loved her so! Therefore I thought of myself first of all. It was inexcusably selfish at that time!

Arnholm. Hm. I suppose every man is a little selfish under such circumstances. But I've never noticed that vice in you, Doctor Wangel.

Wangel (walks uneasily about the room). Oh yes! And I have been since then, too. Why, I am so much, much older than she is. I ought to have been like a father to her and a guide. I ought to have done my best to develop and enlighten her mind. Unfortunately I have done nothing of the sort. You see, I hadn't enough initiative, I preferred her just as she was. So things went from bad to worse with her, and then I didn't know what to do. *(In a lower voice.)* That was why I wrote to you in my trouble, and asked you to come here.

Arnholm (looks at him in astonishment). What, was that why you wrote?

Wangel. Yes, but don't let anyone know.

Arnholm. How on earth, my dear doctor—what good did you expect me to be? I don't understand.

Wangel. No, of course you don't. Because I was on an altogether false track. I thought that at one time Ellida had been fond of you, and that she still secretly cared for you a little—that perhaps it would do her good to see you again, and talk about her home and the old days.

Arnholm. So it was your wife you meant when you wrote that there was someone who was waiting for me, and—and perhaps longing for me.

Wangel. Yes, who else?

Arnholm (hurriedly). No, no. You're right. But I didn't understand.

Wangel. No, of course you didn't. As I said, I was on an absolutely wrong track.

Arnholm. And you call yourself selfish!

Wangel. Ah! but I had such a great sin to atone for. I felt I dared not neglect any means that might give the slightest relief to her mind.

Arnholm. How do you really explain the power this stranger exercises over her?

Wangel. Hm—my dear friend—there are probably sides to the matter that *cannot* be explained.

Arnholm. Do you mean something inexplicable in itself—absolutely inexplicable?

Wangel. In any case inexplicable so far as we know.

Arnholm. Do you believe there is something in it, then?

Wangel. I neither believe nor disbelieve; I simply don't know. That's why I leave it alone.

Arnholm. Yes.   But just one thing; her extraordinary, weird assertion about the child's eyes——

Wangel (*eagerly*). I don't believe a word about the eyes.   I *will* not believe such a thing.   It must be pure imagination on her part, nothing else.

Arnholm. Did you notice the man's eyes when you saw him yesterday?

Wangel. Of course I did.

Arnholm. And you saw no kind of resemblance?

Wangel (*evasively*). Hm—good heavens!   What shall I say? It wasn't quite light when I saw him.   And besides, Ellida had been saying so much about this resemblance, I really don't know if I was capable of observing quite impartially.

Arnholm. No, well, that may be.   But that other matter? All this terror and unrest coming over her at the very time, so it seems, that this strange man was on his way home.

Wangel. That—oh, that's something she must have persuaded and dreamed herself into since the day before yesterday. She was not seized with this quite so suddenly—as she now maintains.   But since she heard from young Lyngstrand that Johnston—or Friman, or whatever his name is—was on his way here, three years ago, in the month of March, she now evidently believes her anguish of mind came upon her at that very time.

Arnholm. Didn't it do that, then?

Wangel. No, indeed not.   There were signs and symptoms of it before this time, though it did happen, by chance, that in that March, three years ago, she did have a rather severe attack.

Arnholm. After all, then——?

Wangel. Yes, but that is easily accounted for by the circumstances—the condition she happened to be in at the time.

Arnholm. So, it points both ways, then.

Wangel (*wringing his hands*). And not to be able to help her! Not to know what to advise her!   To see no way out!

Arnholm. Supposing you made up your mind to leave this place, to go somewhere else, so that she could live in surroundings that would seem more homelike to her?

Wangel. Ah, dear friend! Do you think I haven't offered her that, too? I suggested moving out to Skjoldviken, but she won't hear of it.

Arnholm. Won't she do that either?

Wangel. No, she doesn't think it would be any good; and perhaps she's right.

Arnholm. Hm. Do you think so?

Wangel. As a matter of fact, when I think it all over carefully, I really don't know how I could manage it. I don't think I should be justified, for the sake of the girls, in going away to such a desolate place. After all, they must live where there is at least a prospect of their being provided for some day.

Arnholm. Provided for! Are you thinking about that already?

Wangel. Heaven knows, I must think of that too! But then again, on the other hand, my poor sick Ellida! Oh, my dear Arnholm! in many respects I seem to be standing between the devil and the deep blue sea!

Arnholm. Perhaps you've no need to worry on Bolette's account—— (*Breaks off.*) I should like to know where she— where they have gone. (*Goes up to the open door and looks out.*)

Wangel. Oh, I would so gladly make any sacrifice for all three of them, if only I knew what!

(ELLIDA *enters from the door on the left.*)

Ellida (*quickly, to* WANGEL). You won't go out this morning, will you?

Wangel. No, no, of course not. I'll stay at home with you. (*Pointing to* ARNHOLM, *who is coming towards them.*) But haven't you noticed our friend here?

Ellida (*turning*). Oh, are you here, Mr Arnholm? (*Holding out her hand to him.*) Good morning.

Arnholm. Good morning, Mrs Wangel. So you've not been bathing as usual to-day?

Ellida. No, no, no! That's out of the question to-day. But won't you sit down a moment?

Arnholm. No, thanks, not now. (*Looks at* WANGEL.) I promised the girls to go down to them in the garden.

Ellida. Goodness knows if you'll find them there. I never know where they are.

Wangel. They're sure to be down by the pond.

Arnholm. Oh, I shall find them right enough. (*Nods, and goes out across the veranda into the garden.*)

Ellida. What time is it, Wangel?

Wangel (*looking at his watch*). Just past eleven.

Ellida. Just past. And at eleven or half past to-night the steamer will be here. If only that were over!

Wangel (*going nearer to her*). Dear Ellida, there is one thing I should like to ask you.

Ellida. What is that?

Wangel. The evening before last—up at the Prospect—you said that during the last three years you had so often seen him lifelike before you.

Ellida. Yes, so I have, believe me.

Wangel. But how did you see him?

Ellida. How did I see him?

Wangel. I mean, what did he look like when you thought you saw him?

Ellida. But, Wangel, my dear, why, you know yourself now what he looks like.

Wangel. Did he look exactly like that in your imagination?

Ellida. Yes. He did.

Wangel. Exactly the same as you saw him in reality yesterday evening?

Ellida. Yes, exactly.

Wangel. Then how was it you didn't recognize him at once?

Ellida. Didn't I?

Wangel. No, you said yourself afterwards that at first you didn't know at all who the strange man was.

Ellida (*perplexed*). Yes, I really believe you are right. Don't you think that was strange, Wangel? Fancy my not knowing him at once!

Wangel. It was only the eyes, you said.

Ellida. Oh yes! The eyes—the eyes.

Wangel. Well, but at the Prospect you said that he always appeared to you exactly as he was when you parted out there—ten years ago.

Ellida. Did I?

Wangel. Yes.

Ellida. Then, I suppose he did look much as he does now.

Wangel. No. On our way home, the day before yesterday, you gave quite another description of him. Ten years ago he had no beard, you said. His dress, too, was quite different.

And that scarf-pin with the pearl?   That man yesterday wore nothing of the sort.

Ellida. No, he didn't.

Wangel (looks searchingly at her). Now just think back a little, Ellida dear.   Or perhaps you can't quite remember how he looked when he stood by you at Bratthammer?

Ellida (thoughtfully closing her eyes for a moment). Not quite distinctly.   No, to-day I can't.   Isn't that strange?

Wangel. Not so very strange after all.   You have now been confronted by a new and real image, and that overshadows the old one, so that you can no longer see it.

Ellida. Do you really think that's it, Wangel?

Wangel. Yes.   And it overshadows your sick imaginings, too. That is why it is good that the reality has come.

Ellida. Good?   Do you think it's good?

Wangel. Yes.   The fact that it has come.   It may restore you to health.

Ellida (sitting down on the sofa). Wangel, come and sit down by me.   I must tell you all my thoughts.

Wangel. Yes, do, Ellida dear.

(*He sits down on a chair on the other side of the table.*)

Ellida. It was really a great misfortune—for us both—that we two of all people should have come together.

Wangel (amazed). What are you saying?

Ellida. Oh yes, it was.   And it's quite natural that it could bring nothing but unhappiness, after the way in which we came together.

Wangel. But what was wrong in the way we came together?

Ellida. Listen, Wangel.   It's no use going on, lying to ourselves and to one another.

Wangel. Are we doing that?   Lying, you say?

Ellida. Yes, we are; or at least we suppress the truth.   For the truth—the pure and simple truth is—that you came out there and bought me.

Wangel. Bought—did you say bought!

Ellida. Oh, I wasn't a bit better than you.   I accepted the bargain.   Sold myself to you!

Wangel (looks at her full of pain). Ellida, have you really the heart to call it that?

Ellida. But is there any other name for it?   You could no longer bear the emptiness of your house.   You were on the look-out for a new wife.

Wangel. And a new mother for the children, Ellida.

Ellida. Yes. That too, perhaps, as well, although you didn't in the least know if I were fit to be a mother to them. Why, you had only seen me and spoken to me a few times. Then you wanted me, and so——

Wangel. Yes, you can call it what you like.

Ellida. And I, on my side—why, I was so helpless and bewildered, and so absolutely alone. Oh, it was perfectly natural I should accept the bargain, when you came and proposed to provide for me all my life.

Wangel. But I assure you, my dear Ellida, I didn't look at it in that light at all. I asked you honestly if you would share with me and the children the little I could call my own.

Ellida. Yes, I know you did. But all the same, I should never have accepted! Never have accepted that at any price! Not sold myself! Better the meanest work—better the poorest life—but from one's own choice.

Wangel (rising). Then have the five or six years that we have been living together been so utterly worthless to you?

Ellida. Oh! Don't think that, Wangel. I have been as well cared for here as any human being could wish. But I did not come to your house of my own free will. That is the whole thing.

Wangel (looking at her). Not of your own free will!

Ellida. No. It was not of my own free will that I went with you.

Wangel (in subdued tone). Ah! I remember your words from yesterday.

Ellida. The secret lies in those words. They have thrown a new light on things for me, and so I see it all now.

Wangel. What do you see?

Ellida. I see that the life we two live together—is really no marriage.

Wangel (bitterly). You have spoken the truth there. The life we *now* live is not a marriage.

Ellida. Nor was it before. Never—not from the very beginning *(looks straight in front of her)*. The first—that might have been a complete and real marriage.

Wangel. The first—what do you mean?

Ellida. Mine—with him.

Wangel (looks at her in astonishment). I don't understand you in the least.

Ellida. Ah, dear Wangel, don't let us lie to each other, nor to ourselves.

Wangel. Well—what more?

Ellida. You see—we can never get away from that one thing—that a freely given promise is just as binding as a marriage.

Wangel. But what on earth——

Ellida (rising impetuously). Let me leave you, Wangel!

Wangel. Ellida!   Ellida!

Ellida. Yes, yes!   Oh, let me do that!   Believe me, it will come to that in any case—after the way we two came together.

Wangel (conquering his pain). It has come to this, then?

Ellida. It has come to this.   It could not be otherwise.

Wangel (looking gloomily at her). So I have not won you by our living together.   Never, never quite possessed you.

Ellida. Ah, Wangel—if only I could love you, how gladly I would—as dearly as you deserve.   But I feel so strongly—that that will never happen.

Wangel. Divorce, then?   It is a divorce, a complete, legal divorce that you want?

Ellida. My dear, you don't understand me at all!   It's not formalities like these that I care about.   Such outward things don't really matter, I think.   What I want is that we should release each other, of our own free will.

Wangel (bitterly, nods slowly). To cry off the bargain again—yes.

Ellida (quickly). Exactly.   To cry off the bargain.

Wangel. And then, Ellida?   Afterwards?   Have you thought of what life would be for both of us?   What life would be for both you and me?

Ellida. That doesn't matter.   Things must turn out afterwards as they like.   What I beg and implore of you, Wangel, is the most important.   Set me free!   Give me back my complete freedom!

Wangel. Ellida, it is a fearful thing you ask of me.   At least give me time to collect myself before I come to a decision.   Let us talk it over more carefully.   And you yourself—you must take time to consider what you are doing.

Ellida. But we have no time to lose with this.   I must have my freedom again to-day.

Wangel. Why to-day?

Ellida. Because he is coming to-night.

Wangel (starts). Coming! He! What has this stranger to do with it?

Ellida. I want to face him in perfect freedom.

Wangel. And what—what else do you intend to do?

Ellida. I don't want to hide behind the fact that I am another man's wife; nor make the excuse that I have no choice, because then it wouldn't be a real decision.

Wangel. You talk about a choice. Choice, Ellida! A choice in such a matter!

Ellida. Yes, I must be free to choose—to choose either way. I must be able to let him go away—alone, or to go with him.

Wangel. Do you know what you are saying? Go with him—put your whole life in his hands!

Ellida. But didn't I put my life into *your* hands, without thinking twice about it?

Wangel. Maybe. But he! He, an absolute stranger! A man about whom you know so little!

Ellida. Ah, but after all I knew you even less, and yet I went with you.

Wangel. Then you knew to some extent what life lay before you. But now? In this case, think! What do you know? You know absolutely nothing. Not even who or what he is.

Ellida (looking in front of her). That is true. But that is just the terrible thing.

Wangel. Yes, indeed, it is terrible!

Ellida. That is why I feel I must plunge into it.

Wangel (looking at her). Because it seems terrible?

Ellida. Yes. Just because of that.

Wangel (coming closer). Listen, Ellida. What do you really mean by terrible?

Ellida (reflectively). A terrible thing is something which terrifies and attracts me at the same time.

Wangel. Attracts, you say?

Ellida. Attracts most of all, I think.

Wangel (slowly). You are one with the sea.

Ellida. Terror is in that too.

Wangel. And that terror is in you. You both terrify and attract.

Ellida. Do you think so, Wangel?

Wangel. After all, I have never really known you—never completely. Now I am beginning to understand.

Ellida. And that is why you must set me free! Free me

from every bond to you—and yours. I am not what you took me for. Now you see it yourself. Now we can part like friends —and of our own free will.

Wangel (sadly). Perhaps it would be better for us both if we parted. And yet, I cannot! You are the terror to me, Ellida; the attraction that is strongest in you.

Ellida. Do you mean that?

Wangel. Let us try and live through this day wisely—in perfect peace of mind. I dare not set you free, and release you to-day. I have no right to. No right for your own sake, Ellida. I exercise my right and my duty to protect you.

Ellida. Protect? What is there to protect me from? I am not threatened by any outward power. The terror lies deeper, Wangel. The terror is—the attraction in my own mind. And what can you do against that?

Wangel. I can strengthen and urge you to fight against it.

Ellida. Yes, if I wanted to fight against it.

Wangel. Then you don't want to?

Ellida. Oh! I don't know myself.

Wangel. To-night all will be decided, dear Ellida——

Ellida (bursting out). Yes, imagine! The decision so near— the decision for one's whole life!

Wangel. And then to-morrow——

Ellida. To-morrow! Perhaps my real future will have been ruined.

Wangel. Your real——

Ellida. The whole, full life of freedom lost—lost for me, and perhaps for him also.

Wangel (in a lower tone, seizing her wrist). Ellida, do you love this stranger?

Ellida. Do I love him? Oh, how can I tell! I only know that to me he is a terror, and that——

Wangel. And that——

Ellida (tearing herself away). And that it is to him I feel I belong.

Wangel (bowing his head). I begin to understand better.

Ellida. And what remedy have you for that? What advice to give me?

Wangel (looking sadly at her). To-morrow he will be gone, then your misfortune will be averted. And then I will consent to set you free. We will cry off the bargain to-morrow, Ellida.

Ellida. Oh, Wangel, to-morrow! That will be too late.

Wangel (looking towards the garden). The children—the children! Let us spare them, at least for the present.

(ARNHOLM, BOLETTE, HILDE, *and* LYNGSTRAND *come into the garden.* LYNGSTRAND *says good-bye in the garden, and goes out. The rest come into the room.*)

Arnholm. D'you know we have been making plans.

Hilde. We're going out to the fiord to-night and——

Bolette. No, you mustn't tell.

Wangel. We two have also been making plans.

Arnholm. Oh!—really?

Wangel. To-morrow Ellida is going away to Skjoldviken for a time.

Bolette. Going away?

Arnholm. Well, I must say that's very sensible, Mrs Wangel.

Wangel. Ellida wants to go home again—home to the sea.

Hilde (springing towards ELLIDA). You are going away—away from us?

Ellida (frightened). Hilde! What is the matter?

Hilde (controlling herself). Oh, it's nothing. (*In a low voice, turning from her.*) Well, go if you like!

Bolette (anxiously). Father—oh, I see—*you*, too, are going—to Skjoldviken!

Wangel. Not me, no! I shall run out there every now and again, I expect.

Bolette. And come here to us?

Wangel. I will——

Bolette. Every now and again!

Wangel. Dear child, it must be. (*He crosses the room.*)

Arnholm (whispers). We will talk it over later, Bolette. (*He crosses to* WANGEL. *They speak in low tones up stage by the door.*)

Ellida (aside to BOLETTE). What was the matter with Hilde? She looked quite upset.

Bolette. Have you never noticed what Hilde goes about here, day in, day out, pining for?

Ellida. Pining for?

Bolette. Ever since you came into the house?

Ellida. No, no. What is it?

Bolette. One single loving word from you.

Ellida. Oh! If there should be something for me to do here! (*She clasps her hands together over her head, and looks fixedly in front of her, as if torn by contending thoughts and emotions.*

WANGEL *and* ARNHOLM *come across the room whispering.*
BOLETTE *goes to the side room, and looks in.   Then she throws
open the door.*)

Bolette. Father, dear—the table is laid—if you——

Wangel (*with forced composure*). Is it, child?   That's good.
Come, Arnholm!   We'll go in and drink a farewell cup—with
the 'Lady from the Sea.'   (*They go out through the right.*)

ACT V

(SCENE.—*The distant part of* DOCTOR WANGEL's *garden, and
the carp pond.   The summer night gradually darkens.*   ARNHOLM,
BOLETTE, LYNGSTRAND, *and* HILDE *are in a boat, punting along
the shore to the left.*)

Hilde. Look!   We can jump ashore easily here.

Arnholm. No, no, don't!

Lyngstrand. I can't jump, Miss Hilde.

Hilde. Can't you jump either, Arnholm?

Arnholm. I'd rather not try.

Bolette. Then let's land down there, by the bathing steps.

(*They push off.   At the same moment* BALLESTED *comes along
the footpath, carrying music-books and a French horn.   He
nods to those in the boat, turns and speaks to them.   The
answers are heard farther and farther away.*)

Ballested. What do you say?   Yes, of course it's on account
of the English steamer.   This is her last visit here this year.   But
if you want to enjoy the music, you mustn't wait too long.
(*Calling out.*)   What?   (*Shaking his head.*)   Can't hear what
you say!

(ELLIDA, *with a shawl over her head, enters, followed by* DOCTOR
WANGEL.)

Wangel. But, dear Ellida, I assure you there's plenty of time.

Ellida. No, no, there is not!   He may come any moment.

Ballested (*outside the fence*). Hallo!   Good evening, doctor.
Good evening, Mrs Wangel.

Wangel (*noticing him*). Oh, is it you?   Will there be music
to-night?

Ballested. Yes, the Brass Band Society thought of making
themselves heard.   We've no dearth of festive occasions nowadays.   To-night it's in honour of the English ship

Ellida. The English ship! Is she in sight already?

Ballested. Not yet. But you know she comes from between the islands. You don't see anything of her, and then suddenly she's alongside of you.

Ellida. Yes, that is so.

Wangel (*half to* ELLIDA). To-night is the last voyage, then she won't come again.

Ballested. A sad thought, doctor, and that's why we're going to give them an ovation, as the saying is. Ah yes—ah yes. The lovely summer-time will soon be over now. Soon all ways will be barred, as they say in the tragedy.

Ellida. All ways barred—yes!

Ballested. It's sad to think of. We have been the joyous children of summer for weeks and months now. It's hard to reconcile yourself to the dark days—just at first, I mean. For men *can* accli—a—acclimatize themselves, Mrs Wangel. Yes, indeed they can. (*Bows, and goes off to the left.*)

Ellida (*looking out at the fiord*). Oh, this terrible suspense! This torturing last half-hour before the decision!

Wangel. You are determined, then, to speak to him yourself?

Ellida. I must speak to him myself. I must make my choice of my own free will, you see.

Wangel. You have no choice, Ellida. You have no right to choose—no right without my permission.

Ellida. You can never prevent the choice, neither you nor anyone else. You can forbid me to go away with him—if I should choose to do that. You can keep me here by force—against my will. That you can do. But that I should choose, choose from my very soul—choose him, and not you—in case I had to choose that way—this you cannot prevent.

Wangel. No, you are right. I cannot prevent that.

Ellida. And so I have nothing to help me to resist. Here, at home, there is not one single thing that attracts me and binds me. I am so absolutely rootless in your house, Wangel. The children are not mine—their hearts, I mean—never have been. When I go, if I do go, either with him to-night, or to Skjoldviken to-morrow, I haven't a key to give up, an order to give about anything whatsoever. I am absolutely rootless in your house—I have been absolutely outside everything from the very first.

Wangel. You yourself wanted it like that.

Ellida. No, no, I didn't. I neither wanted nor didn't want it.

I simply left things just as I found them the day I came here. It is you, and no one else, who wanted it.

Wangel. I was trying to do the best for you.

Ellida. Yes, Wangel, I know that so well! But there is retribution in that, something that avenges itself. For now I find no binding power here—nothing to strengthen me— nothing to help me—nothing to draw me towards what should have been the strongest possession of us both.

Wangel. Yes, I see, Ellida. And that is why from to-morrow you shall have back your freedom. Henceforth you shall live your own life.

Ellida. And you call that my own life! No! My real own life lost its bearings when I agreed to live with you. (*Clenches her hand in fear and unrest.*) And now—to-night—in half an hour, the man I failed is coming—the man I should have held on to, just as he has held on to me! Now he is coming to offer me—for the last and only time—the chance of living my life over again, of living my real own life—the life that terrifies and attracts—and I *cannot* forgo that—not freely.

Wangel. That is why it is necessary that your husband—and your doctor—should take the power of acting from you, and act on your behalf.

Ellida. Yes, Wangel, I quite understand. Believe me, there are times when I think it would be peace and deliverance if I could be bound to you with all my soul—and try to brave all that terrifies—and attracts me. But I cannot! No, no, I cannot do that!

Wangel. Come, Ellida, let us walk up and down together for a while.

Ellida. I would like to—but I dare not. He told me I was to wait for him here.

Wangel. Come along! There is enough time.

Ellida. Do you think so?

Wangel. Plenty of time, I tell you.

Ellida. Then let's go, for a little while.

(*They go out in the foreground. At the same time* ARNHOLM *and* BOLETTE *appear by the upper edge of the pond.*)

Bolette (*noticing the two as they go out*). Look there——

Arnholm (*in a low voice*). Hush! Let them go.

Bolette. Can you understand what has been going on between them these last few days?

Arnholm. Have you noticed anything?

Bolette. I should think I have!

Arnholm. Anything peculiar?

Bolette. Well, yes, many small things.   Haven't you?

Arnholm. Well—I don't know exactly.

Bolette. Yes, you have, only you won't admit it.

Arnholm. I think it will do your stepmother good to go on this little journey.

Bolette. Do you think so?

Arnholm. Yes.   I should say too it would be better for all parties that she should get away every now and then.

Bolette. If she does go home again to Skjoldviken to-morrow she will never come back to us here!

Arnholm. My dear Bolette, whatever makes you think that?

Bolette. I am quite convinced of it.   Just you wait.   You'll see that she won't come back again—anyhow not as long as Hilde and I are in the house here.

Arnholm. Hilde?

Bolette. Well, it might be all right perhaps with Hilde, for she is little more than a child.   And I believe that underneath she worships Ellida.   But, you see, it's different with me—a stepmother who isn't so very much older than myself!

Arnholm. Dear Bolette, it may not be so very long before you leave after all.

Bolette (*eagerly*). Really!   Have you spoken to father about it?

Arnholm. Yes, I have.

Bolette. Well, what does he say?

Arnholm. Hm!   Well, your father's so thoroughly taken up with other matters just now——

Bolette. Yes, yes!   I said it would be like that.

Arnholm. But I got this much out of him.   You mustn't reckon on any help from him.

Bolette. No?

Arnholm. He explained his circumstances to me clearly. He thought that such a thing was absolutely out of the question, impossible for him.

Bolette (*reproachfully*). And you had the heart to come and mock me?

Arnholm. I've certainly not done that, Bolette dear.   It depends wholly and solely upon yourself whether you go away or not.

Bolette. What depends upon me?

Arnholm. Whether you are to go out into the world—learn all the things you want to—do all the things you long to do—live a happier life, Bolette.   What do you say to that?

Bolette (*clasping her hands together*). Good heavens!   But it's impossible!   If father won't or can't—and I have no one else on earth I could turn to——

Arnholm. Couldn't you make up your mind to accept a little help from your old—from your former tutor?

Bolette. From you, Mr Arnholm!   Would you be willing to——

Arnholm. Stand by you!   Yes—with all my heart.   Both in word and deed.   You can count upon that.   Then you accept?   Well?   Do you agree?

Bolette. Do I agree!   To get away—to see the world—to learn something really worth learning!   Everything which has seemed to be a great, beautiful impossibility!

Arnholm. Well, all that may now become a reality to you, if only you yourself wish it.

Bolette. And you will help me to all this wonderful happiness! Oh no!   Tell me, *can* I accept such an offer from a stranger?

Arnholm. You can from me, Bolette.   From me you can accept anything.

Bolette (*seizing his hands*). Yes, I almost think I can!   I don't know how it is, but—— (*Bursting out.*) Oh, I could laugh and cry for joy, for sheer happiness!   Then I should really live after all. I began to be so afraid life would pass me by.

Arnholm. You need not be afraid of that, Bolette.   But now you must tell me quite frankly—if there is anything—any tie which binds you here.

Bolette. Binds me?   No, there isn't anything.

Arnholm. Nothing whatever?

Bolette. No, nothing at all.   That is—father is a tie to some extent.   And Hilde, too.   But——

Arnholm. Well, you'll have to leave your father sooner or later.   And some time or other Hilde also will go her own way in life.   That's only a question of time.   Nothing more.   But apart from that there is nothing else that binds you, Bolette? No other kind of tie?

Bolette. None whatever.   As far as that goes, I could leave at any moment.

Arnholm. Well, if that is so, my dear Bolette, you shall go away with me!

Bolette (*clapping her hands*). O heavens above, how wonderful!

Arnholm. I hope you have every confidence in me?

Bolette. Indeed I have!

Arnholm. And you dare to trust yourself and your future absolutely and fearlessly in my hands, Bolette? Do you? Dare you do this?

Bolette. Of course. Why shouldn't I? Could you imagine anything else? You, who have been my old tutor—my tutor in the old days, I mean.

Arnholm. Not because of that. I don't pay much attention to that side of the matter. But—well, so you are really free, Bolette! There is nothing that ties you. And so I ask you, if you could—tie yourself to me for life?

Bolette (steps back frightened). What are you saying?

Arnholm. For your whole life, Bolette. Will you be my wife?

Bolette (half to herself). No, no, no! That is impossible, utterly impossible!

Arnholm. Is it really so absolutely impossible for you to——

Bolette. But surely you can't mean what you are saying, Mr Arnholm! (*Looking at him.*) Or—yet—was that what you meant when you offered to do so much for me?

Arnholm. You must listen to me one moment, Bolette. I suppose I have greatly surprised you!

Bolette. Oh, how could such a thing from you—how could it but—but surprise me!

Arnholm. Perhaps you are right. Of course you didn't—you could not know it was for your sake I came here.

Bolette. Did you come here for—for my sake?

Arnholm. Yes, I did, Bolette. In the spring I received a letter from your father, and in it there was a phrase that made me think—hm—that you kept your former tutor in—in a little more than friendly remembrance.

Bolette. How could father write such a thing?

Arnholm. He did not mean it like that. But I worked myself into the belief that here was a young girl longing for me to come back again.—No, you mustn't interrupt me, Bolette dear! And—you see, when a man like myself, who is no longer quite young, has such a belief—or fancy, it makes an overwhelming impression. There grew within me a living, a grateful affection for you. I thought I must come to you, see you again, and tell you I shared the feelings that I imagined you had for me.

Bolette. And now that you know it is not so—that it was a mistake?

Arnholm. It makes no difference, Bolette. Your image, as I carry it inside myself, will always be coloured and stamped with the impression that this mistake aroused in me. Perhaps you can't understand this; but still it is so.

Bolette. I never thought such a thing possible.

Arnholm. But now you have seen that it is possible, what do you say now, Bolette? Couldn't you make up your mind to be—yes—to be my wife?

Bolette. Oh, it seems so utterly impossible, Mr Arnholm. You, who have been my tutor!   I can't imagine ever standing in any other relationship towards you.

Arnholm. Well, if you think you really cannot—then our old relationship remains unchanged, my dear Bolette.

Bolette. What do you mean?

Arnholm. I mean, of course, that I shall keep my promise all the same.   I will make sure that you get out into the world and see something of it.   Learn about things you really want to know; be safe and independent.   I shall provide for your future also, Bolette.   In me you will always have a good, faithful, trust-worthy friend.   That you may be sure of.

Bolette. Good heavens!   Mr Arnholm, all that is so utterly impossible now.

Arnholm. Is that impossible too?

Bolette. Surely you can see that!   After what you have just said to me, and after my answer—oh, you must see yourself that it is impossible for me now to accept such a tremendous amount from you.   I can't accept a thing from you—not a thing after this.

Arnholm. Then you would rather stay at home here, and let life pass you by?

Bolette. Oh, it is torture to think of.

Arnholm. Will you renounce knowing something of the outer world?   Renounce playing your part in all that you yourself say you are longing for?   To know there is so infinitely much, and yet never really to understand anything of it?   Think carefully, Bolette.

Bolette. Yes, yes!   You are right, Mr Arnholm.

Arnholm. And then, when one day your father is no longer here, then perhaps to be left helpless and alone in the world; or live to give yourself to another man—whom you, perhaps, will also feel no affection for——

Bolette. Oh yes!   I see how true all you say is.   But still— and yet perhaps——

Arnholm (quickly). Well?

Bolette (looking at him hesitatingly). Perhaps it might not be so impossible after all.

Arnholm. What, Bolette?

Bolette. Perhaps it might be possible—to accept—what you proposed to me.

Arnholm. Do you mean that, after all, you might be willing to—that at all events you could give me the happiness of helping you as a steadfast friend?

Bolette. No, no, no! Never that, for that would be utterly impossible now. No—Mr Arnholm—far better to take the whole of me.

Arnholm. Bolette! You will after all?

Bolette. Yes, I believe I will.

Arnholm. And after all you will be my wife?

Bolette. Yes, if you still think that—that you will have me.

Arnholm. Still think—— (*Seizing her hand.*) Oh, thank you, thank you, Bolette. Everything else that you said—your former doubts—these don't frighten me. If I don't possess your whole heart, I shall know how to win it. Oh, Bolette, I will wait upon you hand and foot!

Bolette. And then I shall see something of the world? Shall live! You have promised me that?

Arnholm. And I will keep my promise.

Bolette. And I can learn everything I want to?

Arnholm. I, myself, will be your teacher just as before, Bolette. Do you remember the last school year?

Bolette (quietly and absently). Imagine—to know one's self free, and to get out into the strange world, and then, not to need to be anxious about the future—not to be harassed about one's stupid livelihood!

Arnholm. No, you will never need to waste a moment's thought on things like that. And that will be nice, too, Bolette, won't it? Eh?

Bolette. Yes. Indeed it will. That's quite true.

Arnholm (putting his arms about her). Oh, you just see how comfortably and easily we shall settle down together! And how well and safely and trustfully we shall both get on with one another, Bolette.

Bolette. Yes. I'm also beginning to—I really believe—it will work. (*Looks out to the right, and hurriedly frees herself.*) Oh, don't say anything about this.

Arnholm. What is it, dear?

Bolette. Oh, it's that poor—— (*Pointing.*) Look out there.

Arnholm. Is it your father?

Bolette. No. It's the young sculptor. He's down there with Hilde.

Arnholm. Oh, Lyngstrand! What's the matter with him?

Bolette. Why, you know how weak and delicate he is.

Arnholm. Yes. Unless it's simply imaginary.

Bolette. No, it's real enough! He won't last long. But it's perhaps best for him.

Arnholm. Why should *that* be best, dear?

Bolette. Well, because—because—nothing would come of his art anyhow. Let's go before they come.

Arnholm. Willingly, my dear Bolette.

(HILDE *and* LYNGSTRAND *appear by the pond.*)

Hilde. Hi, hi! Won't your honours wait for us?

Arnholm. Bolette and I would rather go on a little in advance. (*He and* BOLETTE *go out to the left.*)

Lyngstrand (*laughs quietly*). It's rather nice here now. Everybody goes about in pairs—always two and two together.

Hilde (*looking after them*). I could almost swear he's proposing to her.

Lyngstrand. Really? Have you noticed anything?

Hilde. Yes. It's not very difficult—if you keep your eyes open.

Lyngstrand. But Miss Bolette won't have him. I'm certain of that.

Hilde. No. She thinks he's got so dreadfully old-looking, and she thinks he'll soon be bald.

Lyngstrand. It's not only because of *that*. She wouldn't have him anyhow.

Hilde. How do you know?

Lyngstrand. Well, because there's someone else she's promised to keep in her thoughts.

Hilde. Only to keep in her thoughts?

Lyngstrand. While he is away, yes.

Hilde. Oh, then I suppose it's you she's to keep in her thoughts?

Lyngstrand. Possibly.

Hilde. Has she promised you that?

Lyngstrand. Yes—she really did promise me that! But mind you don't tell her you know.

Hilde. Oh, I'll be mum!   I'm as silent as the grave.

Lyngstrand. I think it's awfully kind of her.

Hilde. And when you come home again—are you going to be engaged to her, and then marry her?

Lyngstrand. No, that wouldn't do very well.   I daren't think of such a thing during the first years.   And when I am able to, she'll be rather too old for me, I fancy.

Hilde. And yet you want her to continue to think of you?

Lyngstrand. Yes, it would be a great help to me.   Because I'm an artist, you see.   And as she has no real calling herself, she could do that quite easily.   But all the same, it's kind of her.

Hilde. Do you think you'll be able to get on more quickly with your work if you know that Bolette is here thinking of you?

Lyngstrand. Yes, I think so.   To know there is a spot on earth where a young, gentle, reserved woman is quietly dreaming about you—I think it must be so—so—well, I really don't exactly know what to call it.

Hilde. Perhaps you mean—thrilling?

Lyngstrand. Thrilling!   Oh yes, thrilling was what I meant, or something like it.   (*Looks at her for a moment.*)   You are so clever, Miss Hilde.   You really are very clever.   When I come home again you'll be about the same age as your sister is now. Perhaps, too, you'll look like your sister looks now.   And perhaps, too, you'll have the same personality as she has now. Then, perhaps, you'll be both yourself and your sister—in one body, so to speak.

Hilde. Would you like that?

Lyngstrand. I don't really know.   Yes, I almost think I should.   But just now, for this summer, I would rather you were like yourself alone, and exactly as you are.

Hilde. Do you like me best as I am?

Lyngstrand. Yes, I like you very much, just as you are.

Hilde. Hm.   Tell me, you who are an artist, do you think I'm right always to wear bright-coloured summer dresses?

Lyngstrand. Yes, I think you're quite right!

Hilde. You think bright colours suit me, then?

Lyngstrand. Yes.   They suit you charmingly—to my taste.

Hilde. But tell me, as an artist, how do you think I should look in black?

Lyngstrand. In black, Miss Hilde?

Hilde. Yes, all in black.   Do you think I should look nice?

Lyngstrand. Black's hardly suitable for the summer. However, you'd probably look remarkably nice in black, especially with your figure.

Hilde (*looking straight in front of her*). All in black, up to my throat, black frilling round that, black gloves, and a long black veil hanging down behind.

Lyngstrand. If you were dressed like that, Miss Hilde, I would wish I were a painter, and I'd paint you as a young, beautiful, heart-broken widow!

Hilde. Or as a young, sorrowing, bride.

Lyngstrand. Yes, that would be better still. But you can't want to be dressed like that?

Hilde. I don't really know, but I think it's thrilling.

Lyngstrand. Thrilling?

Hilde. Thrilling to think of, yes. (*Suddenly pointing to the left.*) Oh, just look *there*!

Lyngstrand (*looking*). The big English steamer—and right by the pier!

(WANGEL *and* ELLIDA *come in past the pond.*)

Wangel. No, I assure you, dear Ellida, you are mistaken. (*Seeing the others.*) What, are you two here? It's not in sight yet, is it, Mr Lyngstrand?

Lyngstrand. The big English ship?

Wangel. Yes.

Lyngstrand (*pointing*). There she is already, doctor.

Ellida. Oh, I knew it.

Wangel. It's come!

Lyngstrand. Come like a thief in the night, as one might say, so quietly and noiselessly.

Wangel. You must go to the pier with Hilde. Be quick! I'm sure she wants to hear the music.

Lyngstrand. Yes, we were just going there, doctor.

Wangel. We may follow you. We'll come soon.

Hilde (*whispering to* LYNGSTRAND). They're hunting in couples, too!

(HILDE *and* LYNGSTRAND *go out through the garden. Music is heard in the distance out at the fiord during the following.*)

Ellida. He has come! He is here! Yes—I feel it.

Wangel. You'd better go in, Ellida. Let me talk to him alone.

Ellida. Oh, that's impossible—impossible, I say. (*With a cry.*) Ah, do you see him, Wangel?

(THE STRANGER *enters from the left, and remains on the pathway outside the fence.*)

The Stranger (*bowing*). Good evening. You see I am here again, Ellida.

Ellida. Yes, yes. The time has come now.

The Stranger. And are you ready to start, or not?

Wangel. You can see for yourself that she is not.

The Stranger. I'm not asking about travelling clothes, or anything of that kind, or about packed trunks. I have all that is needed for a journey with me on board. I've also secured a cabin for her. (*To* ELLIDA.) I merely ask you if you are ready to come with me, to come with me—of your own free will?

Ellida. Oh, don't ask me! Don't tempt me!

(*A ship's bell is heard in the distance.*)

The Stranger. That is the first bell for going on board. Now you must say 'Yes' or 'No.'

Ellida (*wringing her hands*). To decide—decide for one's whole life! Never to be able to undo it again!

The Stranger. Never. In half an hour it will be too late.

Ellida (*looking shyly and searchingly at him*). What makes you hold on to me so resolutely?

The Stranger. Don't you feel, as I do, that we belong together?

Ellida. Do you mean because of the promise?

The Stranger. Promises bind no one, neither man nor woman. If I hold on so persistently to you, it is because I *cannot* do otherwise.

Ellida (*in a low, trembling voice*). Why didn't you come before?

Wangel. Ellida!

Ellida (*bursting out*). Oh, what is it that attracts, and tempts, and lures me into the unknown? All the power of the sea is concentrated in this one thing!

(THE STRANGER *climbs over the fence.*)

Ellida (*stepping back to* WANGEL). What is it? What do you want?

The Stranger. I see it and I hear it in your voice, Ellida. You will choose me in the end.

Wangel (*going towards him*). My wife has no choice in this. I am here to choose for her and to defend her. Yes, defend! If you don't go away from here—away from this country—and never come back again—do you know what risks you will be taking?

Ellida. No, no, Wangel, not that!

The Stranger. What will you do to me?

Wangel. I will have you arrested as a criminal, at once, before you go on board. I know all about the murder at Skjoldviken.

Ellida. Ah, Wangel, how can you?

The Stranger. I was prepared for that, and so—(*takes a revolver from his breast pocket*)—I provided myself with this.

Ellida (*throwing herself in front of* WANGEL). No, no, don't kill him, kill me instead!

The Stranger. Neither you nor him, don't worry. This is for myself, because I will live and die a free man.

Ellida (*with growing excitement*). Wangel, let me tell you this—tell you so that he can hear it. You can indeed keep me here! You have the means and the power to do it. And you intend to do it. But my mind—all my thoughts, all the longings and desires of my soul—you cannot bind these! They will rush and press out into the unknown that I was created for, and that you have kept from me!

Wangel (*in quiet sorrow*). Yes, I see that plainly, Ellida. Little by little you are slipping from me. The craving for the boundless, the infinite, the unattainable will drive your soul into the darkness of night in the end.

Ellida. Yes, I can feel it hovering over me like black noiseless wings.

Wangel. It shall not come to that. No other deliverance is possible for you. At least I can see no other. And so—so I cry off our bargain at once. Now you can choose your own path in perfect—perfect freedom.

Ellida (*stares at him awhile as if stricken dumb*). Is it true—true what you say? Do you mean that—mean it with all your heart?

Wangel. Yes—with all my sorrowful heart—I mean it.

Ellida. And can you do it? Can you manage to carry it out?

Wangel. Yes, I can. I can because I love you so dearly.

Ellida (*in a low, trembling voice*). And have I become so near—so dear to you?

Wangel. The years and the living together have done that.

Ellida (*clasping her hands together*). And I—I have been so blind to it.

Wangel. Your thoughts were elsewhere. But now—now you are completely free of me and mine. Now your own true life may resume its real bent again, for now you can choose of your own free will, and on your own responsibility, Ellida.

Ellida (*clasps her head with her hands, and stares at* WANGEL). Of my own free will, and on my own responsibility! Responsibility, too? That changes everything.

(*The ship bell rings again.*)

The Stranger. Do you hear, Ellida? It has rung now for the last time. Come.

Ellida (*turns towards him, looks firmly at him, and speaks in a resolute voice*). I shall never go with you after this!

The Stranger. You won't?

Ellida (*clinging to* WANGEL). Oh, I shall never go away from you after this.

Wangel. Ellida, Ellida!

The Stranger. So it is all over?

Ellida. Yes. Over for ever.

The Stranger. I see. There is something here stronger than my will.

Ellida. Your will has not a vestige of power over me any longer. To me you are like a dead man—who has come home from the sea, and who returns to it again. I no longer dread you. And I am no longer drawn to you.

The Stranger. Good-bye, Mrs Wangel! (*He swings himself over the fence.*) From now on you are nothing but a shipwreck in my life that I have survived. (*He goes out.*)

Wangel (*looks at her for a while*). Ellida, your mind is like the sea—it ebbs and flows. Why this change?

Ellida. Ah, don't you understand that the change came—was *bound* to come when I could choose in freedom?

Wangel. And the unknown—doesn't that lure you any longer?

Ellida. No, it neither lures nor frightens me. I could have seen it—gone out into it, if I had wanted to. I could have chosen it. And that is why I was able to reject it.

Wangel. I am beginning to understand you little by little. You think and conceive in pictures—in visible figures. Your longing and aching for the sea, your attraction towards this strange man, these were the expression of an awakening and growing desire for freedom—nothing else.

Ellida. I don't know about that. But you have been a good physician for me. You found, and you *dared* to use the right remedy—the only one that could help me.

Wangel. Yes, in dire need and danger we doctors dare a great deal. And now you are coming back to me again, Ellida?

Ellida. Yes, dear, faithful Wangel—now I am coming back to you again. Now I can. For now I come to you of my own free will, and on my own responsibility.

Wangel (*looks lovingly at her*). Ellida! Ellida! To think that now we can live wholly for each other——

Ellida. And with memories common to both of us. Yours, as well as mine.

Wangel. Yes, indeed, my dear.

Ellida. And for our two children, Wangel?

Wangel. You call them *ours!*

Ellida. They are not mine yet, but I shall win them.

Wangel. Ours! (*Happily and quickly kisses her hands.*) I can't tell you how grateful I am for that word!

(HILDE, BALLESTED, LYNGSTRAND, ARNHOLM, *and* BOLETTE *come into the garden. At the same time a number of young townspeople and visitors pass along the footpath.*)

Hilde (*aside to* LYNGSTRAND). Now look! Why, she and father look exactly as if they were an engaged couple!

Ballested (*who has overheard*). It is summer time, little missie.

Arnholm (*looking at* WANGEL *and* ELLIDA). The English steamer is leaving.

Bolette (*going to the fence*). You can see her best from here.

Lyngstrand. The last trip of the season.

Ballested. Soon all ways will be barred, as the poet says. It is sad, Mrs Wangel. And now we're to lose you too for a time. To-morrow you're off to Skjoldviken, I hear.

Wangel. No, nothing is coming of that. We've both changed our minds—to-night.

Arnholm (*looking from one to the other*). Oh—really!

Bolette (*coming forward*). Father, is that true?

Hilde (*going towards* ELLIDA). Are you going to stay with us after all?

Ellida. Yes, dear Hilde, if you'll have me.

Hilde (*struggling between tears and laughter*). Oh, listen to that —if I will——!

Arnholm (*to* ELLIDA). But this is quite a surprise——

Ellida (*smiling earnestly*). Well, you see, Mr Arnholm—do you remember we talked about it yesterday? When you have once become a land-creature you can no longer find your way back again to the sea, nor to the sea-life either.

Ballested. Why, that's exactly the case with my mermaid.

Ellida. Very like it—yes.

Ballested. Only with this difference—that the mermaid dies of it, while human beings can acclam—acclimatize themselves. Yes, yes. I assure you, Mrs Wangel, they can ac-climatize themselves.

Ellida. Yes, in freedom they can, Mr Ballested.

Wangel. And when they act on their own responsibility, dear Ellida.

Ellida (*quickly holding out her hand to him*). Exactly.

(*The big steamer glides noiselessly down the fiord. The music is heard nearer land.*)